I0901089

IMAGES of America

AROUND ALEDO

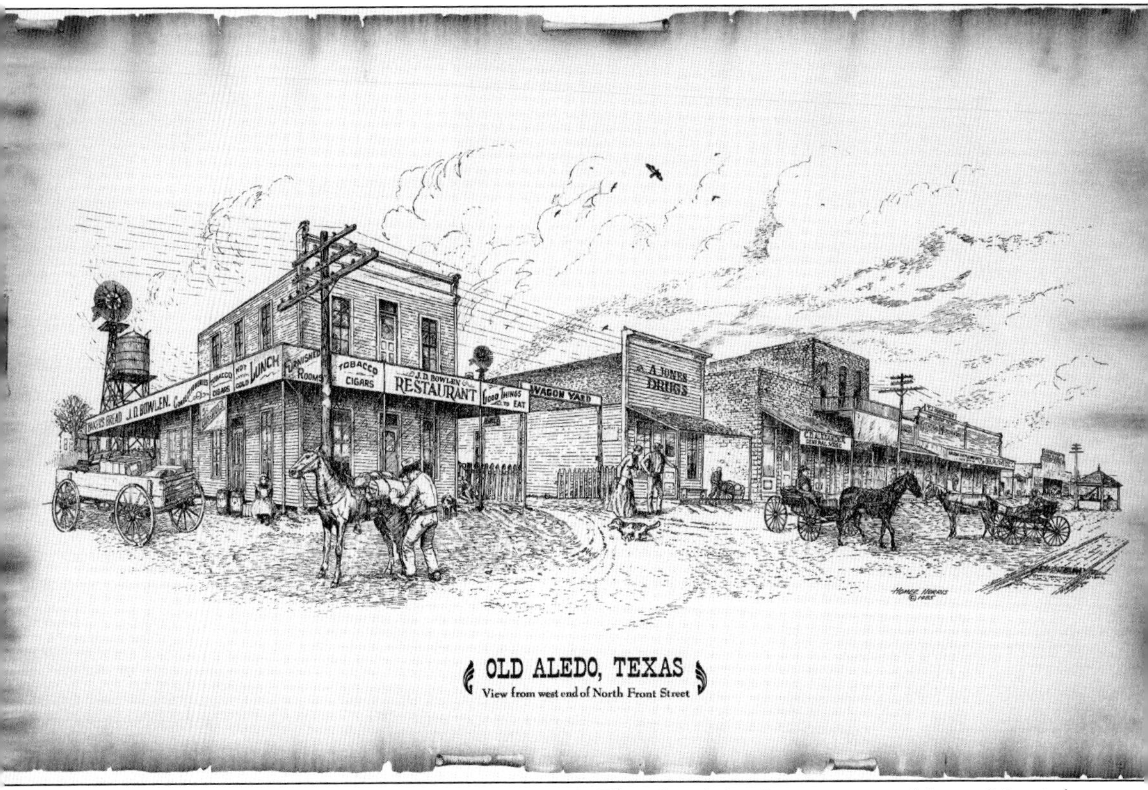

NORTH FRONT STREET, ALEDO, AROUND 1906. This sketch by Annetta artist Homer Norris has become an iconic image of the fledgling community, which developed as a rail stop on the Texas and Pacific Railway line that entered eastern Parker County in the 1870s. The public well, on the right, was a popular gathering spot. (Courtesy of Homer Norris.)

ON THE COVER: Bowlen's on North Front Street in Aledo was operated by proprietor John D. "Chink" Bowlen, born in 1875 in Massachusetts. Chink lived on the first floor with his wife, Kate, a Tennessee native 16 years his junior. An enterprising man who sported an impressive walrus-style mustache, Bowlen offered haircuts, shaves, meals, rooms to rent, mercantile items, confections, cigars and tobacco, and buggies for hire. Aledo residents recalled that Bowlen would interrupt a haircut to rent a buggy to a young man who wished to go courting. The building was moved to Fort Worth in the 1920s and painted a vivid red. Ball's Trading Post occupied the building for many years. The structure was torn down after 1950. (Courtesy of Homer Norris.)

IMAGES
of America

AROUND ALEDO

Susan McKeague Karnes
Foreword by Homer Norris

ARCADIA
PUBLISHING

ISBN 978-0-7385-7911-4

Published by Arcadia Publishing
Charleston, South Carolina

Printed in the United States of America

Library of Congress Control Number: 2010922842

For all general information contact Arcadia Publishing at:
Telephone 843-853-2070
Fax 843-853-0044
E-mail sales@arcadiapublishing.com
For customer service and orders:
Toll-Free 1-888-313-2665

Visit us on the Internet at www.arcadiapublishing.com

For my parents,
Gordon Clark and Louise Marea McKeague,
and my grandparents,
Thomas Emmett and Louise Marea Coln Jones
and
Robert Irwin and Mary Christine Clark McKeague

Contents

FOREWORD

Aledo was thousands of years from having a name when Upper Pleistocene–period hunters roamed the Clear Fork Valley. Gravel deposits yield the bones of mammoths, camels, bison, and big cats with 6-inch fangs. The mammoths had 9-foot tusks, and the bison *latifrons* had a horn span of 6 feet. I have dug up some of the mammoth ivory and a bison *anticus* skull with a 3-foot horn span.

Those ancient hunters risked their lives going in close range to large game, as do modern citizens, driving into herds of vehicles on the highways—all to provide food for loved ones. These ancients were not hazy myths and legends, but living, loving people whose remains sleep in the sandy slopes along our streams.

We have evidence of bands in the Clovis, Folsom, Plano, and the long Archaic period of habitation here. This was followed by those excellent horsemen, the Comanche and Kiowa, who ruled the plains so impressively. Every time I left a hayfield, shimmering in the summer sun, and dropped off into our living streams, I forgot all cares and reverted back to the age of the flint artifacts found on the gravel bars. In a world of shady cool and the smell of willow, connection with the ancient ones transcended all mundane concerns.

In the early 1850s, covered wagons rolled into this area, bringing folks from Kentucky and Georgia. They brought a walking plow, a few seeds, and a lot of faith. Conditions had not changed much by the time I was a young boy in the early 1930s. Lest we should become soft, the Great Depression came to discipline us.

Aledo would not have public electricity until World War II; wagon travel was still common in my boyhood, and we would go to the front door to watch a car pass. To us, the mere idea of a traffic jam in Aledo was about as feasible as Buck Rogers traveling in space. We knew a world of biscuits cooked in a wood range, adventure books read wide-eyed by a kerosene lamp, and ice cream freezers cranked by hand. To us, radio was more exciting than television. Despite hard realities, life was rich and good. When we snuggled into bed and went to sleep, listening to whippoorwills and wolves, we knew that Mama was right: everything would turn out fine.

Now we want either the central heat or air conditioning to be on at all times. If our feet touch earth, it is because we slipped off the sidewalk on the way to the car. Comfort is the key word. Comfort is honorable, but have we become so far removed from the earth that we rob ourselves of a better reality?

The Aledo I grew up in has been largely vaporized. Old Bob Ball no longer sits by our hearth and tells about cattle drives. Mama no longer puts a drop of kerosene on our tongue to cure a noisy cough. The old ones have gone on. I've watched a whole town of people slip away, usually taking their wit, wisdom, and tales of struggle and adventure with them. Blessed are those who chronicle and point us back to the people, the simple faiths and philosophies that can set us more solidly on this land.

—Homer Norris
Annetta, Texas
November 2009

ACKNOWLEDGMENTS

This book would not exist if not for Homer Clyde "Tot" Norris and Reubene Gressett Scott, two gifted storytellers who live in eastern Parker County, love its history, and write about it. Reubene's homespun, humorous *Ramblin' Reubene* column in the *Community News* first introduced me to the area's history. Homer Norris, a remarkable artist and writer who captures vignettes of local life on canvas and in his *Parker County Prairie Sketchbook* series, offered a second nostalgic portal. Reubene's folk humor evokes the likes of Will Rogers; Homer's humble brilliance touches the heart. I defy anyone's imagination to elude the magic woven by those two voices.

I owe deep and special thanks, also, to my editor at Arcadia Publishing, the ever-patient and encouraging Luke Cunningham; and Jean Bennett, Evlyn Wiley Broumley, Randy Keck, Doyle Marshall, Aledo mayor Kit Marshall, Brenda McClurkin and Cathy Spitzenberger of the University of Texas at Arlington Special Collections, John Scovil and his staff at the Doss Cultural and Heritage Center, and Vickie Ballow Slagle and members of the East Parker County Genealogy and Historical Society (EPCGHS).

Many friends, neighbors, and eastern Parker County residents offered generous assistance, including Rose Barton, Steve Bolton, Jack Borden, Beverly Branch, Jim Calhoun, John Chapman, Pam and John Chase, Don Collins, Leila Collins, Lori Cope, Chris Cornwall, Diane McFarland Cornwall, Kay W. Davis, Helen Bennett Dill, John Dycus, Bill and Leta Eastman, Pam Flowers, Josef Gratts, Kimberly Hardick, Sally Harrison, Barney B. Holland Jr., Terry Hyles, Mary Lynne Bigby Jones, Mary Kemp, Josephine and Richard King, B. J. Lacasse, Nelda McGlinchey, Jackie McLellan, Melissa Moorman, Jan Orr-Harter, Jerry Reid, Mitzi Riley, Mary Roberts, Ann and Tom B. Saunders, Barbara Smiley, Dan Smith, Lance Tahmahkera, Leon Tanner, Weldon Turner, Jon Vandagriff, Mason Wallis, Lyn Walsh, Stacey Jandrucko and Malcolm Louden of the Walsh Foundation, and Loweda, Jim, and Renna Wood.

International award-winning author and Aledo resident Sherrie McLeroy led me to the most enjoyable writing project of my career. I owe her a debt of gratitude.

At age five, I announced my intention to grow up, move to Texas, and marry a cowboy—a far-fetched aim for a child of the Chicago suburbs born into a fourth-generation Illinois family. For almost 30 years I've been firmly rooted in Texas. If a 5-acre "ranch" and weekend cowboy qualify, my life's dream is in place. I thank the warm, welcoming folks of Parker County for making the achievement a rich satisfaction.

INTRODUCTION

At first glance, the history of eastern Parker County seems to be the quintessential tale of the American West, rife with cowboys and Indians, conflict and compromise, depredation and deprivation. Of course, the actual story began much earlier than this. Ice Age climate changes crafted the soil foundations of Texas prairies, and melting glaciers created the Trinity and Brazos watersheds. Mammoths, bison, and camels thrived, and eventually, the first people arrived.

For hundreds of years, the Kiowa and Nüma-nu (Comanche) inhabited the land. Nomadic hunters and gatherers, masters of the plains and the horse, these Native American bands lived in seasonal encampments of teepees and followed herds of buffalo.

Early settlers from nearby Southern states arrived in the mid-19th century, attracted by the clear waters and sandy loam soil along the broad Clear Fork of the Trinity River, Mary's Creek, and the Bear Creeks. By 1855 farms, ranches, and tiny settlements dotted the land, and residents formed a county named for state representative Isaac Parker, with Weatherford as its seat.

A few pioneers in the new settlements of Center, Alma, Dicey, Newburg, and Elm Springs owned slaves; most did not. The majority, however, were sympathetic to the Confederate cause. As the Civil War erupted, the county voted 535 to 61 in favor of secession. By late 1861, most men under the age of 45 had joined the cause, leaving women, children, and the older and infirm to defend homes and property.

As the war began, raids by the Native Americans were already common. Settlers dreaded full moons, since raiding parties often would take advantage of the moonlight to steal horses and other valuables. With the Civil War, however, came heightened conflict, exacerbated by the absence of able-bodied husbands and sons. From 1858 until 1872, when peace between whites and the Plains Indians finally prevailed, Parker County endured more raids (many marked by violence and death) than any other county in Texas, according to 19th-century historian J. W. Wilbarger. Henry Smythe estimated property damage at more than $6 million.

Many died at the hands of raiding parties. An estimated 400 settlers were taken into captivity, a practice perhaps encouraged by a mutual hostage market and exchange between the Plains Indians and the government. And the raids ran both ways. Settlers organized posses and brandished their own form of justice. Some took scalps of their Comanche or Kiowa conquests.

In the end, the tenacious settlers persevered, and their communities began to grow. By 1870, there were schools at Bear Creek, Alma, and O'Neal Springs. Freight wagons ambled to market, piled high with buffalo hides.

In 1875, Comanche chief Quanah Parker recognized that the buffalo had been decimated, the prairie belonged to settlers, and the Comanches' future depended on peaceful assimilation. He struck an accord with the U.S. government and led his people into the difficult transition from their nomadic ways to farming on government-issued land in Oklahoma.

After an arduous Civil War and postwar period, by 1878, the Fort Worth–Yuma cattle trail and stagecoach line crossed Parker County, and in 1879, a Texas and Pacific Railway line connected Fort Worth to Weatherford via stations in eastern Parker County. Settlements started to flourish.

Aledo

Alma, an early community located near present-day FM1187 and Kelly Road, is considered the precursor to Aledo. Named for a young McConnell daughter who died, the settlement centered around Alma Hall, a small structure used by the Baptists, Methodists, and Masons.

In the late 1870s, the Texas and Pacific Railway Company expanded its line into Parker County from Fort Worth, 2 miles north of Alma. A settlement grew near the stop, called Medearis or Medera, after the adjacent Medearis land grant (Texas and Pacific passengers sometimes requested the Hood Ranch station). Residents settled on a name that reflected that of the county, Parker Station, but confusion regarding mail bound for the county seat caused post office officials to request a name change. In 1882, the burg became Aledo, a bow to a railroad executive's Illinois hometown.

The new town was platted on the Sanchez land grant. Business lots measured 25 by 150 feet, residential lots 50 by 150 feet. Businesses faced the tracks on either North Front Street or South Front Street.

Along the former, Bowlen's offered rooms, haircuts, and buggies for hire. The proprietor of Overmier's General Store sold dippers of his well water to train passengers. Newt Markum built a drugstore, and on the first floor of his building, J. J. Sears sold axle grease, bacon, and coffins; the Masons met upstairs. Sears owned the bank on the east end of North Front Street, a lumberyard, and farms around town. When occasion demanded, he served as undertaker. On South Front Street, M. C. Griffin repaired harnesses, collars, wagons, and wheels, and he also shod horses in his blacksmith shop.

Alma Hall was moved to Aledo (effectively marking the demise of the Alma community) and placed on a parcel of land purchased by the Methodist Episcopal Church South in 1892.

As the 19th century dawned, the Church of Christ and the Baptists built churches. H. F. Leach owned the first telephone switchboard; only party lines were available. Soon the automobile arrived, and by 1910, there were 73 registered in Parker County. Prosperous rancher Charles McFarland delighted many a child by offering a lift to the schoolhouse in his two-cylinder Buick.

Farming remained the primary occupation. Miles Wilkerson arrived with his family in 1908. "It was prairie land filled with wooded valleys," he later said. Common crops were cotton, corn, grains, and hay. The Wilkerson family raised sudan, baled oats, and thrashed wheat.

Aledo citizens built their first school building, a two-room plank structure with a shed on the west side. Esther Gray led a suffragette parade down the streets of the city. In 1917, soldiers from Camp Bowie practiced firing French 75mm guns southwest of town. In 1919, a fatal nitroglycerin explosion on the nearby Kuteman Cutoff created a media sensation.

Aledo entered the 1920s with a population of 400, twelve businesses, and one bank. Despite Prohibition, whiskey abounded, thanks to hidden stills. Ray Smyth recalled finding a 5-gallon jug; one week later, its contents had eaten a hole through the lid. A Clear Fork flood in 1921 devastated fields and buildings, and the bank failed when an officer of the institution misused funds. J. J. Sears liquidated his assets rather than fail his depositors.

"Old man Sears is due a lot of credit," said Ray Smyth. "He carried people on his book. Between the Baptist Church and the Sears house was Sears Park. People forget that kind of thing."

By 1925, residents drove Bankhead Highway, the first all-weather transcontinental road in the nation. In 1928, Willow Springs School consolidated with Aledo.

The Great Depression hit Aledo hard. Merchants and farmers struggled to provide for their families. A massive storm caused extensive damage to the area. There were bright spots, though, and life went on. Elizabeth "Bettie" Hamaker, the postmistress, handled mail duties, while her husband, James, who had fought in the Battle of Gettysburg, met the train and carried the mail from the depot. Ray Smyth built a mill that employed up to 100; for years it remained the only employer in Aledo, a fact for which men would thank Smyth for the remainder of his life.

In the 1940s, the Aledo Civic Club formed, and it hosted Gene Autry, who owned a ranch east of town, at a benefit box supper that raised more than $1,200—a princely sum for the time. As World War II impacted the country, the McFarland Ranch School closed in 1943, when its only student married a soldier. Lt. Gen. William Hood Simpson, a descendant of early settler and Texas state legislator Judge A. J. Hood, rose to prominence as he led the Ninth Army in Europe.

In 1946, as the first school stadium was built, a group of Parker County men founded the National Cutting Horse Association. By 1951, pens and feeding lots on the north side of the railroad tracks held up to 10,000 head of cattle for market. Tragedy spurred the formation of the Aledo Volunteer Fire Department, and the Aledo Independent School District was created.

The community incorporated in 1963 and named Bob Daugherty its first mayor. As Aledo approached its 100-year mark, people welcomed the arrival of the first new bank to be chartered in town since 1925. Residents celebrated the centennial with a parade and danced in the shadow of the historic buildings on North Front Street and South Front Street.

Annetta

The community of Annetta formed around 1876 at A. B. Fraser's station and store, built to serve freighters carrying buffalo hides to markets in the east. Fraser named the station Anneta after his daughter. When the Texas and Pacific Railroad extended west of Fort Worth, S. A. Winslow offered right-of-way through his property on the condition that a rail station be established. Upon its completion, Fraser built a post office and general store. The railroad adopted the name Anneta from the nearby way station.

Until the late 20th century, Anneta's population hovered around 50, mostly farmers of cotton, grains, pecans, and other crops. In the 1970s, the area became popular as a desirable rural residence. By 1979, the original spelling had morphed to Annetta. To avoid inclusion in Fort Worth extraterritorial jurisdiction, the community incorporated as three cities: Annetta, Annetta South, and Annetta North. Annetta South lies south of the original community, which was situated in the northern section of present-day Annetta and the central portion of Annetta North.

Dicey

One of the oldest settlements in Parker County, dating to the 1850s, the community established one of the earliest churches in Parker County. Originally named Power, its residents honored the wife of pioneer W. G. Puryear by later choosing the name Dicey.

A post office was established at Dicey in 1891. From the 1920s through the mid-1940s, the town reported a population of more than 60 residents, and two grocery stores served the area. The post office was closed in 1929. The creation of Lake Weatherford in 1957 appropriated much of the original community.

Willow Park

Many consider Willow Park a new community, given its origins in the development of the El Chico Ranch and 1963 incorporation, but the city is derived from one of the oldest settlements in the county. City historian Kay W. Davis traced its roots to farmers who settled, in the 1850s, in an area near present-day Interstate 20 and FM5. The original name—Elm or Allum Springs—evolved to Willow Springs.

Farmers and sharecroppers raised cotton, corn, peanuts, and dairy cows well into the 20th century. In 1935, Fort Worth businessman W. K. Stripling and partners built the El Chico Lodge retreat, said to have hosted Jack Dempsey, Gene Autry, and Roy Rogers.

Around 1940, Highway 80 was completed; a scenic roadside park and pond proved popular. In 1955, the El Chico Ranch was developed as El Chico Estates. Within 20 years of its incorporation, Willow Park had a golf course, fire department, and several churches. The El Chico Lodge served as a city hall, as well as a sanctuary for two church congregations, before sale to a private owner in 1979.

Proximity to Interstate 20 has triggered further development. While the historic community of Willow Springs fades from memory, the cemetery remains in use and reflects the area's founding families, including Bierschenk, Brazell, Gratts, Froman, Mikus, Ray, and Yeary.

One

EARLY FAMILIES

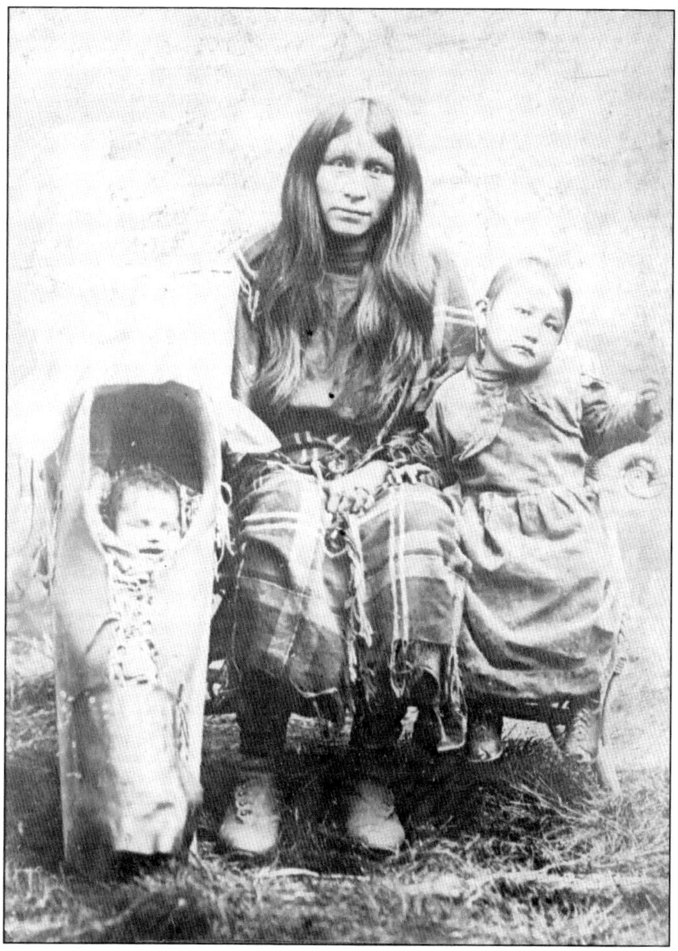

NÜMA-NU, THE PEOPLE. Long before settlers arrived in eastern Parker County in the mid-19th century, bands of Kiowa and Nüma-nu, or Comanche, roamed the land, hunting the buffalo. Nüma-nu means "the people." Pictured here are a Comanche mother and her children, date unknown. (Courtesy of Lance Tahmahkera.)

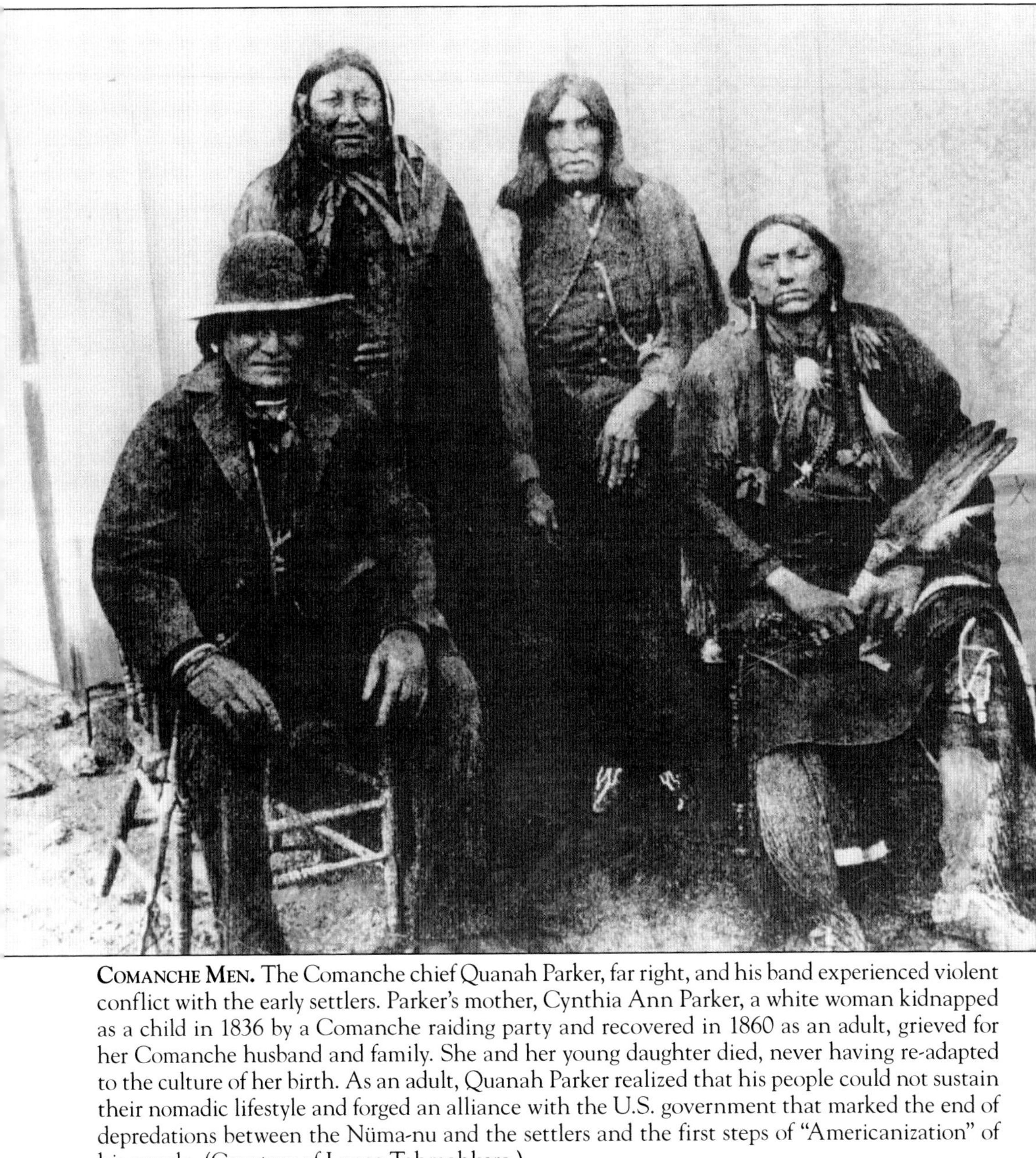

COMANCHE MEN. The Comanche chief Quanah Parker, far right, and his band experienced violent conflict with the early settlers. Parker's mother, Cynthia Ann Parker, a white woman kidnapped as a child in 1836 by a Comanche raiding party and recovered in 1860 as an adult, grieved for her Comanche husband and family. She and her young daughter died, never having re-adapted to the culture of her birth. As an adult, Quanah Parker realized that his people could not sustain their nomadic lifestyle and forged an alliance with the U.S. government that marked the end of depredations between the Nüma-nu and the settlers and the first steps of "Americanization" of his people. (Courtesy of Lance Tahmahkera.)

Kiowa Woman. An undated photograph shows a young Native American of the Great Plains. (Courtesy of Lance Tahmahkera.)

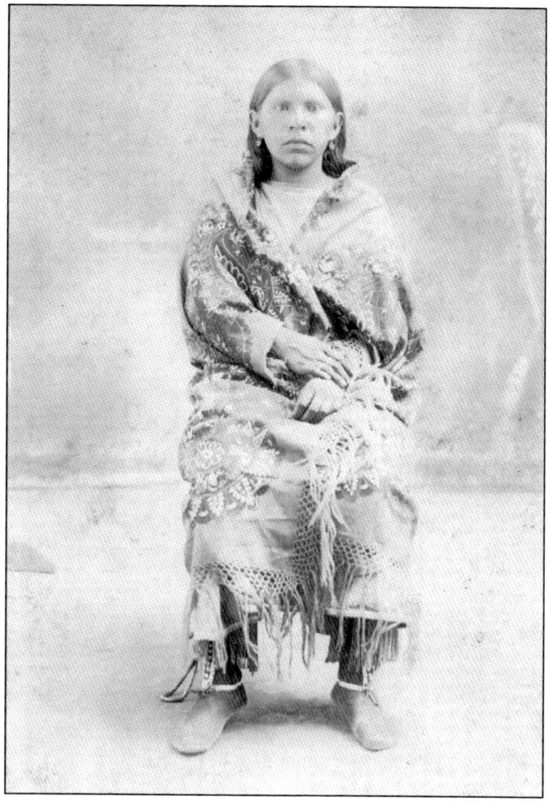

The Brown Family. In 1856, Thomas and Catherine Beamer Brown and their family emigrated from Monroe County, Virginia, in a covered wagon. Brown burned countless cords of mesquite wood in a kiln by the Clear Fork to bake the brick for his home between Alma and Center. The exterior walls were three courses deep. Adam Clark Brown, pictured in a dark hat, came to Parker County when he was three and recalled helping make bricks by toting buckets of water. (Courtesy of Homer Norris.)

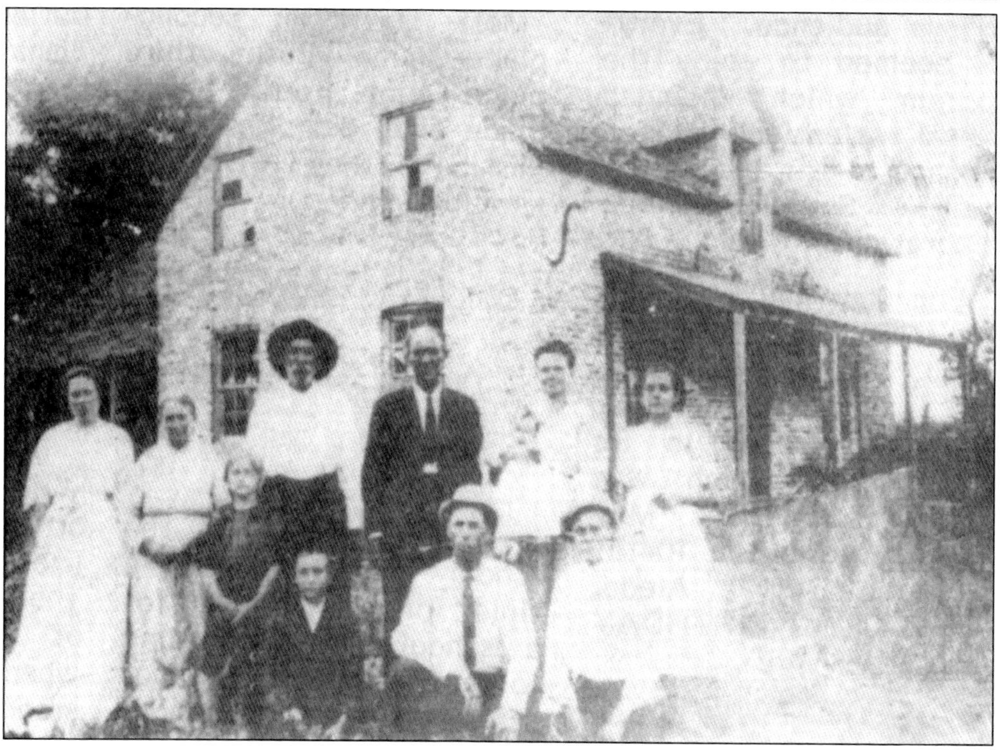

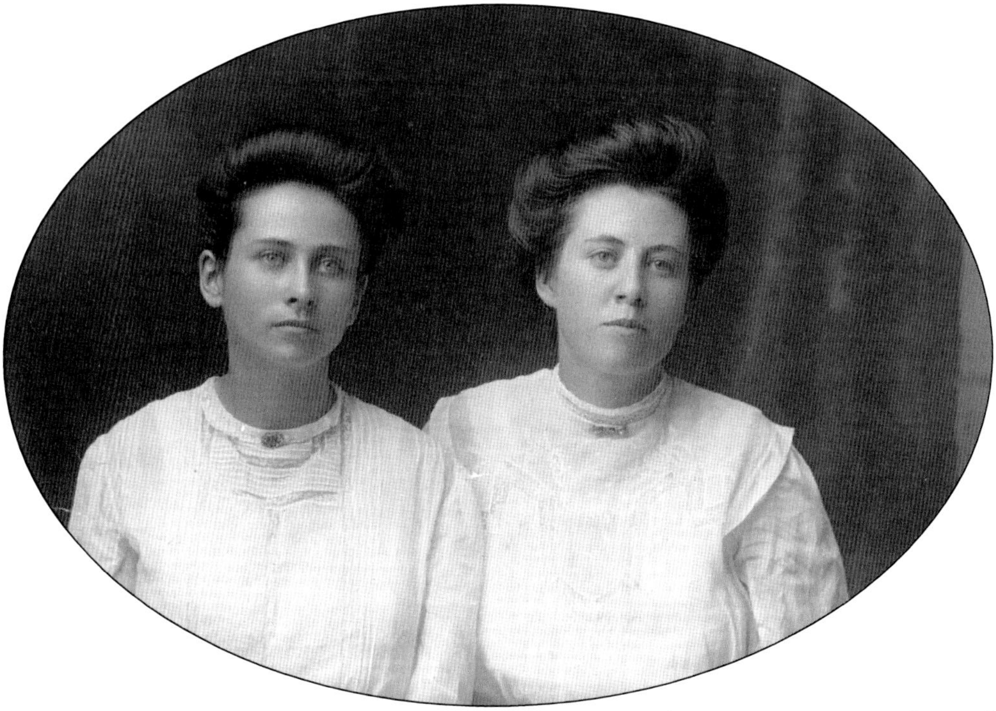

ANNIE AND LEORA BROWN. The daughters of Adam Clark and Elona Brown are pictured around 1910. Annie, left, married dairyman W. E. Conway of Crowley, Texas. Leora, right, taught school in Graford, Texas, before marrying Georgia native A. W. Eastman and settling on a farm near her parents. (Courtesy of Bill and Leta Eastman.)

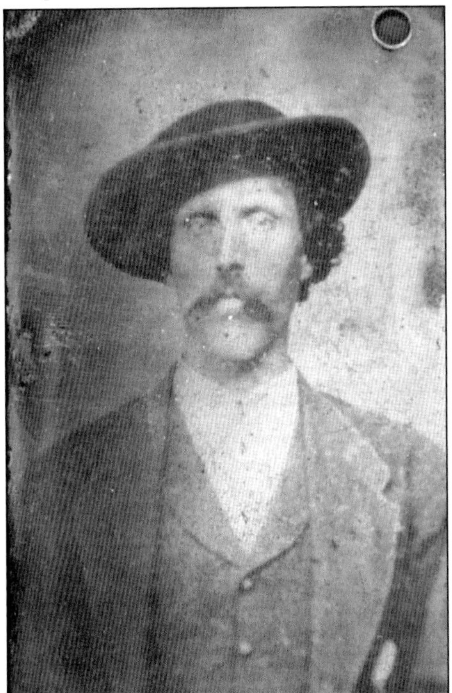

JOHN HARRISON ROBERTSON. Born in 1847 in Missouri, he was a small boy when his family arrived in Texas. Robertson married Mary Independence Blocker in 1870, the daughter of a Parker County First Family, John B. and Lucinda Duff Blocker. The First Families of Parker County are those who arrived prior to the end of the Civil War, and they are honored by Parker County Texas History and Heritage, Inc. Robertson served in the Frontier Reserves and patented land north and east of present-day Lake Weatherford. (Courtesy of Kay W. Davis.)

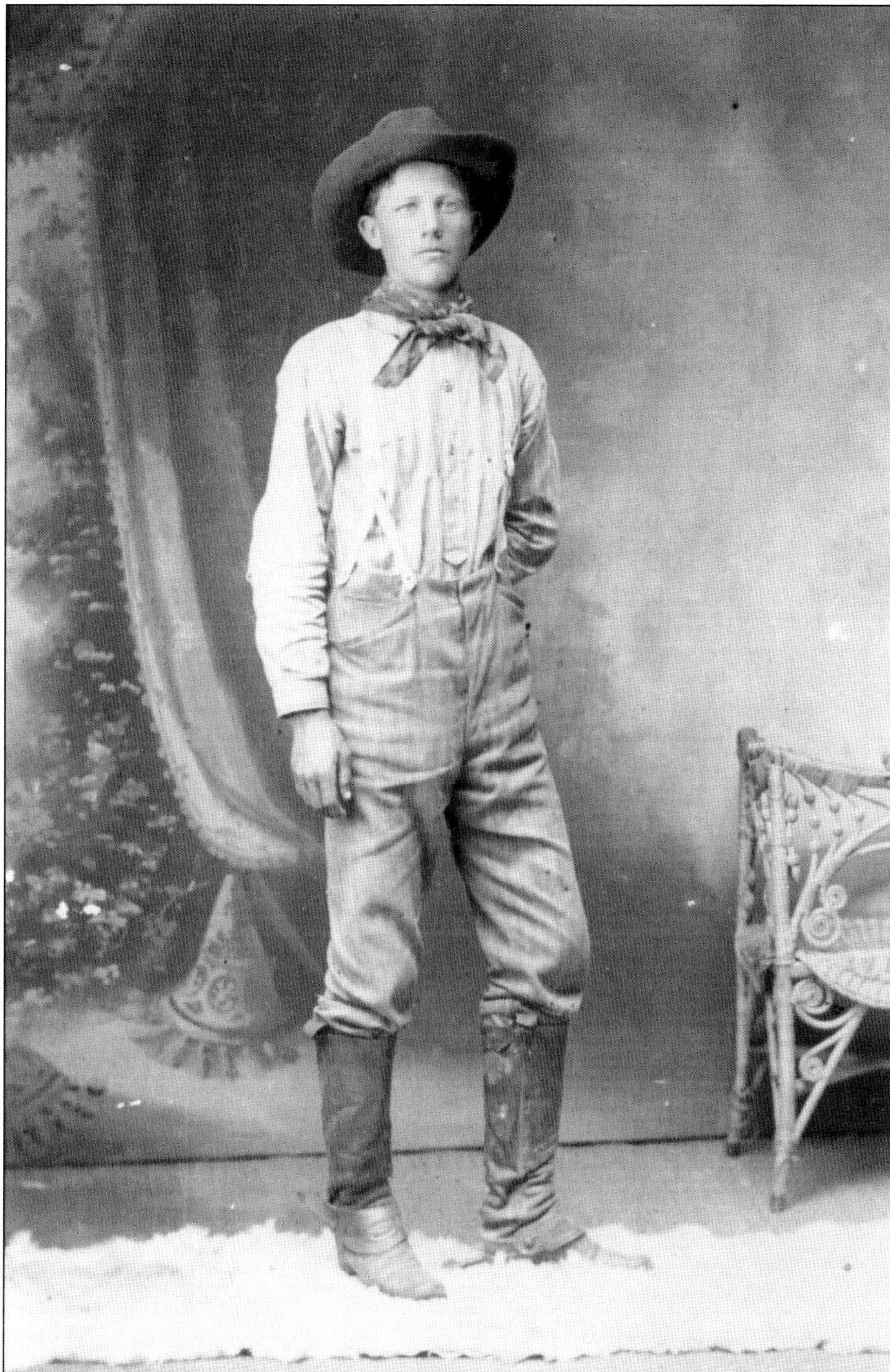

ALBERT M. ROBERTSON. The oldest child of early settlers James Monroe and Elizabeth Ann Harrison Robertson (1819–1880), one of Parker County's First Families, Albert died of an illness while serving the Confederacy in the War Between the States. He is buried in Willow Springs Cemetery. Elizabeth patented the family land in Parker County. (Courtesy of Kay W. Davis.)

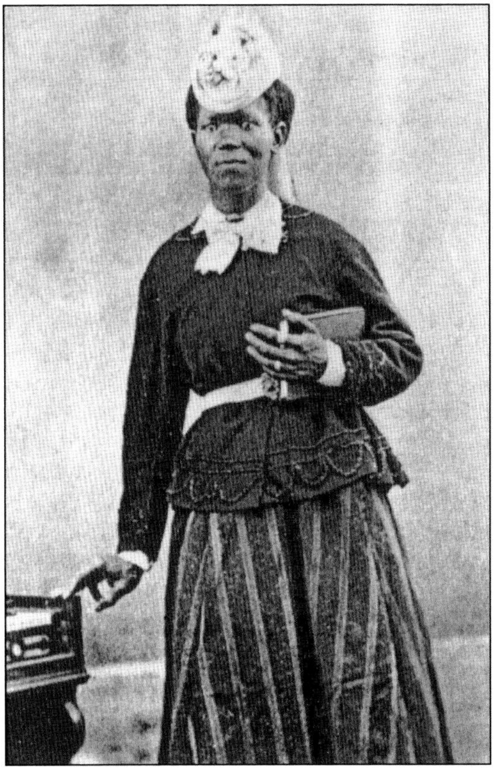

Rosa Cass. Born into slavery on Christmas Day in 1861 at Mary's Creek, at age 16, Rosa Cass married 41-year-old Lawson D. Gratz (below). She was the daughter of Mahala, a well-known slave of C. B. Rider. She died in 1934. (Courtesy of Josef Gratts.)

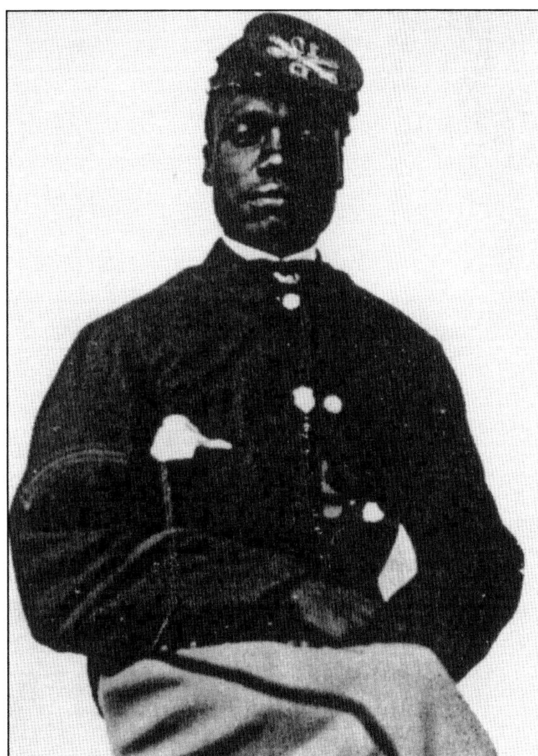

Lawson D. Gratz. The only known Buffalo Soldier and African American Union Civil War veteran who is buried in Parker County was born in 1839 in Kentucky. Gratz (or Gratts, as the family now spells it) served as first sergeant of Company C, 114th Colored Infantry, fought during the sieges of Petersburg and Richmond, and was present at Appomattox Courthouse when Gen. Robert E. Lee surrendered. Gratz reenlisted in 1867 in the 10th U.S. Cavalry; its black troops became known as Buffalo Soldiers and were instrumental in maintaining order among the Native American tribes. Gratts owned land in Annetta, where he lived until his death in 1909. (Courtesy of Josef Gratts.)

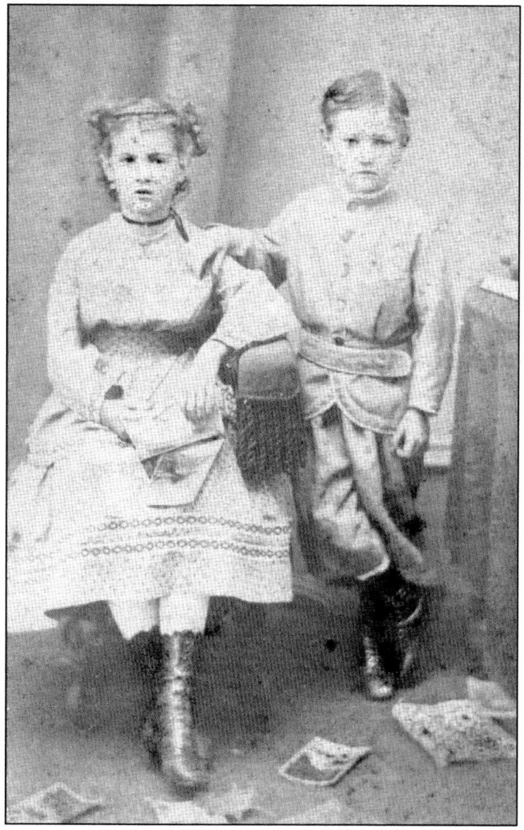

MINNIE AND C. F. CODER, AROUND 1869. Before the end of the century, C. F. Coder owned a farm in the Mary's Creek community. His property included an early stagecoach way station on a trail where several stages were robbed in the late 19th century. (Courtesy of the Doss Heritage and Cultural Center.)

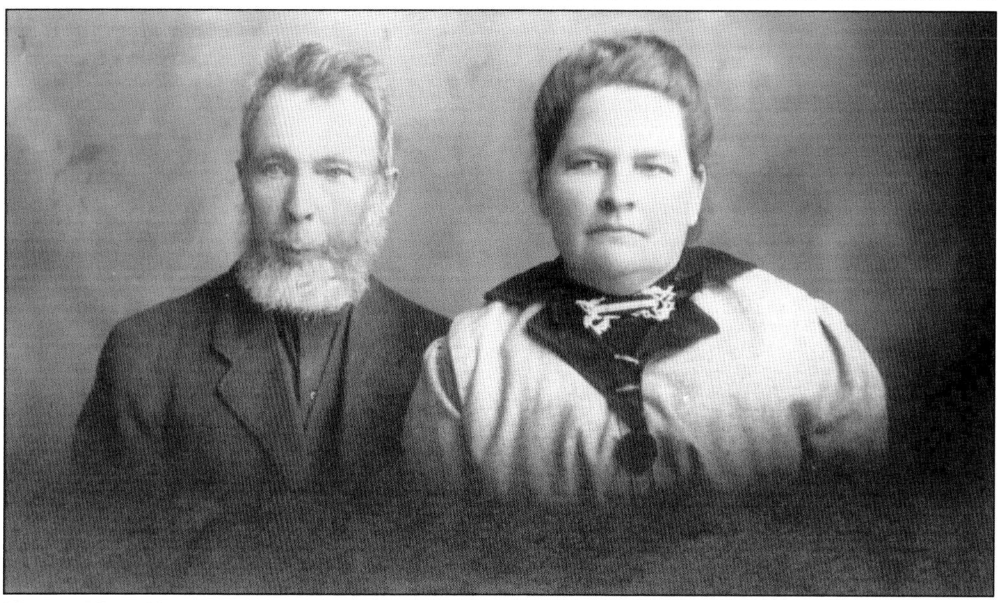

HENRY NEW YEAR AND LUCINDA E. GRIFFITH NORRIS. Henry New Year Norris was born on New Year's Day in 1845, thereby earning his unusual moniker. In 1866, he left his hometown in Illinois for Texas by skating down a frozen river. A mechanic and carpenter, he helped to build many homes and stores in Aledo. (Courtesy of Evlyn Wiley Broumley.)

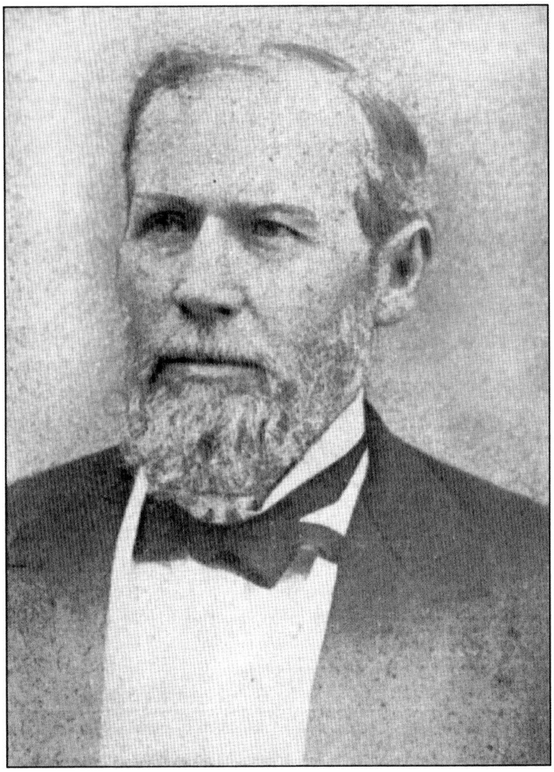

JUDGE A. J. HOOD. Born in 1820, South Carolina native Azariah Jesse Hood migrated to Cherokee County, Texas, around 1846. A few years later, after representing that area during two terms of the state legislature, he moved his family to Parker County, opened a law office in Weatherford, and later served as district judge. At the height of Comanche raiding, he joined Col. John R. Baylor's expedition and served as colonel. (Courtesy of Evlyn Wiley Broumley.)

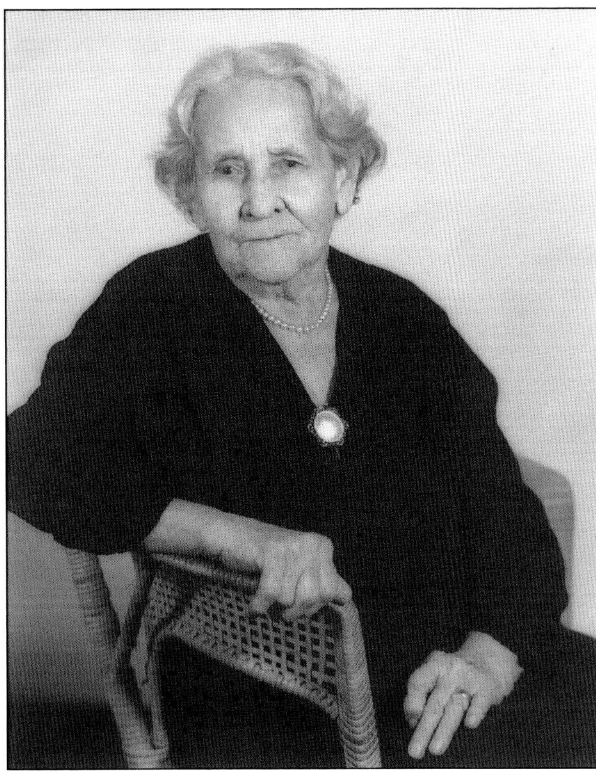

ELIZABETH HOOD SIMPSON, 1940s. The daughter of A. J. Hood lived well into her 90s and recounted tales of interaction with Comanches and Kiowas during the early days of the county. One of her sons, William Hood Simpson, led the Ninth Army during World War II and was promoted to a four-star general for his outstanding record. (Courtesy of Jackie McLennan.)

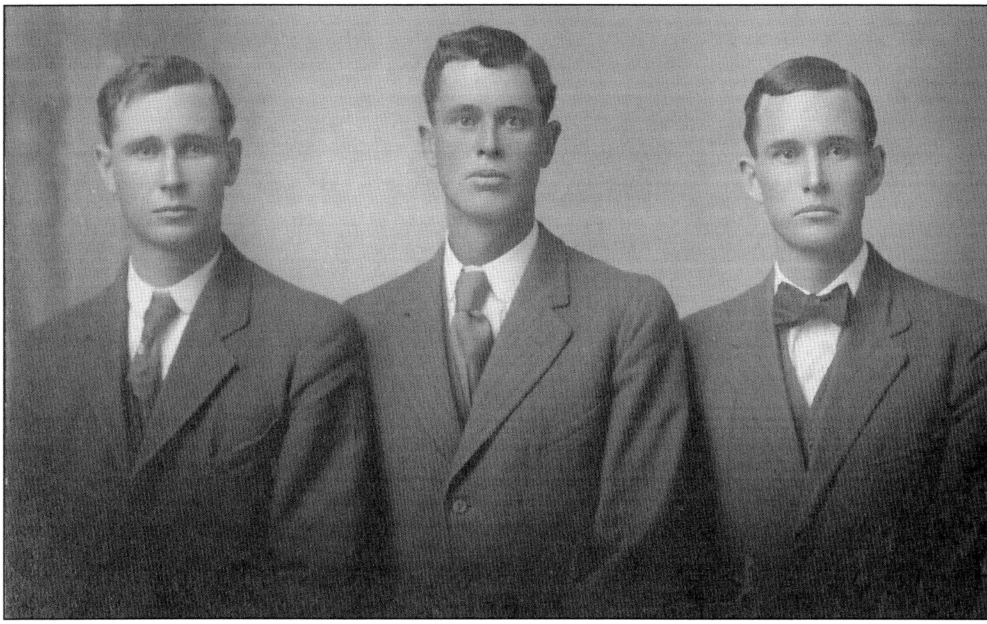

The Hood Boys. From left to right, Constant, Jesse, and Bruce Hood, pictured around 1905, were the sons of Constant, settler A. J. Hood's son, and Constant's wife, Elizabeth. (Courtesy of Jackie McLennan.)

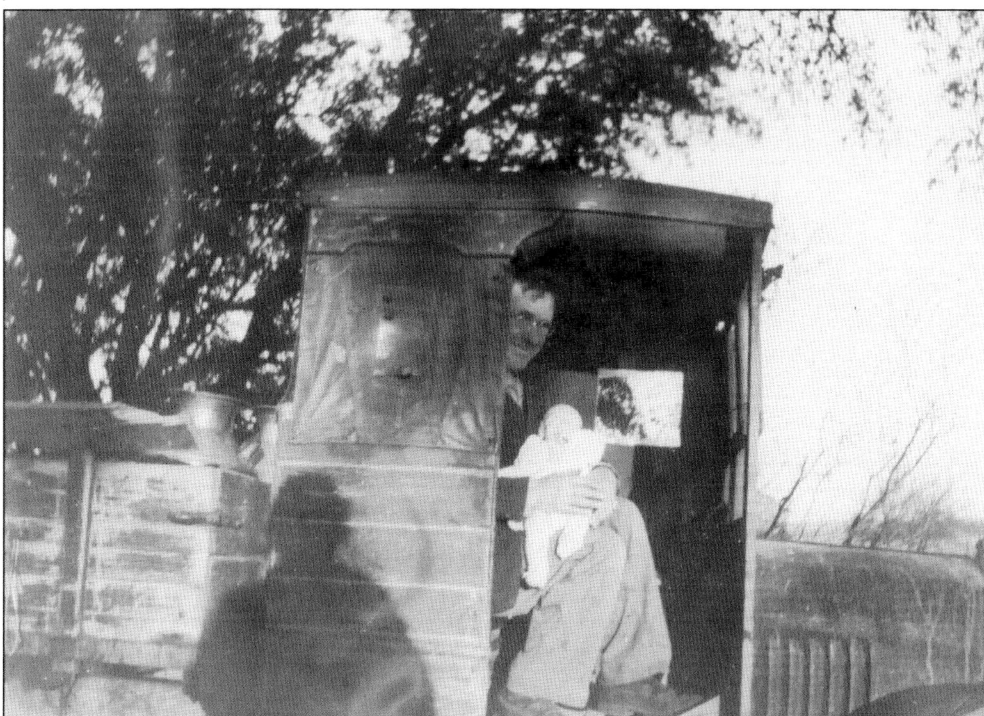

John McGlinchey and Neil Collins. After driving cattle for Union forces during the Civil War, McGlinchey arrived in eastern Parker County around 1878 and lived in the Center community. He is pictured here with his infant nephew in January 1927. (Courtesy of Don Collins.)

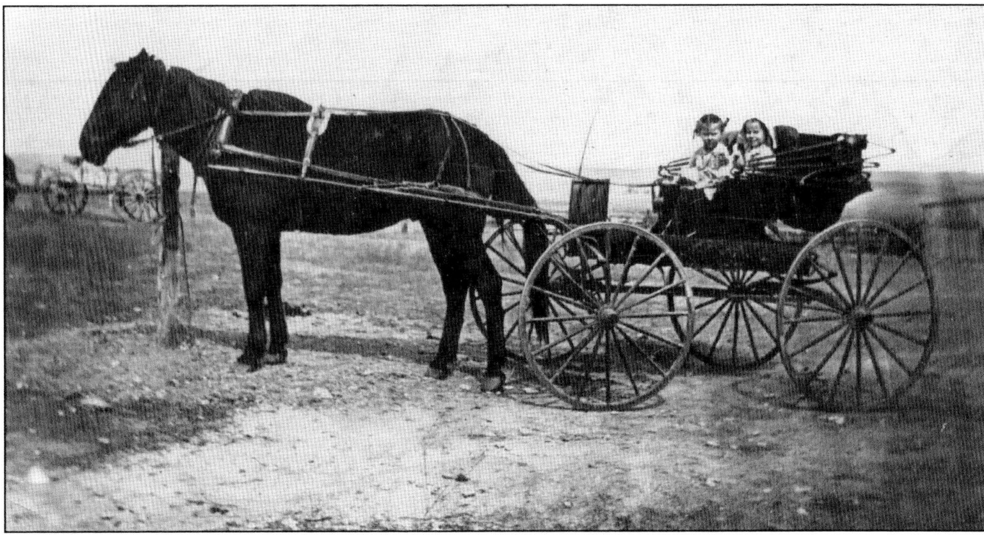

Bettie (Left) and Annie Reynolds. The girls, daughters of T. W. and Louisa Froman Reynolds, were the granddaughters of A. S. "Bid" Froman, who died in a highly publicized 1891 shoot-out with Will Rivers. Both men died, and the *Weatherford Democrat* reported, "Both men stood well." (Courtesy of Homer Norris.)

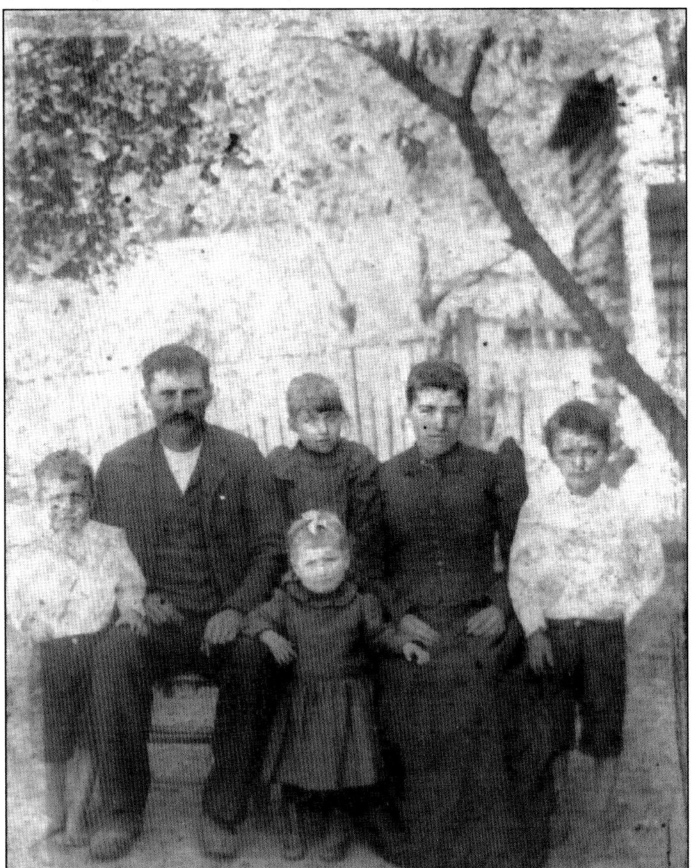

John Morgan Ballow Family, 1896. Traveling from Boone County, Kentucky, in a covered wagon, the Ballows settled near Bear Creek along present-day Goforth Road. Listed as a chicken peddler in the U.S. Census records, Ballow farmed and raised poultry and hogs until his death in 1936. Shown here, from left to right, are William Jackson, John Morgan, daughters Evy and Osie, Sallie Crain, and Ferdinand. (Courtesy of Vickie Ballow Slagle.)

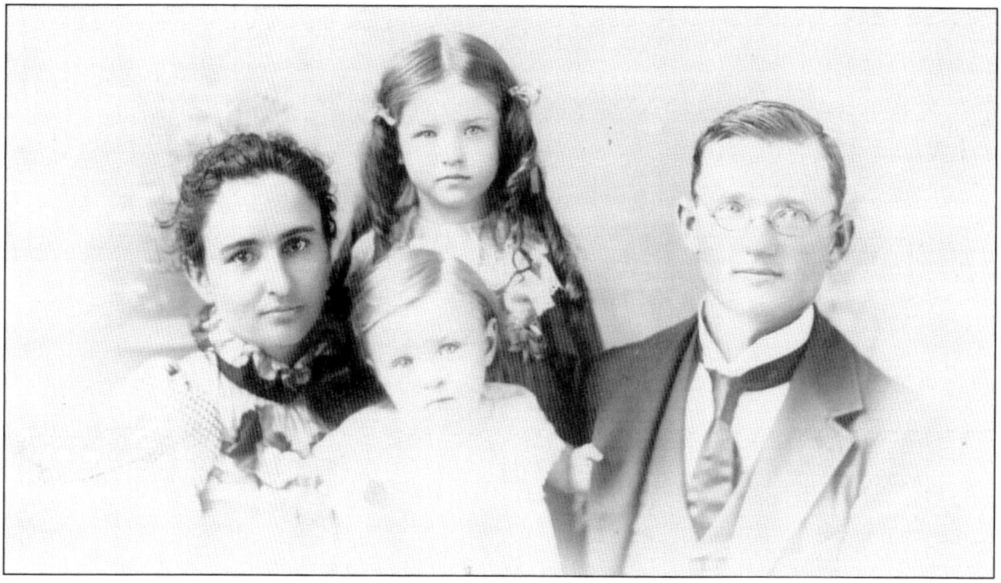

C. E. Bloss and Family. Bloss taught at the Aledo School in the early 20th century. He is pictured here with his wife, Dixie; daughter, Mary; and son, Paul. (Courtesy of Vickie Ballow Slagle.)

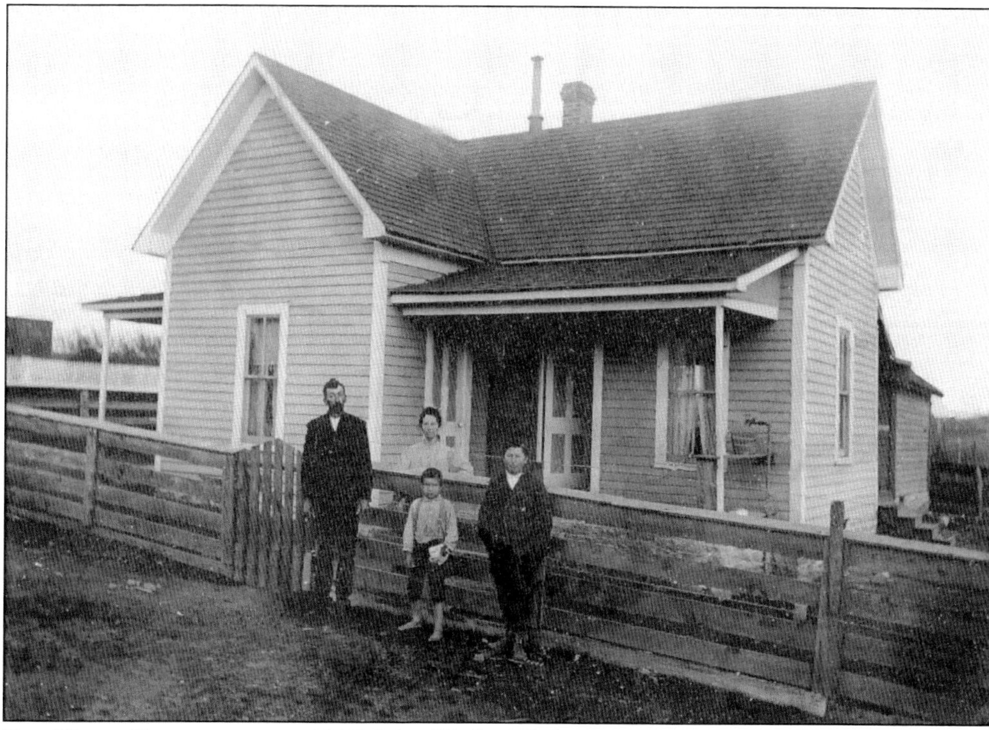

The Wallis Family, around 1905. John Wesley Wallis arrived in eastern Parker County around the late 1880s or early 1890s. He and his wife, Octavia, owned a 200-acre farm in Annetta and a home in Aledo, where he also worked as a blacksmith on the east end of North Front Street. The family moved to the farm when the boys were old enough to ride their horse to the Aledo School. Pictured are, from left to right, Wallis, Clyde, Octavia, and Claude. The J. J. Sears building can be seen in the background of the photograph. (Courtesy of Mason Wallis.)

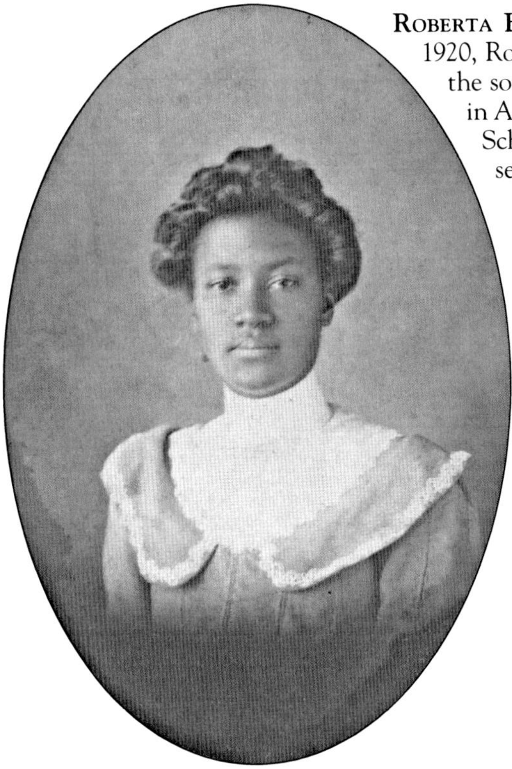

Roberta Evelyn Payne Gratts, around 1903. By 1920, Roberta would be married to Lawson Gratts II, the son of Buffalo Soldier Lawson Gratz, and living in Annetta. The couple's children attended Swann School, a nearby African American school, during segregation. (Courtesy of Josef Gratts.)

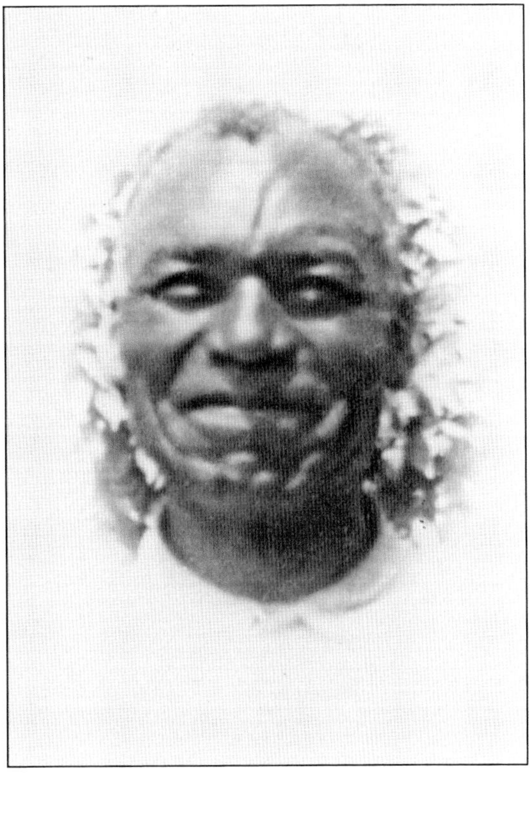

Lawson Gratts II. Born in 1883 to Civil War veteran and Buffalo Soldier Lawson Gratz and wife Rosa, Lawson became a respected farmer in the Annetta area. He died in 1953. (Courtesy of Josef Gratts.)

THE FARMER FAMILY. Present-day Farmer Road, or FM 3325, is named for the early Mary's Creek settler John D. Farmer. Shown here are the Farmer children in 1894—Inez, Tom, and baby Louie. Inez died soon after the portrait was made. (Courtesy of Mary Lynne Bigby Jones.)

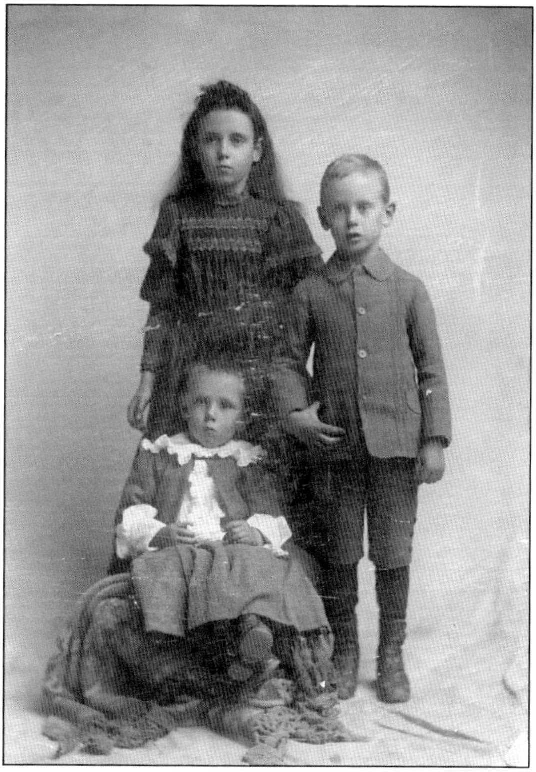

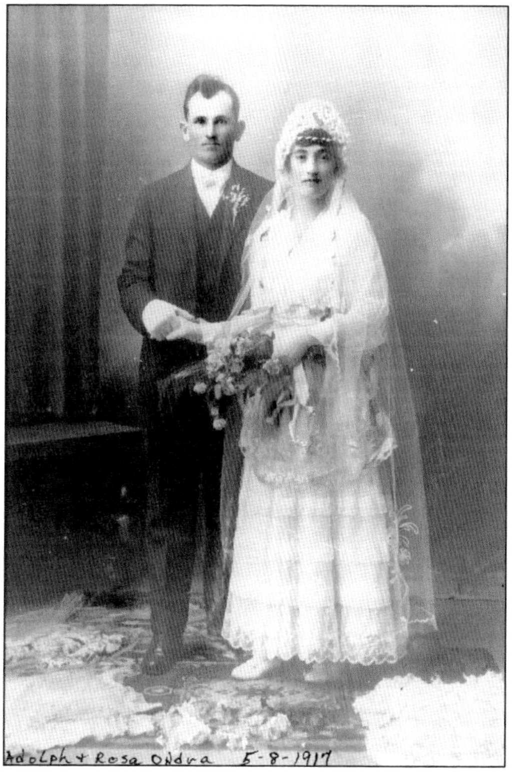

ADOLF AND ROSA ONDRA. Ondra emigrated from Austria and met his wife in Parker County. The couple had seven children and lived in the Dicey community before settling in Aledo. The couple is shown in their 1917 wedding portrait. (Courtesy of Josephine Ondra King.)

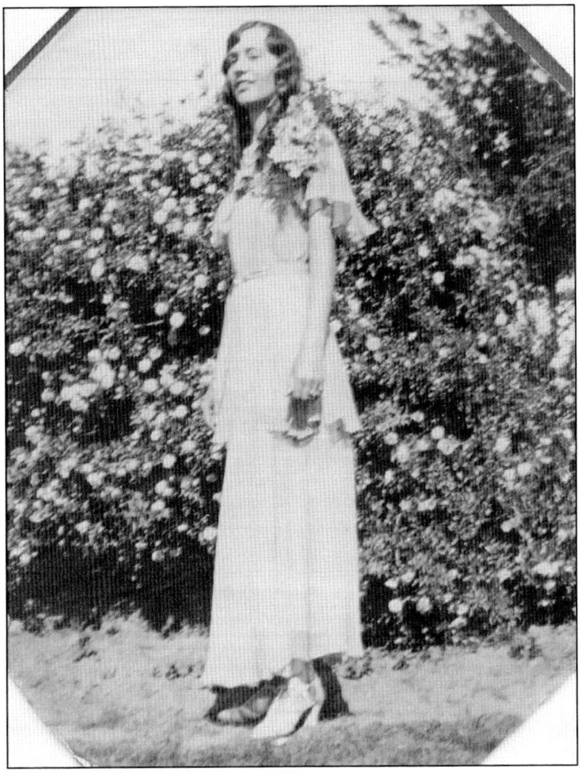

ELVA MAE MITCHELL RAY, 1932. Pictured here in her high school graduation portrait, Elva married Hubert Owen Ray. Hubert's ancestor Jeremiah Ray settled in eastern Parker County soon after the Civil War. One of his former slaves from Georgia recognized the Ray mules while Jeremiah was buying supplies from Fort Worth, sat on the back of the wagon until his return, and accompanied Ray back to Parker County. The man and his family became one of Annetta's founding families. (Courtesy of Roy Ray.)

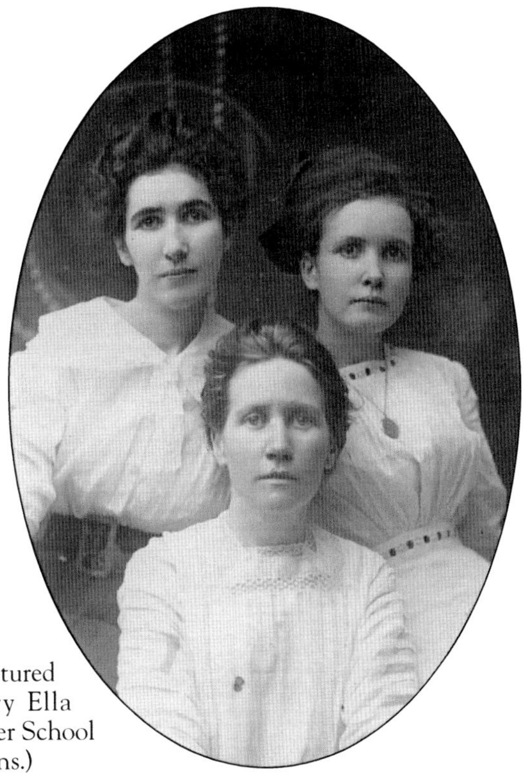

McGLINCHEY DAUGHTERS, AROUND 1908. Pictured are Sallie (left), Anne (right), and Mary Ella McGlinchey. Mary would later teach at Center School and Aledo Academy. (Courtesy of Don Collins.)

Two

SCHOOL DAYS

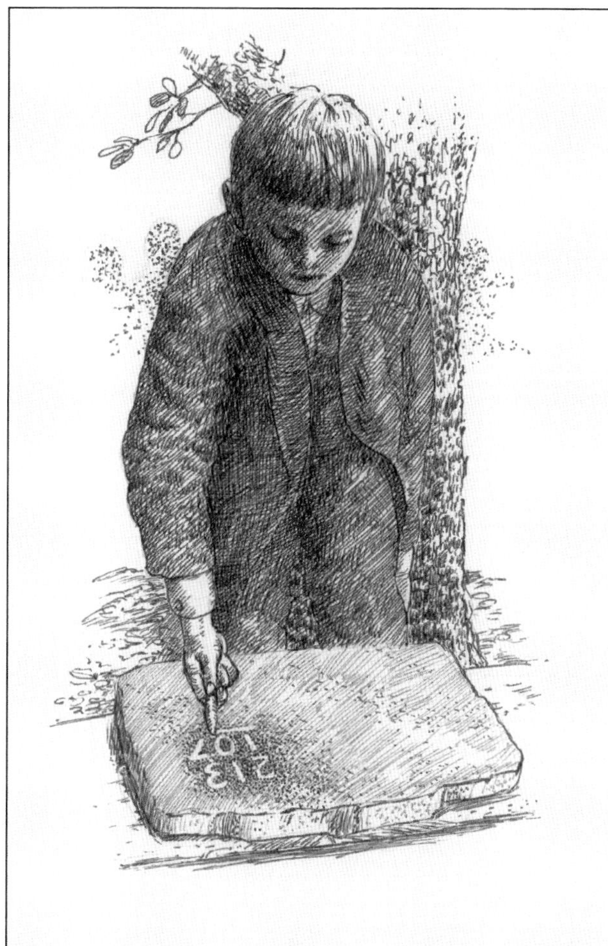

EARLY SCHOOLS. One-room schools dotted the eastern Parker County landscape in the mid- and late-1800s. Thomas Ulvan Taylor, born in 1858 on South Bear Creek, attended the first school in southeastern Parker County, one held under a live oak tree. Nine children attended, sat on split log benches, and used flat rocks for slates. Taylor eventually became the first dean of the engineering school at the University of Texas at Austin. (Sketch by Homer Norris; courtesy of Homer Norris.)

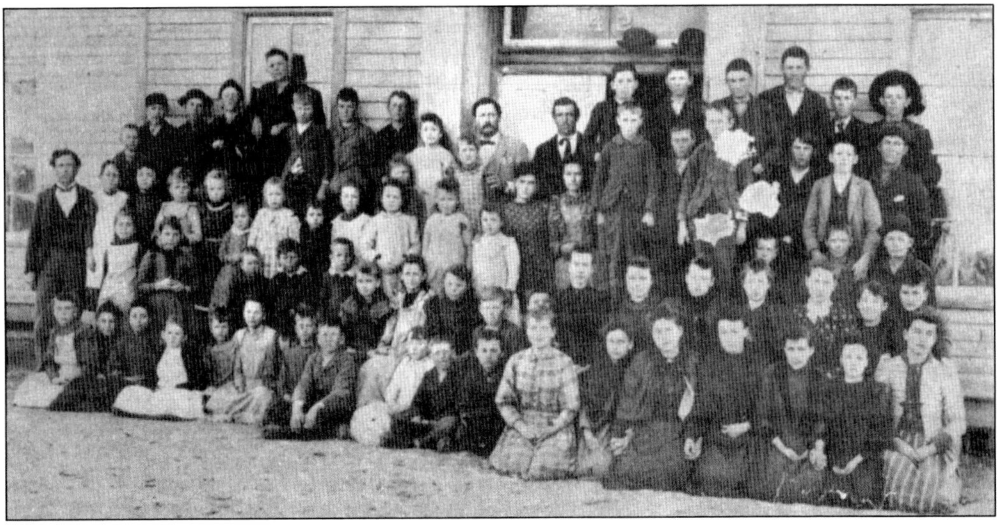

Aledo School, 1893. By the 1880s, Jim and Amanda Brown McConnell had donated land for a two-room school that educated more than 50 students. Teachers and brothers Paul Chastain and Claude Chastain are pictured here with the student body of 1893. From left to right are (first row) Anna Miles, ? Calahan, Beatrice Gill, Susie Davis, Nettie Shaver, Estie Glass, Mae Thompson, unidentified, ? May, Lula Underwood, ? May, Floyd Watson, Hallie Blackwell, Myrtle Jackson, Kate Tennison, unidentified, Louie Nichols, Lela Wingo, and Bert McCoy; (second row) Lottie Wilder, Dora Fox, Odis Wingo, Bun Milburn, Fielding Fields, Minnie Overmier, Allie Murchison, Jennie Milburn, two unidentified, Minnie Miles, Mae Milburn, Ada Shaver, Maud McConnel, Florence Carr, Ora Pitchford, and Camelia Nichols; (third row) Claude Chastain, Annie Brown, Alice Nichols, Myrtle Pitchford, Lena Fields, Myrtle Fox, Ora Witcher, Gussie Overmier, Nell Rhoade, Sadie Murchison, Willie Shaver, Clara Watson, unidentified, ? Calahan, Tom Brown, Will Wingo, Ally Jackson, unidentified, Will Davis, and unidentified; (fourth row) Gordon Glass, Ed Davis, Clarence Watson, two unidentified, Loyd Glass, Tom Cagle, Walter Watson, Lulla Murchison, Addie Carr, Paul Chastain, Sam Shaver, three unidentified, Henry Fox, Dan Pitchford, and Odie Watson. (Courtesy of Bill and Leta Johnson Eastman.)

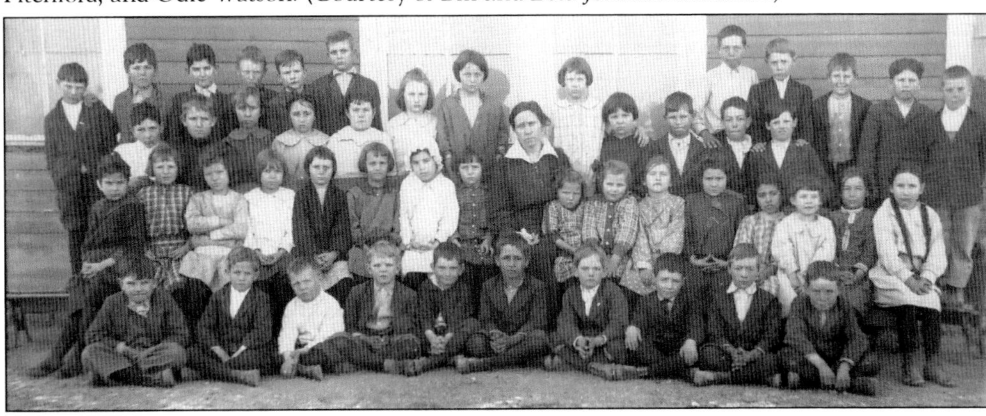

Aledo Academy, 1913–1914. Mary McGlinchey taught classes at Center School and then at Aledo School, including this first-grade class. The building had been remodeled to include two classrooms, a coatroom, and a hall on the first floor. A partition on the second floor allowed the space to be used as two classrooms or as a large room suitable for plays and programs. The red building with white trim housed a library/music room under the belfry. (Collection of Esther Brown Gracy, pictured somewhere in the photograph; courtesy of Bill and Leta Johnson Eastman.)

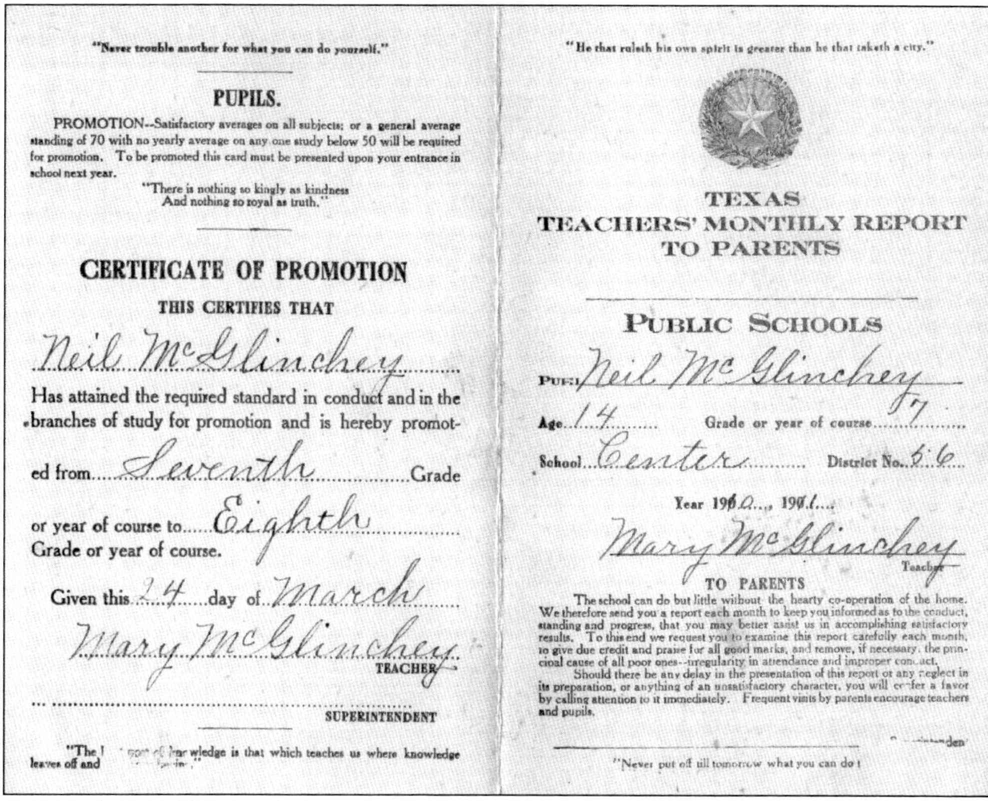
"Never trouble another for what you can do yourself."

PUPILS.

PROMOTION--Satisfactory averages on all subjects; or a general average standing of 70 with no yearly average on any one study below 50 will be required for promotion. To be promoted this card must be presented upon your entrance in school next year.

"There is nothing so kingly as kindness
And nothing so royal as truth."

CERTIFICATE OF PROMOTION

THIS CERTIFIES THAT

Neil McGlinchey

Has attained the required standard in conduct and in the branches of study for promotion and is hereby promoted from Seventh Grade or year of course to Eighth Grade or year of course.

Given this 24 day of March

Mary McGlinchey
TEACHER

SUPERINTENDENT

"The [illegible] of knowledge is that which teaches us where knowledge leaves off and [illegible]."

"He that ruleth his own spirit is greater than he that taketh a city."

TEXAS
TEACHERS' MONTHLY REPORT
TO PARENTS

PUBLIC SCHOOLS

Pupil Neil McGlinchey

Age 14 Grade or year of course 7

School Center District No. 56

Year 1910, 1911

Mary McGlinchey
Teacher

TO PARENTS

The school can do but little without the hearty co-operation of the home. We therefore send you a report each month to keep you informed as to the conduct, standing and progress, that you may better assist us in accomplishing satisfactory results. To this end we request you to examine this report carefully each month, to give due credit and praise for all good marks, and remove, if necessary, the principal cause of all poor ones--irregularity in attendance and improper conduct.

Should there be any delay in the presentation of this report or any neglect in its preparation, or anything of an unsatisfactory character, you will confer a favor by calling attention to it immediately. Frequent visits by parents encourage teachers and pupils.

Superintendent

"Never put off till tomorrow what you can do [illegible]"

Center School Report Card, 1910. Neil McGlinchey earned high marks as a 14-year-old seventh-grade student in Mary McGlinchey's class at Center School. The school was located in the Center community, between present-day FM1187 and Kelly Road, near the Reynolds and McGlinchey homes. The influence of the farm-based economy is reflected in the five-month school calendar that allowed students to assist in seasonal harvests. (Courtesy of Don Collins.)

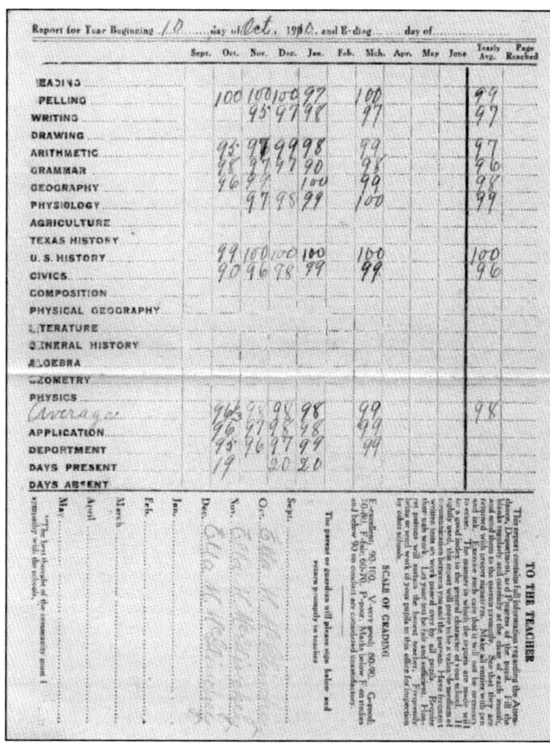
Report for Year Beginning 10 day of Oct. 1910, and Ending ... day of ...

	Sept.	Oct.	Nov.	Dec.	Jan.	Feb.	Mch.	Apr.	May	June	Yearly Avg.	Page Reached
Reading												
Spelling		100	100	100	97		100				99	
Writing			95	97	98		97				97	
Drawing												
Arithmetic		95	97	99	98		99				97	
Grammar		98	97	97	90		98				96	
Geography		96	99		100		99				98	
Physiology			97	98	99		100				99	
Agriculture												
Texas History												
U. S. History		99	100	100	100		100				100	
Civics		90	96	98	99		99				96	
Composition												
Physical Geography												
Literature												
General History												
Algebra												
Geometry												
Physics												
Average		96⅓	98	98	98		99				98	
Application		96	97	98	98		99					
Deportment		95	96	97	99		99					
Days Present		19		20	20							
Days Absent												

TO THE TEACHER

SCALE OF GRADING

The parent or guardian will please sign below and return promptly to teacher

Sept. Oct. Nov. Dec. Jan. Feb. March April May

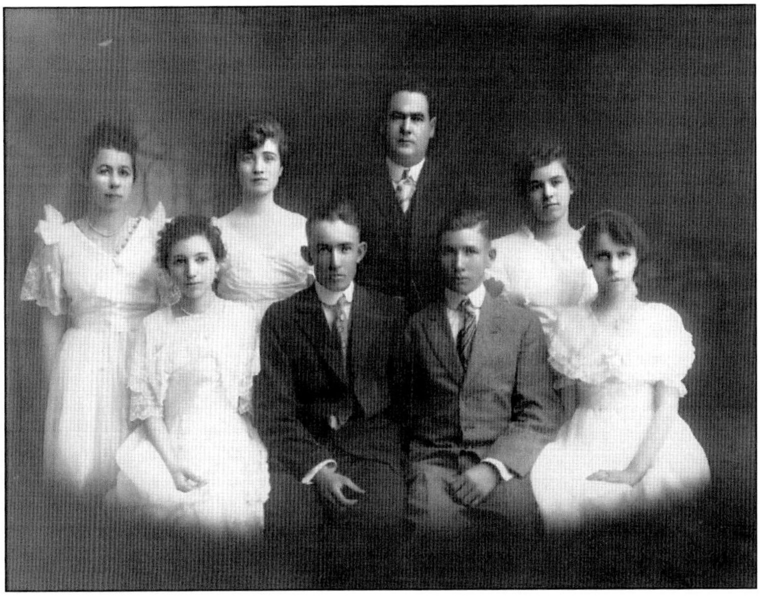

ALEDO ACADEMY CLASS OF 1917. From left to right are (first row) Leona Nichols, Raymond Brady, Zan McGlinchey, and Jewell Gill; (second row) Marie Farris, Myrtle Rickard, Prof. J. N. Johnston, and Thelma Wilkerson. (Courtesy of Nelda McGlinchey.)

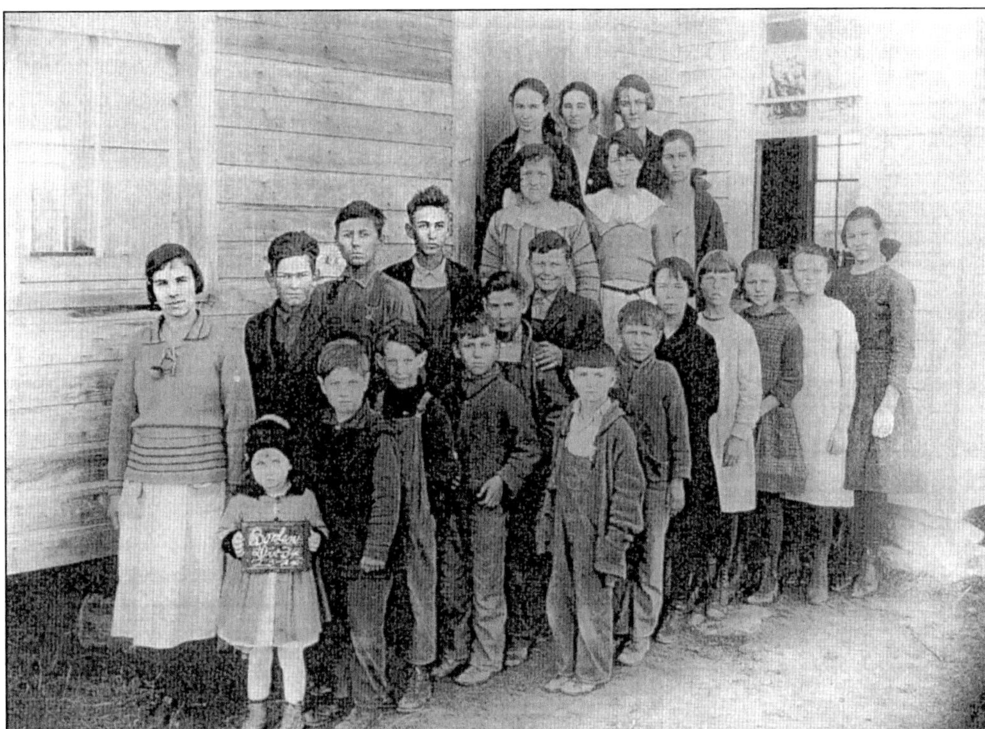

BORDEN SCHOOL, 1923–1924. When the Borden School closed, students attended Dicey School. The small student in front is holding a chalkboard that reads "Borden Dicey, 23–24." Pictured from left to right are (first row) Nathan Vick, Norbert Kubelka, Frances Prichard, Gertrude Spain, Julie Kubelka, Artie Snider, and Rosa Kubelka; (second row) Corine Fawks, Johnny Crenshaw, Roy Spain, Robert Kubelka, Weldon Vick, and Joseph Kubelka; (third row) Thelma Fawks, C. B. Borden, Frankie Kubelka, John Vick, Lee Snider, Virginia Spain, and Fannie Vick; (fourth row) Rosanna Vick, Eva Vick, and Virginia Prichard. (Courtesy of Vickie Slagle/EPCGHS.)

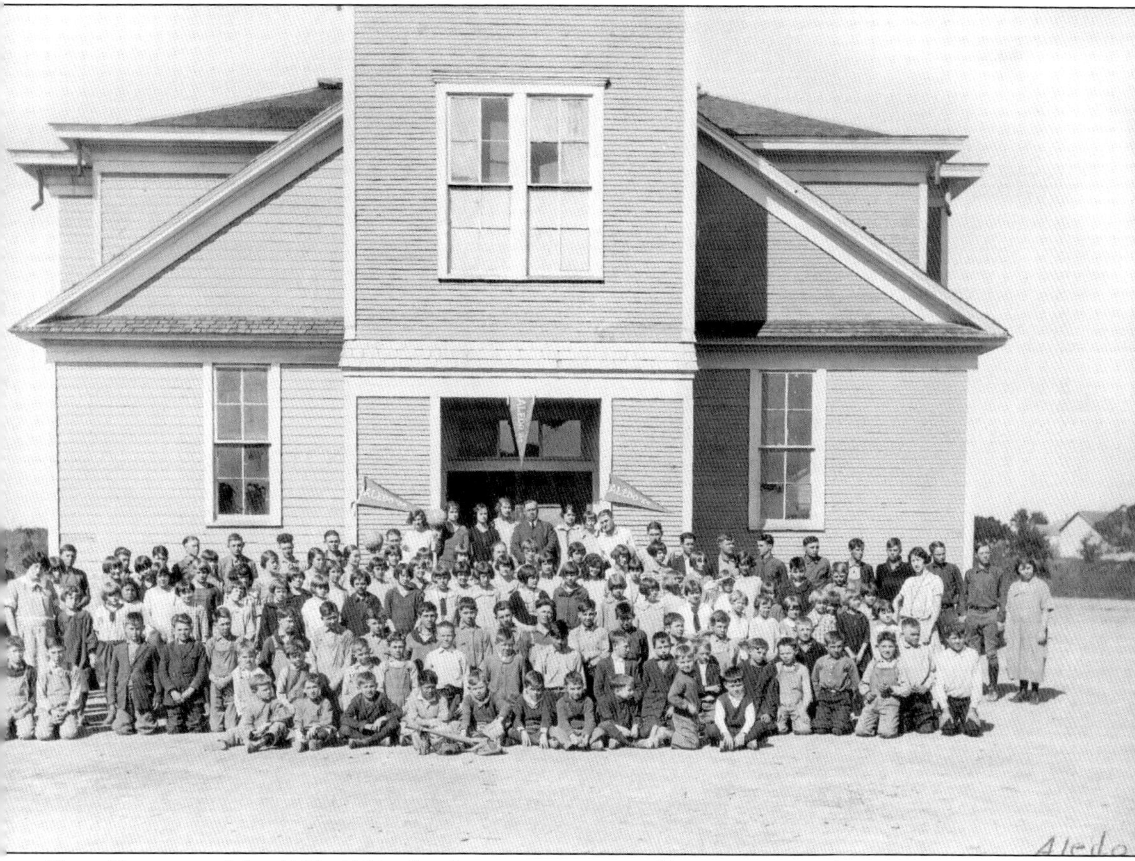

FOND FAREWELL. The 1923–1924 school year was a memorable one. Principal A. M. Sprinkle was asked to resign after teaching the concept of cellular evolution in his class, and the old plank school served its last students. The following school year, a three-story brick structure opened its doors to a new generation of students. Principal James W. Ward and teachers Thelma Bagley, Estelle Bagley, Louise Gilbert, and Katherine Milburn comprised the faculty. (Esther Brown Gracy collection; courtesy of Bill and Leta Johnson Eastman.)

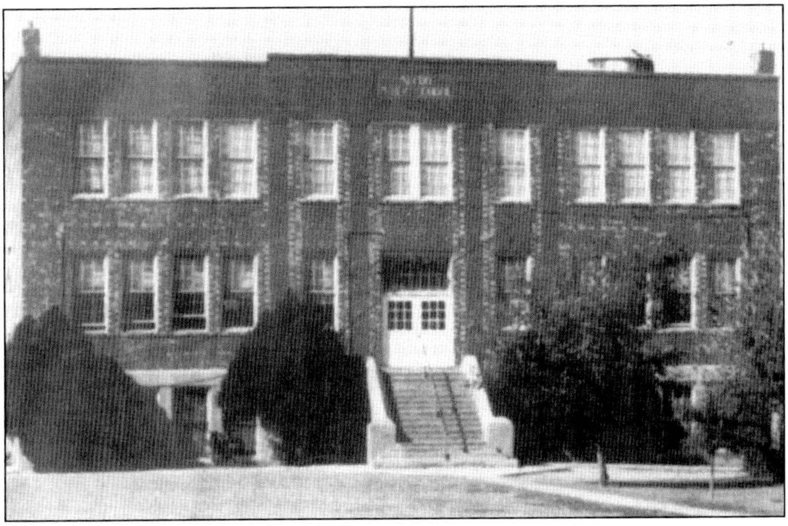

Aledo School. The *Weekly Herald* in June 1924 praised the Aledo community for the spacious new school building that cost $25,000 to build. This photograph was taken in 1957. (Courtesy of Vickie Ballow Slagle.)

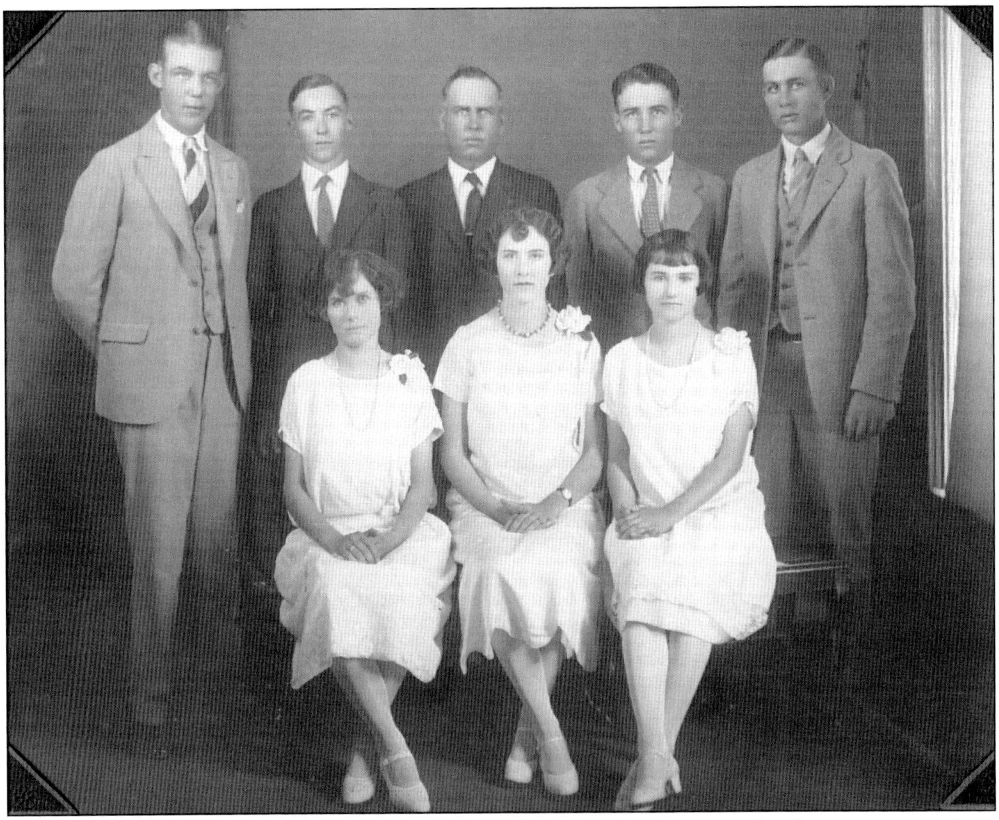

The Class of 1925. Those who sat for this graduation portrait were the first to accept their diplomas on the stage of the new school. More than 200 students enjoyed the modern building's amenities, which included eight classrooms, a homemaking room, a library, an auditorium, a laboratory, a shop, restrooms, two coal rooms, and a Delco system that provided electricity. Seen here from left to right are (first row) Verda Lee Sutton, Esther Brown, and Leanna Bloss; (second row) B. F. McMurray, M. B. Wilkerson, Principal Ward, Rhea Kelley, and Noel Reynolds. (Courtesy of Bill and Leta Eastman.)

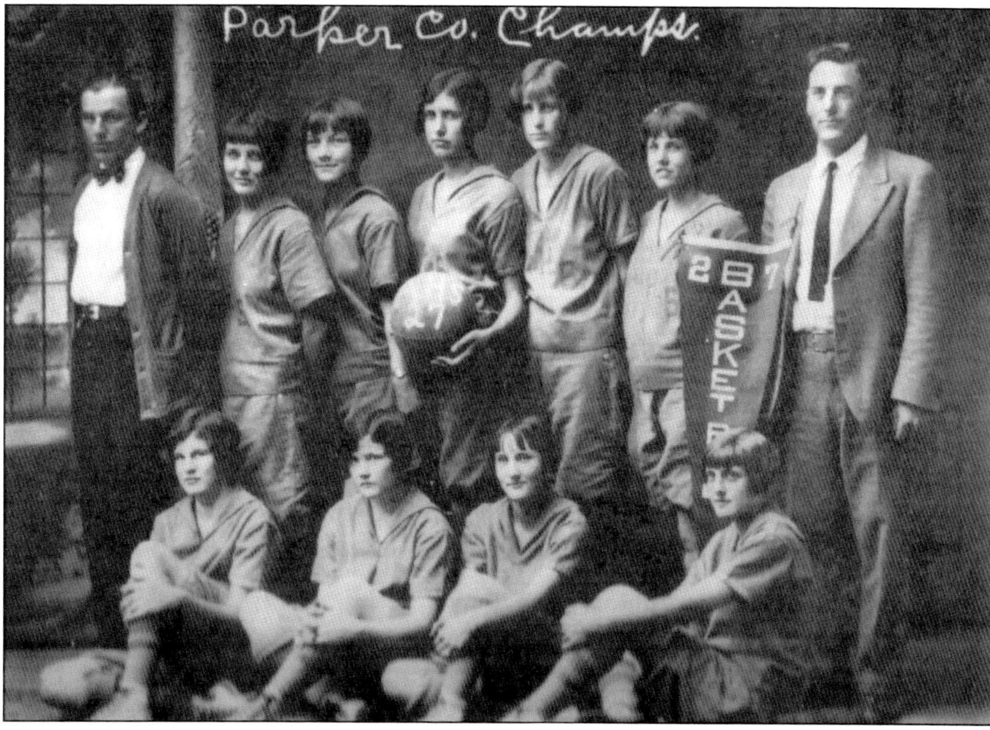

State Champions. The Aledo girls' basketball team won the 1927 state championship. Three players earned All-State honors: Maureen Kelly, Gertrude Kelly, and Mamye Hardin. Other players were Mattie Kelly, Cleo Bennett, Ima Lucas, Bethany Frady, and Harriet Griffin. Grover McAlister coached the team, which played on an outdoor court. (Courtesy of Vickie Ballow Slagle.)

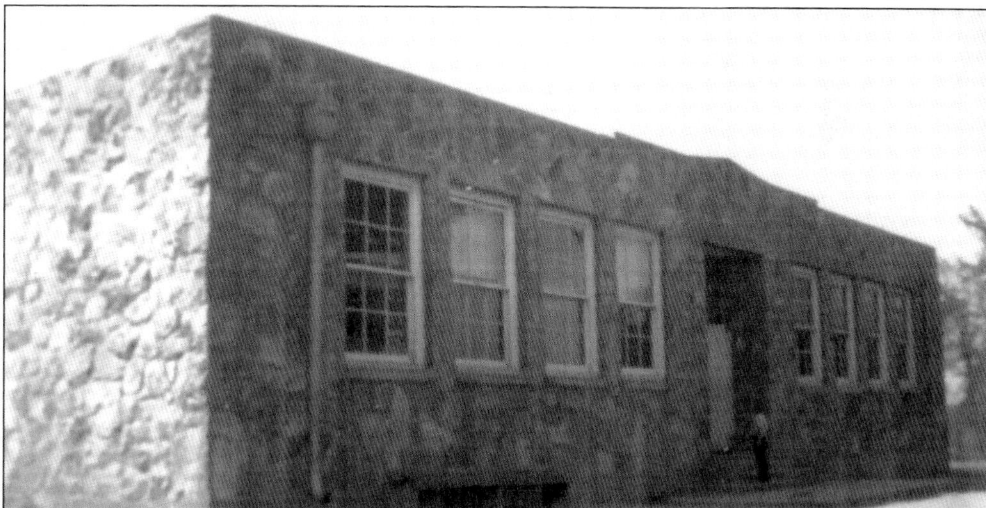

Annetta School. This undated photograph shows the third school built in the community, which contained two classrooms and an auditorium and stood adjacent to Annetta Methodist Church. The first school, a one-room building, was situated near Old Annetta Road, east of FM5. Its high windows with hinged shutters provided protection against possible raids by Native Americans. The modest structure was eventually moved and employed as a hay barn. The second school sat southwest of Airport Road and FM5. (Courtesy of Vickie Ballow Slagle.)

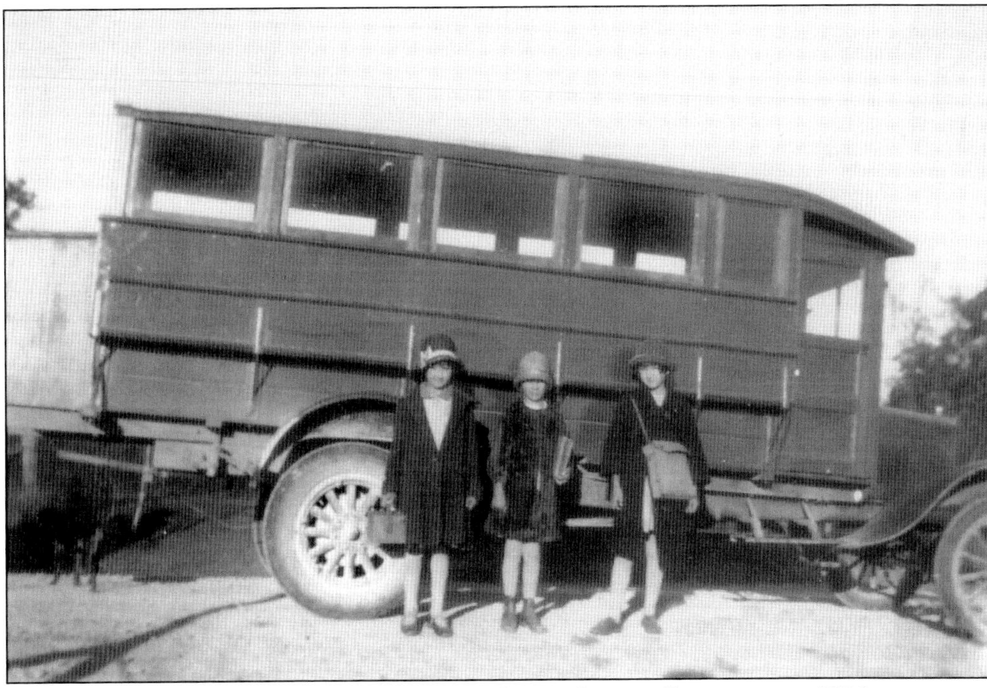

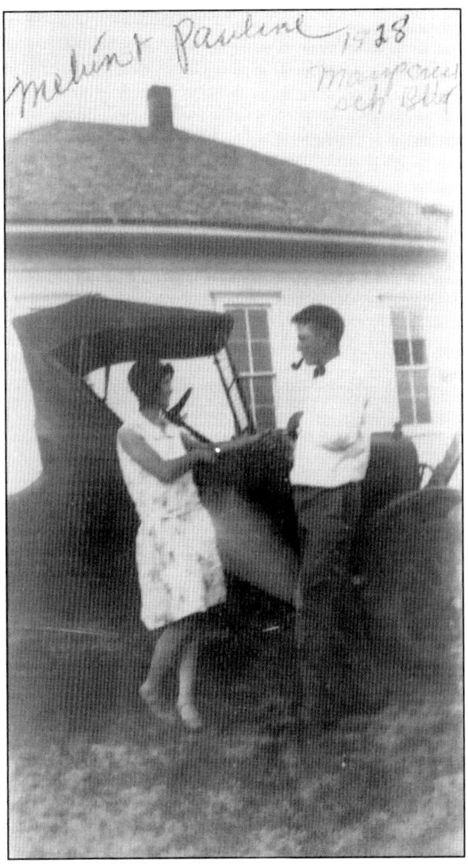

ALEDO SCHOOL BUS, AROUND 1928. From left to right, Alyne, Margaret, and Janie Ondra pose in front of the school bus, a converted Model T truck owned by Charlie Tallent, which also hauled hay. (Courtesy of Josephine Ondra King.)

PRAIRIE HILL SCHOOL, 1928. Students who lived in the Mary's Creek community near present-day Farmer Road, or FM 3325, attended Prairie Hill School, a small building situated to the east of the road and north of Old Weatherford Road. The original structure burned in 1903. Here, Melvin Wiley and Pauline Smith pose in front of the second school building. (Courtesy of Evlyn Wiley Broumley.)

AHS CLASS OF 1937. Aledo graduates pose with their teachers to mark the milestone. Pictured from left to right are (first row) ? Johnson, Charlie Smith, Clara Lee Ball, and Hata Lou Baker; (second row) Leroy Coder, Clyde Barnwell, Glen Eastman, teacher Floyd Bradshaw, James Edwards, Jack Burt, and Chester Wiley; (third row) Ira West and teacher Ed Wilhite. (Courtesy of Loweda Wood.)

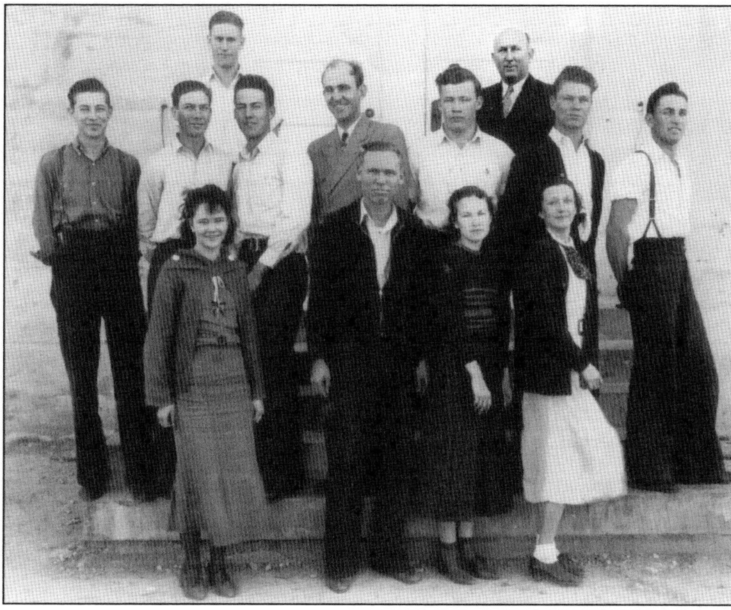

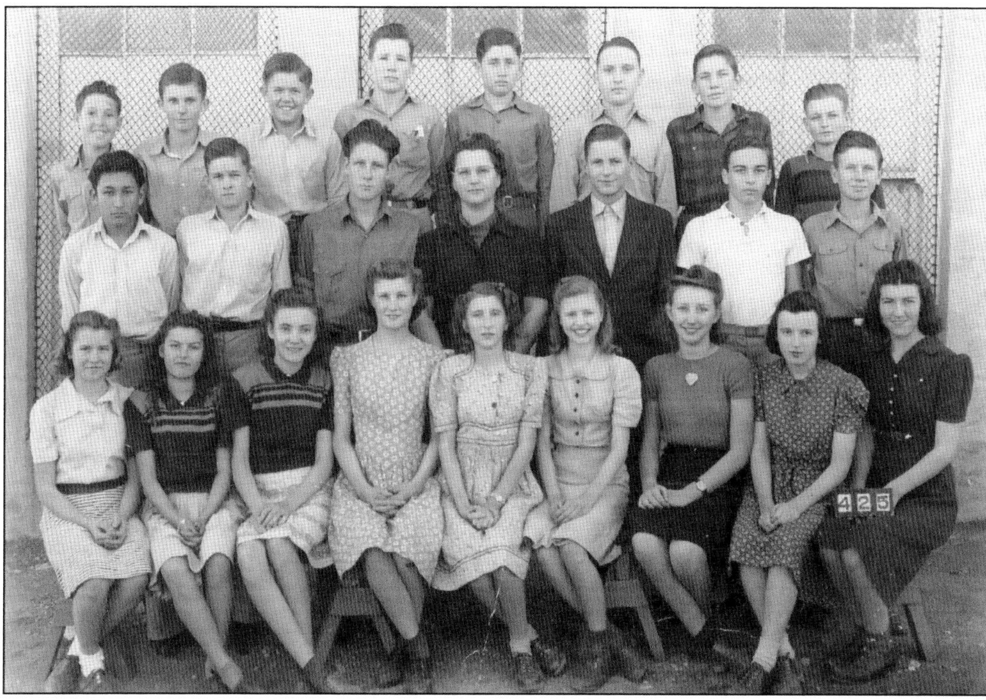

FUTURE SUPERINTENDENT. McAnally Middle School is named after a former student who became superintendent of the Aledo Independent School District. Charles McAnally is pictured here with his 1940s-era classmates. The class included, from left to right, (first row) Betty Lee Johnson, Nellie Hogan, Mary Frances Nichols, unidentified, Verna Shaw, Betty Lou Whitmire, Frances Hudson, Betsy Jo Dearing, and ? Paramore; (second row) unidentified, Glen Riley, Jack Wingo, teacher Mary Johnson (who later married Cortez Wiley), Frank Neverlik, J. C. Robertson, and Charles Norris; (third row) Marvin Blackwell, Billy Ed Ross, Charles McAnally, Billy Edwards, Jimmy Bishop, Clifford Farmer, Richard Pittman, and Paul Parkey. (Courtesy of Homer Norris.)

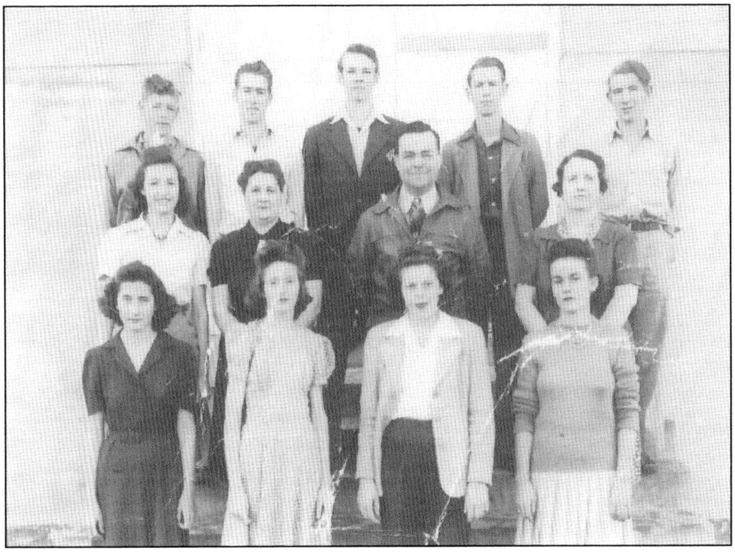

AHS Class of 1944. Pictured from left to right are (first row) Betty Goff, Betty Greenfield, Myrna Morten, and Billie Grace Carver; (second row) Faye Ames, Emma Ross, Willis Apple, and Vivian Davis; (third row) John Hogan, Clayton Wallis, Carl King, and two unidentified. (Courtesy of Loweda Wood.)

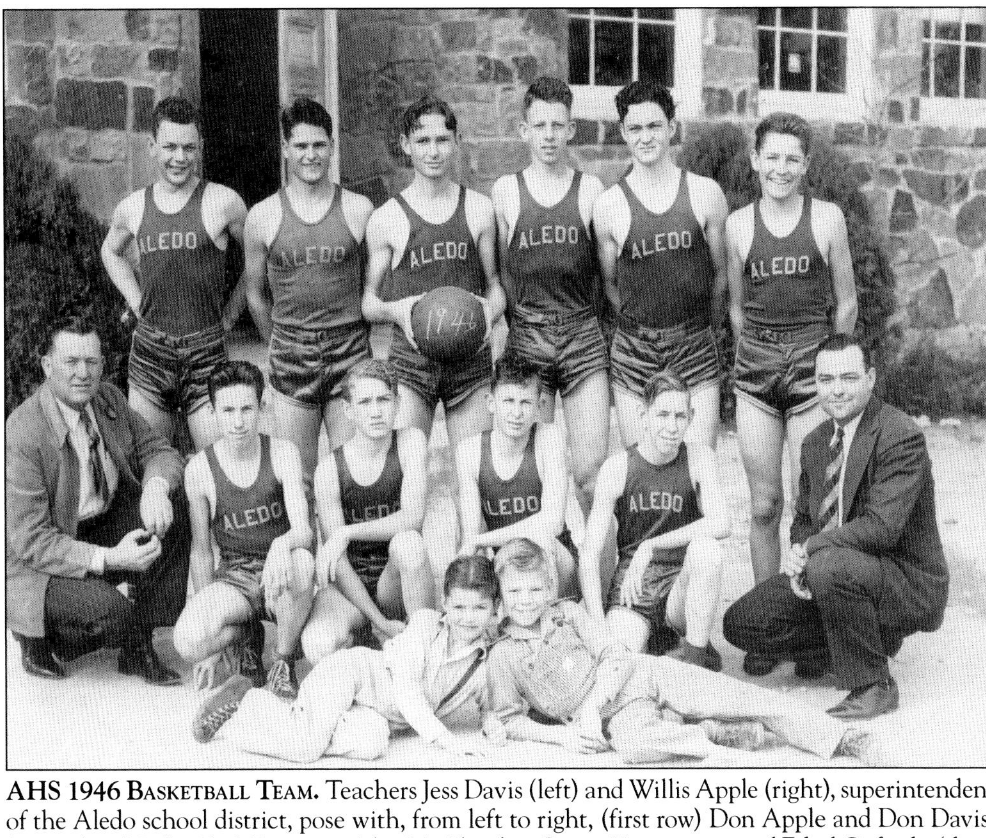

AHS 1946 Basketball Team. Teachers Jess Davis (left) and Willis Apple (right), superintendent of the Aledo school district, pose with, from left to right, (first row) Don Apple and Don Davis; (second row) Billy Clark Eastman, Alex McGlinchey, James Harrington, and Edsel Goforth; (third row) Billy Wayne Goodloe, Fred Johnson, Raymond King, Richard King, Junior Dixon, and Ted Reynolds. (Courtesy of Evlyn Wiley Broumley.)

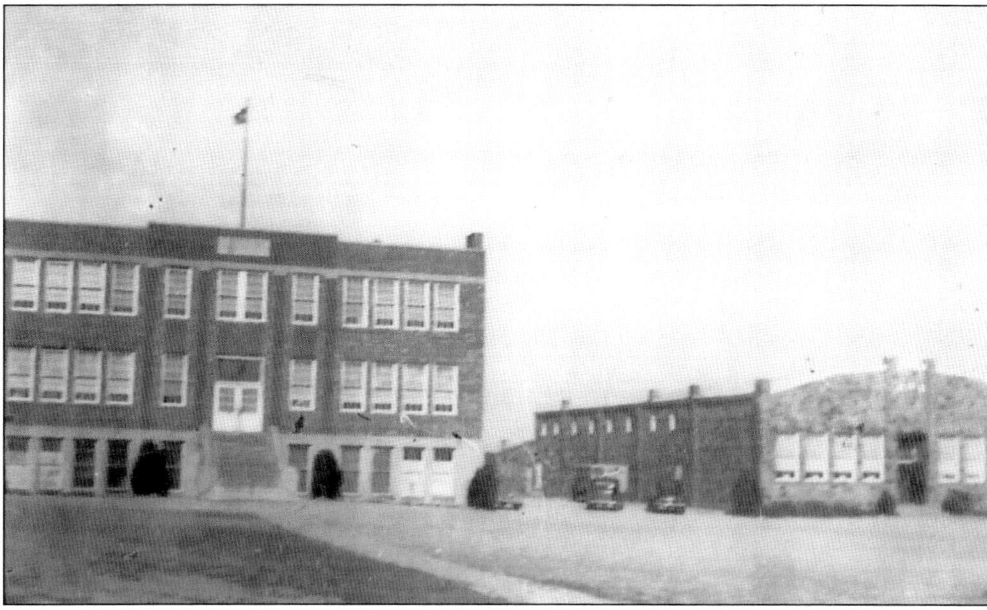

ALEDO HIGH SCHOOL AND THE OLD ROCK GYM. The two structures served Aledo ISD students for many years. A modern middle school now stands on the site. (Courtesy of Loweda Wood.)

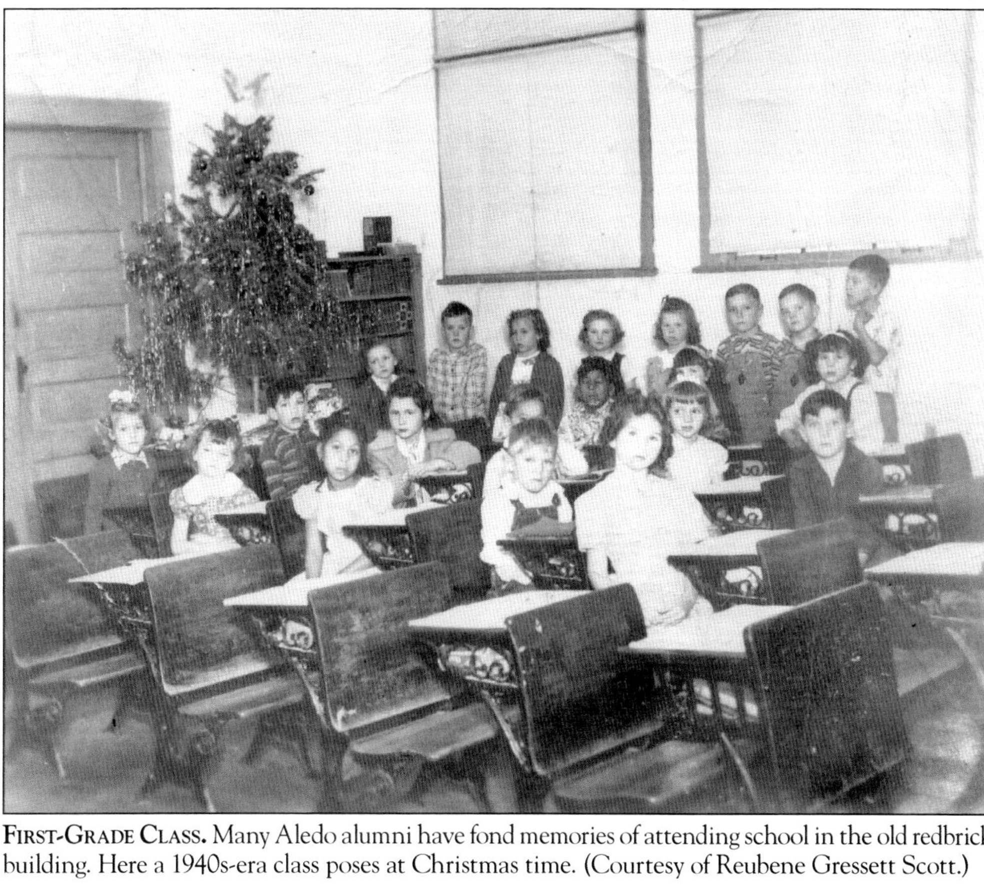

FIRST-GRADE CLASS. Many Aledo alumni have fond memories of attending school in the old redbrick building. Here a 1940s-era class poses at Christmas time. (Courtesy of Reubene Gressett Scott.)

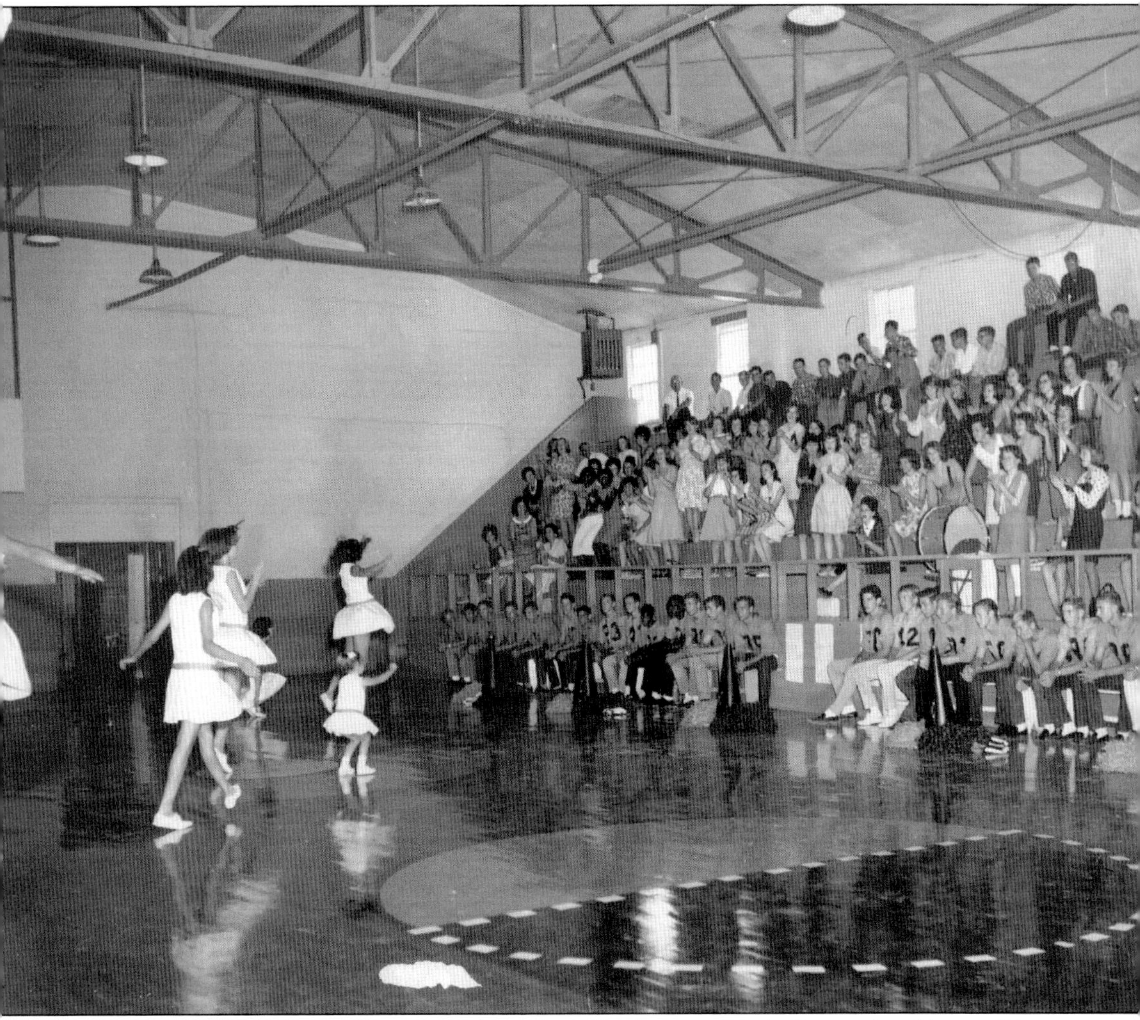

Pep Rally. Cheerleaders, fans, and athletes have fond memories of rallies in the old gym. (Courtesy of Reubene Gressett Scott.)

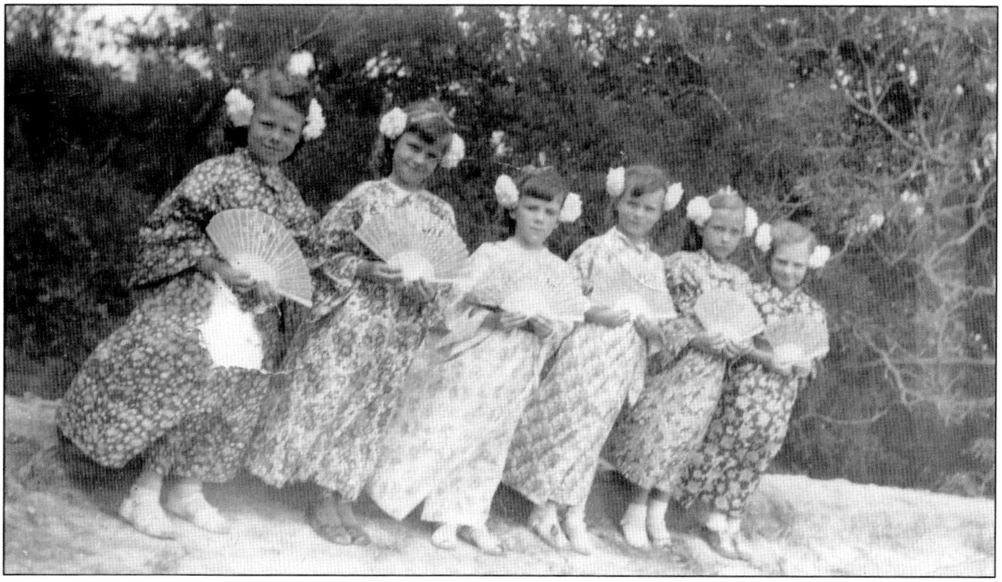

First-Grade Play, 1948. From left to right, the stars of the show were Judy Scott, Judy Bennett, Doris Heady, Margaret Parish, Virginia Miller, and Grace Coder. (Courtesy of Reubene Gressett Scott.)

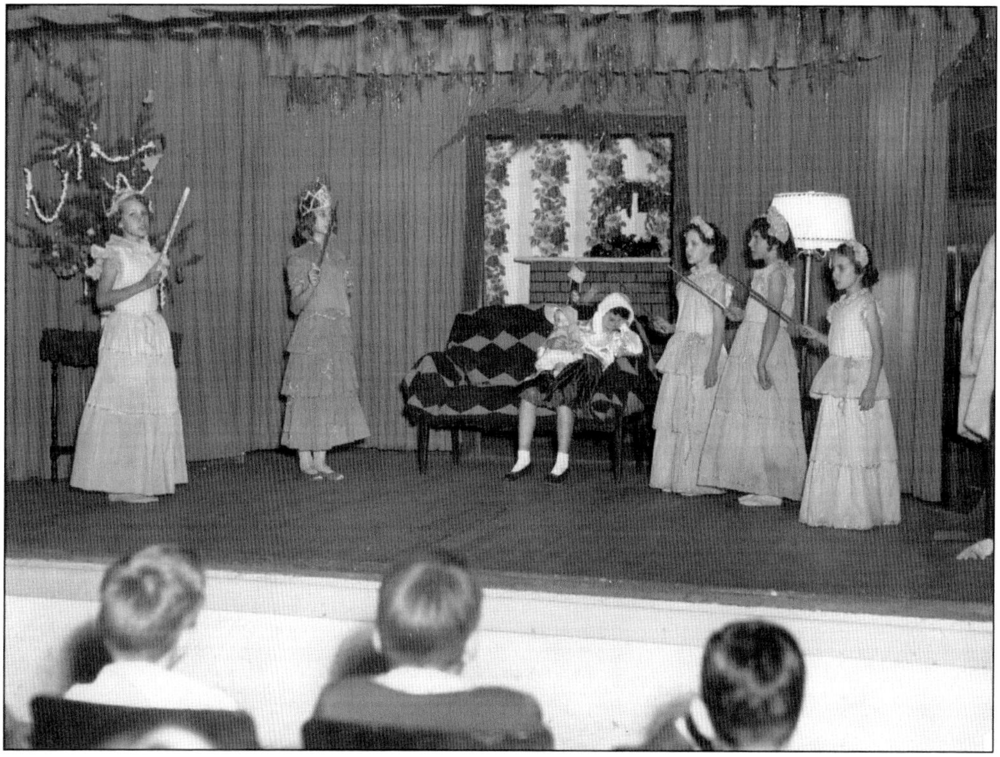

School Play. Fifth and sixth graders in a 1950 or 1951 Christmas production included, from left to right, Linda Morton (Gaskill), Lillian Seedig (Haile), Helen Bennett (Dill), Lou Collins, Mary Ann Kos (Beverung), and Fern Allen Jennings (Green). The girls' dresses were made of crepe paper; Lillian was the head of the fairies. (Courtesy of Vickie Slagle/EPCGHS.)

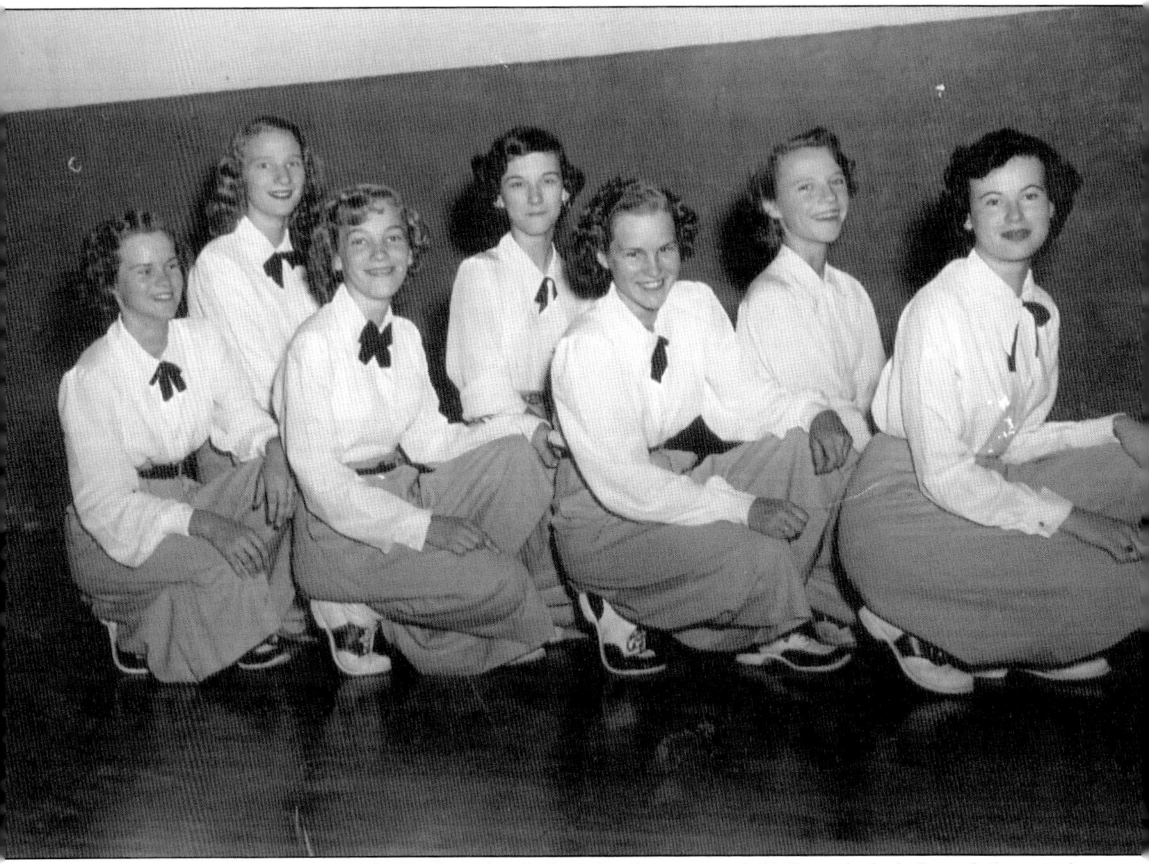

Saddle Shoe Gang. Aledo High School cheerleaders around 1951 included, from left to right, Lula Johnson, Carolyn Lee, Jan Griffin, Elizabeth Tyson, Leta Johnson, Vada Ames, and Nancy Curtis. (Courtesy of Vickie Ballow Slagle.)

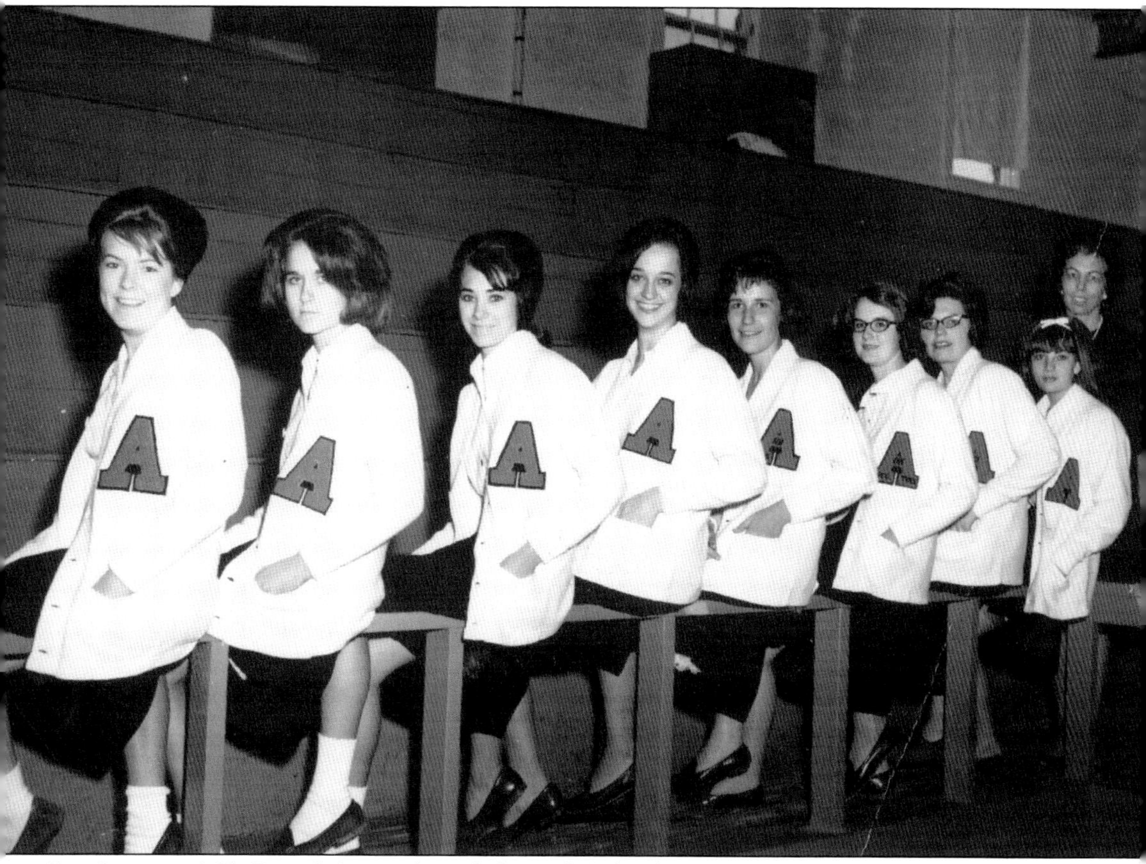

Pep Squad, 1965. From left to right, Aledo High School pep squad members included Betty Miller, Rebecca Allen, Mary Scott, Charlotte Woods, Peggy Edwards, Shirley Chandler, Janet Marshall, and Pam Whisenant. Sponsor Ann Reagan, at far right, also taught home economics. (Courtesy of Reubene Gressett Scott.)

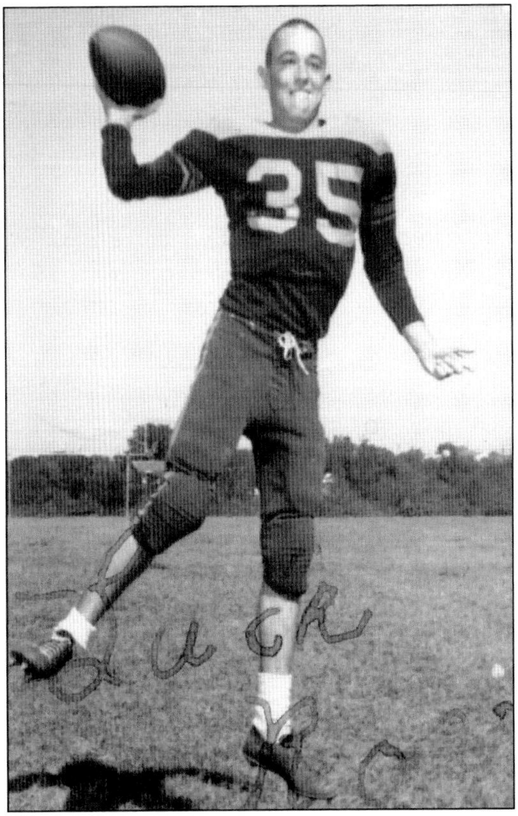

Football Star. Roy Ray played for the Bearcat football team from 1956 to 1960 and as starting quarterback from 1959 to 1960. (Courtesy of Reubene Gressett Scott.)

School Namesakes. Longtime Aledo ISD educators attended a school district board meeting in January 2000 during which schools were named for each. Pictured from left to right are Willard Stuard, Mattie Coder, Elaine Vandagriff, and Charles McAnally. (Courtesy of Kit Marshall.)

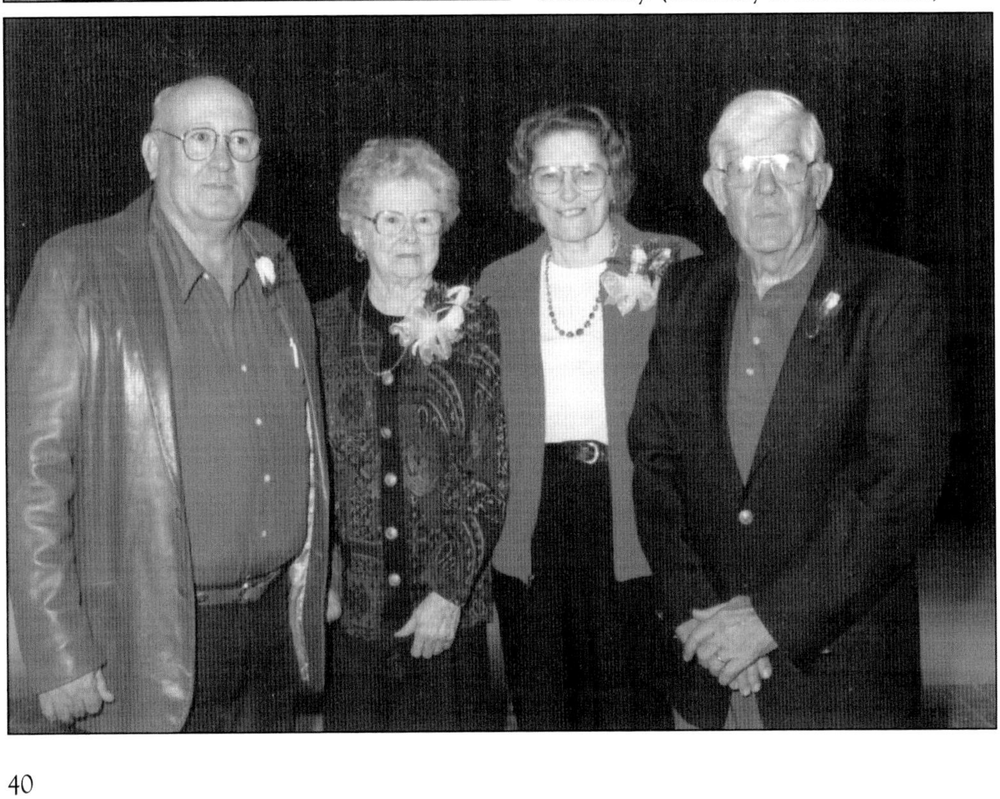

Three

CHURCH LIFE

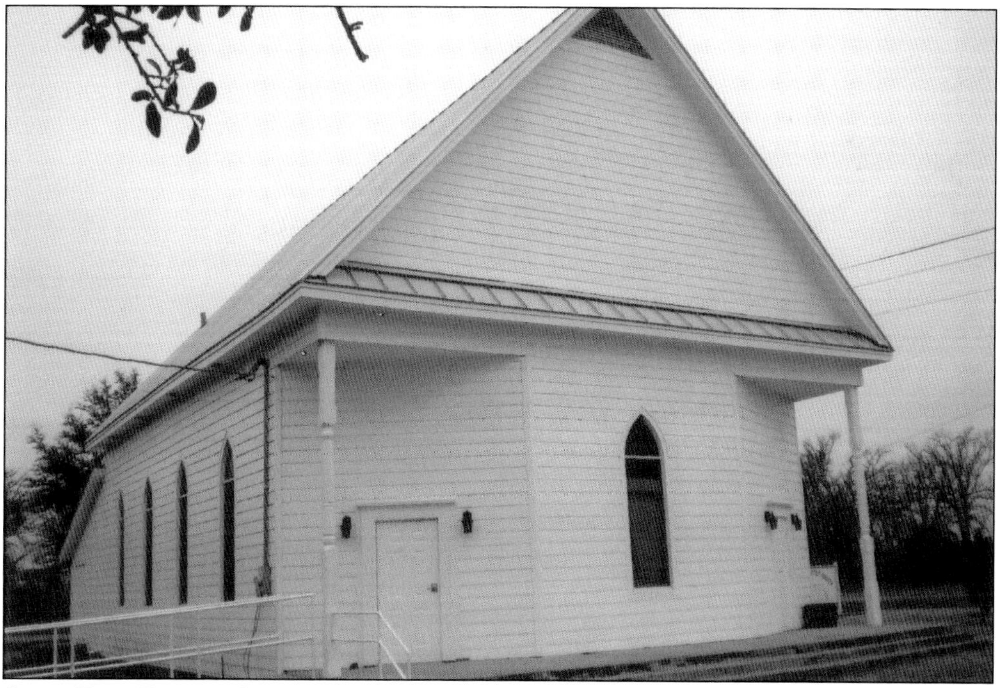

CLEAR FORK BAPTIST CHURCH. Organized in 1858, the congregation met in the home of Andy Green. Scant records remain, but the church has been a mainstay in the Dicey area since its inception. The current building was constructed around 1901. (Photograph by the author.)

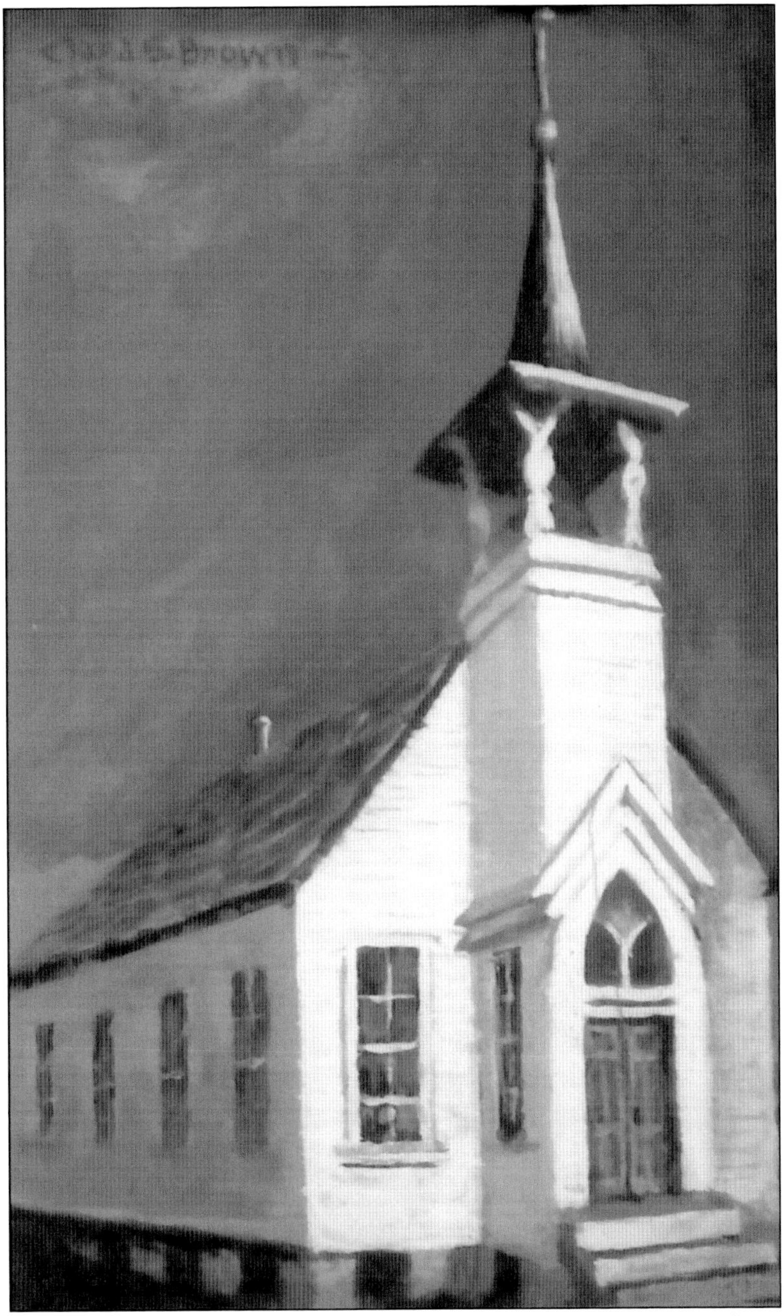

ALMA HALL. The first church in southeastern Parker County was in the Alma settlement, on land given by Samuel Milton and Mary Jane McConnell. Built around 1878 and, like its community, named for Alma McConnell, who died at age 15, the hall was owned in equal shares by the Alma Church and the Alma Masonic Lodge No. 466. Methodists, Baptists, and Masons used the building before it was moved to the present site of Aledo United Methodist Church around 1880 and became the Methodist Episcopal Church South of Aledo. The belfry shown in this earliest view of the structure was added after the move. (Painting by Clara Smyth Brown; Photograph by the author.)

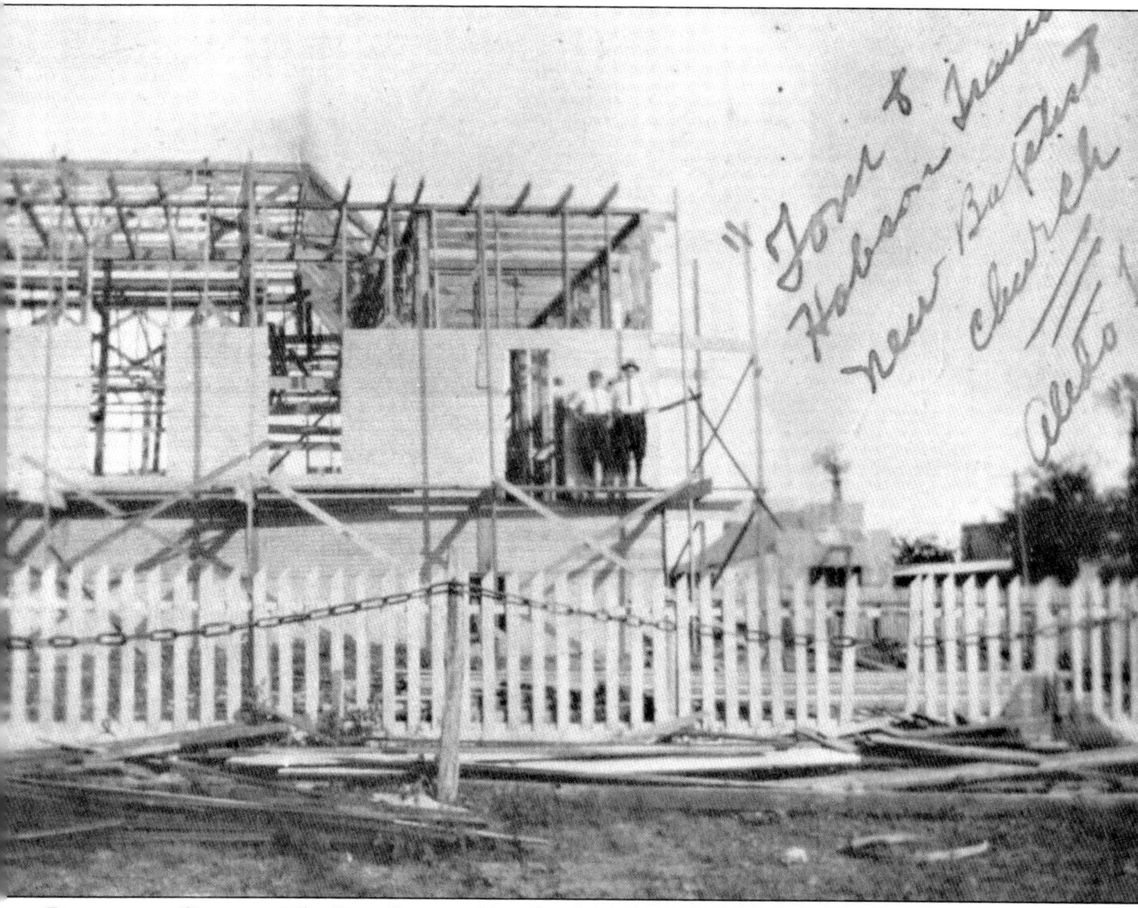

BUILDING A CHURCH. The First Baptist Church of Aledo is shown here under construction in 1913. (Courtesy of Homer Norris.)

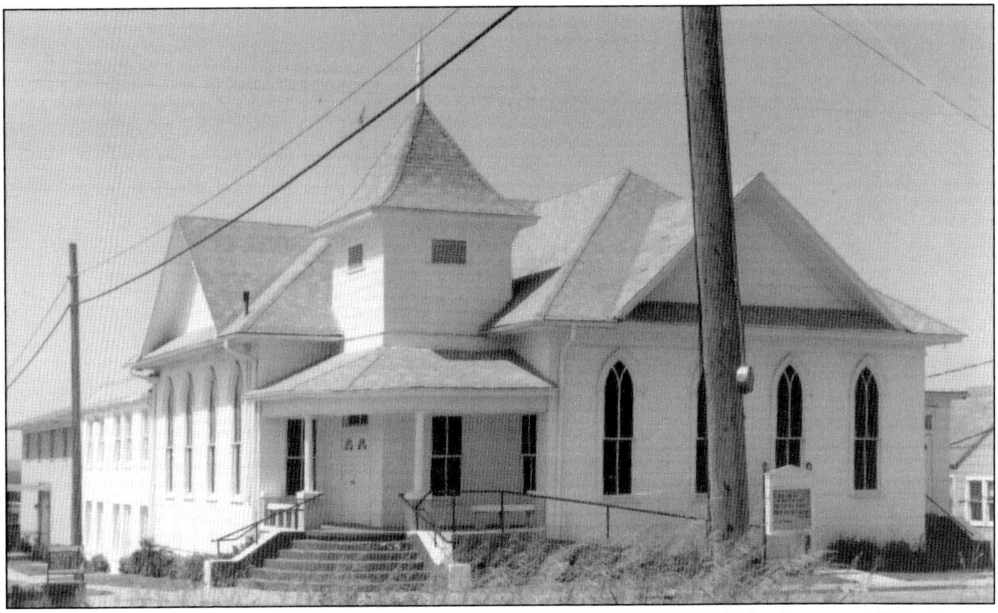

FIRST BAPTIST CHURCH OF ALEDO, 1980S. First Baptist Church of Aledo dates to 1879, when a small group organized as the Missionary Baptist Church "at Almer Hall" and worshipped at Alma Hall under elder Isaac McMurray. When Alma Hall was moved closer to the new railroad tracks and emerging settlement of Aledo, it became the Methodist sanctuary. The Baptist congregation worshipped in the schoolhouse until their sanctuary was completed in 1891. In 1884, Ebinezer and Alma Hall congregations consolidated, and Aledo Baptist Church met in conference. In 1913, a larger sanctuary was built at a cost of $2,700, and it remains in use today as a youth center. In May 1971, the church was officially named the First Baptist Church of Aledo. A Texas Historical Commission Marker was placed at the site in 1983. (Courtesy of Homer Norris.)

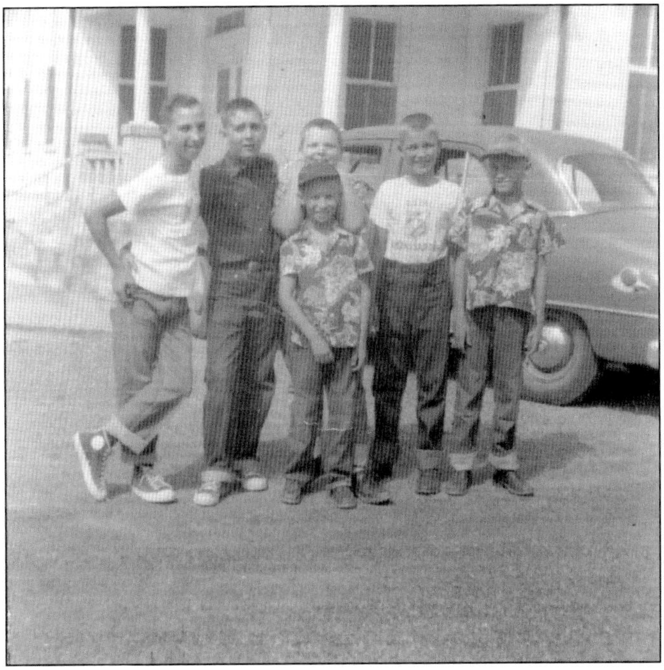

FELLOWSHIP AND FUN. Community life often centered around church. Pictured in 1954 from left to right are Ronny Wood, Doyle Dixon, Mike Scott, Jerald Parish, Jimmy Bennett, and Terry Scott. (Courtesy of Reubene Gressett Scott.)

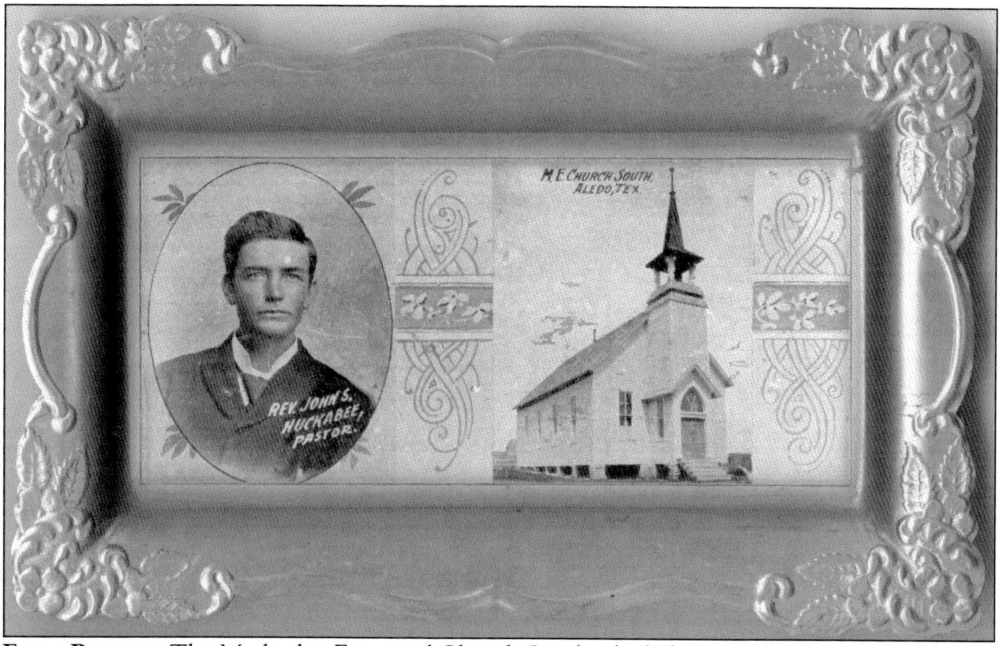

FUND-RAISING. The Methodist Episcopal Church South of Aledo, predecessor to Aledo United Methodist Church, is shown on this small tray, which was sold as a fund-raiser through New Method, Inc., of Chicago. Rev. John S. Huckabee was pastor in Aledo from 1900 to 1904, after serving a congregation in Millsap in 1896 and before transferring in 1904 to the Georgetown district, thus dating the tray. (Courtesy of Nelda McGlinchey.)

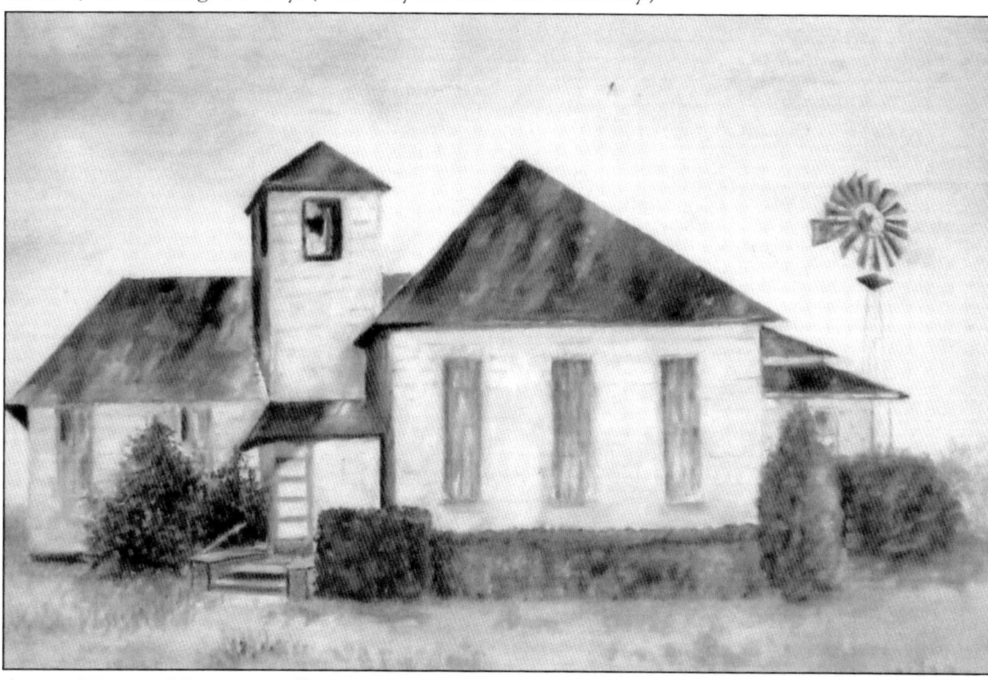

ALEDO UNITED METHODIST CHURCH, 1916–1953. An addition was completed in 1916, as shown above in a painting by longtime member Hilda McGlinchey. The church was torn down in 1953 and replaced with a newer sanctuary. (Painting by Hilda McGlinchey; photograph by the author.)

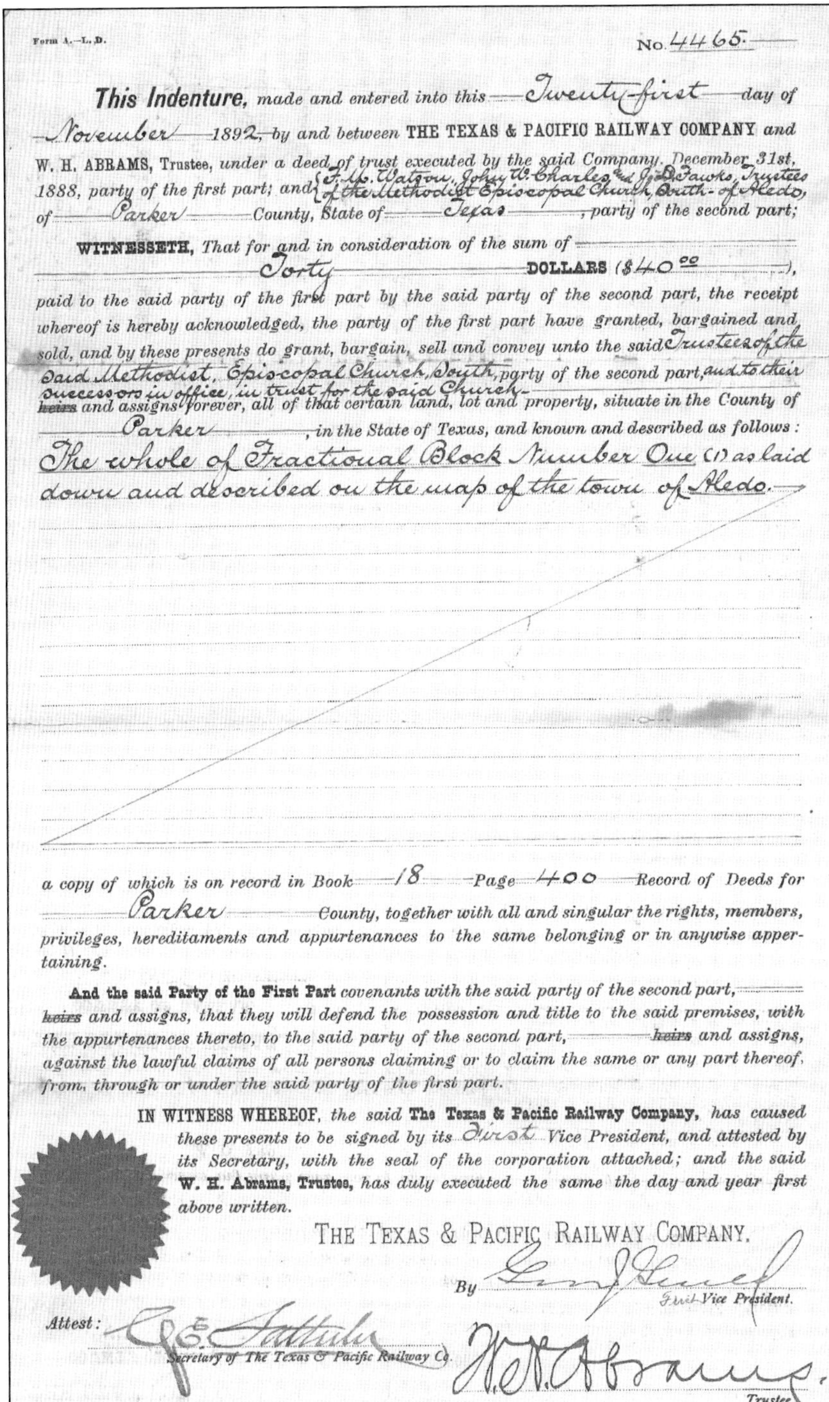

Form A.—L. D.

No. 4465.

This Indenture, *made and entered into this* Twenty-first *day of* November 1892, *by and between* THE TEXAS & PACIFIC RAILWAY COMPANY *and* W. H. ABRAMS, Trustee, *under a deed of trust executed by the said Company, December 31st, 1888, party of the first part; and* F. M. Watson, John W. Charles and J. D. Fawks, Trustees of the Methodist Episcopal Church, South - of Aledo, *of* Parker *County, State of* Texas *, party of the second part;*

WITNESSETH, *That for and in consideration of the sum of* Forty **DOLLARS** ($40.00), *paid to the said party of the first part by the said party of the second part, the receipt whereof is hereby acknowledged, the party of the first part have granted, bargained and sold, and by these presents do grant, bargain, sell and convey unto the said* Trustees of the said Methodist Episcopal Church, South, *party of the second part,* and to their successors in office, in trust for the said Church ~~heirs~~ *and assigns forever, all of that certain land, lot and property, situate in the County of* Parker *, in the State of Texas, and known and described as follows:*

The whole of Fractional Block Number One (1) as laid down and described on the map of the town of Aledo.

a copy of which is on record in Book 18 *Page* 400 *Record of Deeds for* Parker *County, together with all and singular the rights, members, privileges, hereditaments and appurtenances to the same belonging or in anywise appertaining.*

And the said Party of the First Part *covenants with the said party of the second part,* ~~heirs~~ *and assigns, that they will defend the possession and title to the said premises, with the appurtenances thereto, to the said party of the second part,* ~~heirs~~ *and assigns, against the lawful claims of all persons claiming or to claim the same or any part thereof, from, through or under the said party of the first part.*

IN WITNESS WHEREOF, *the said* **The Texas & Pacific Railway Company,** *has caused these presents to be signed by its* First *Vice President, and attested by its Secretary, with the seal of the corporation attached; and the said* **W. H. Abrams, Trustee,** *has duly executed the same the day and year first above written.*

THE TEXAS & PACIFIC RAILWAY COMPANY.

By [signature] First Vice President.

Attest: [signature]
Secretary of The Texas & Pacific Railway Co.

W. H. Abrams.
Trustee.

METHODIST CHURCH DEED. F. M. Watson, John W. Charles, and J. D. Fawks served as trustees for the Methodist Episcopal Church South of Aledo in its purchase of land from the Texas and Pacific Railway Company. The church bought its present tract for $40 in 1892, as shown on this deed of sale. (Courtesy of Nelda McGlinchey.)

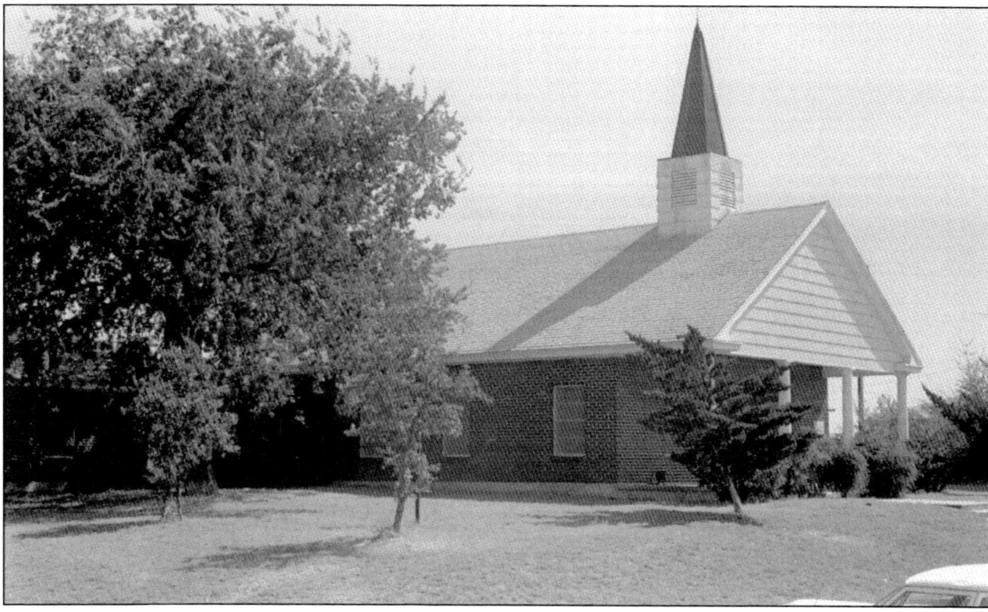

Aledo United Methodist Church, 1972. Founded in 1878 at Alma Hall, the church relocated to Aledo around 1880 as a Methodist Episcopal church South. The church became Aledo Methodist Church in 1939 and Aledo United Methodist in 1968. Until the 1970s, the church was led by circuit ministers who also tended other churches in the area. (Courtesy *Fort Worth Star-Telegram* Photograph Collection, Special Collections, the University of Texas at Arlington.)

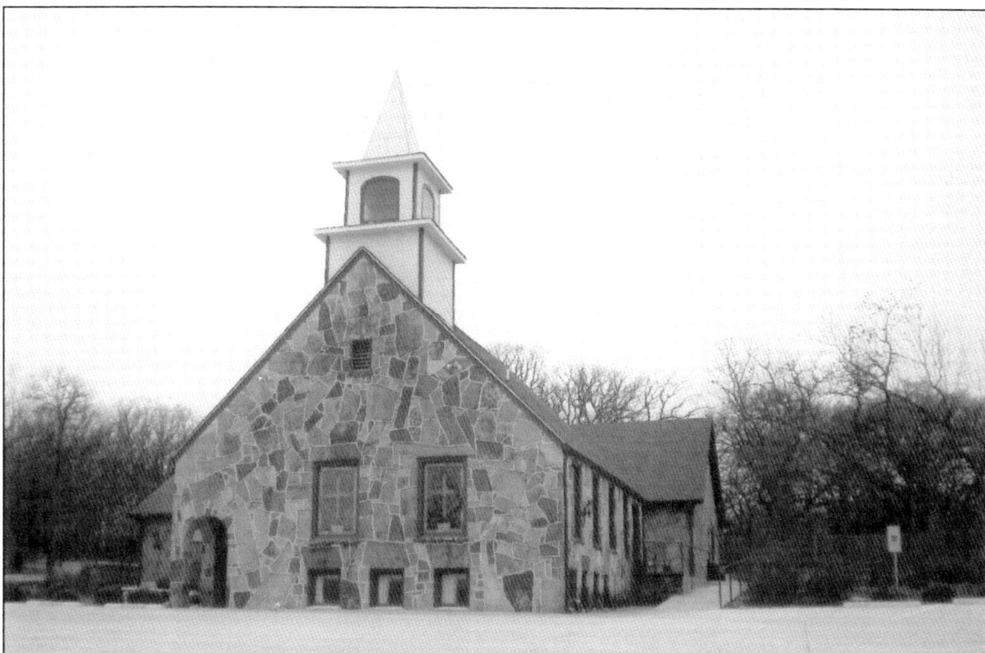

Annetta Methodist Church. Established in 1886, the congregation has worshipped in this stone structure since 1936. By 1989, membership had dwindled to J. D. and Theola Duncan, her brother, and a preacher, but recent population growth has revitalized the church, which added an addition in the early 2000s. (Photograph by the author.)

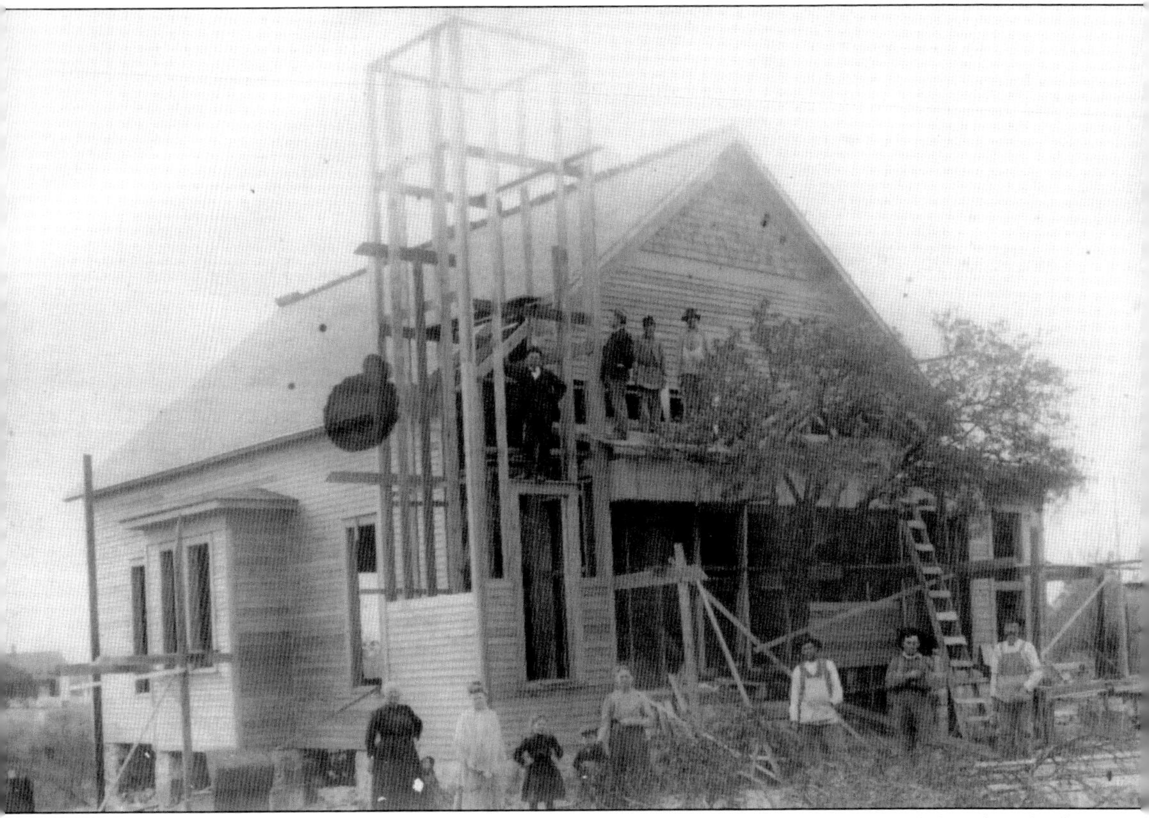

Aledo Church of Christ, 1909. Those responsible for the construction of the church that also would serve the Aledo Christian Church for several years pose for posterity's sake. The man in the tower, Volney Hildreth Sr., was a well-known rancher who owned a ranch east of Aledo. Facing the camera with a nail apron is Henry New Year Norris. To the right of Norris is Allie Gill. The structure faintly seen behind the church to left is the Probes family home. Behind it stood Aledo School, near the old rock gym. The redbrick school had not yet been built. Eventually, the Aledo Church of Christ bought the building from the Aledo Christian Church and worshipped there until building a new church in 1971. The structure is now privately owned. (Courtesy of Homer Norris.)

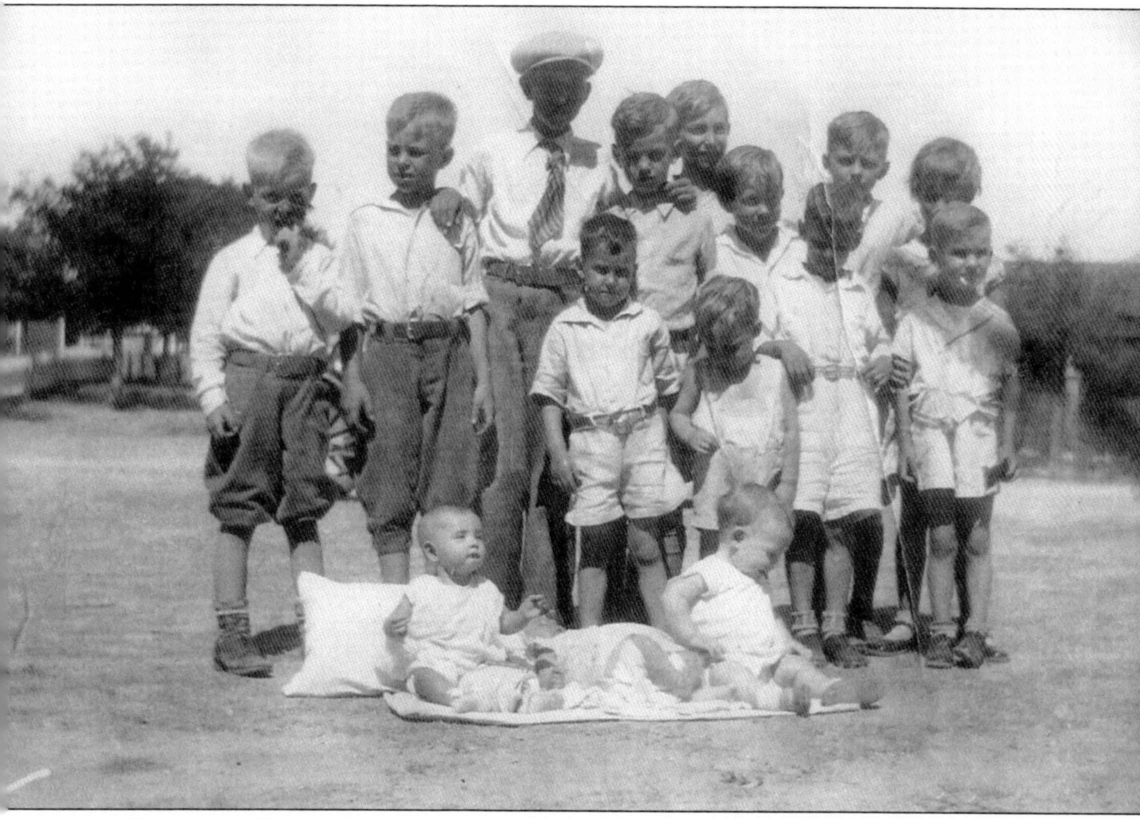

ALEDO CHURCH OF CHRIST CHILDREN, EARLY 1930s. The church formed when G. Dallas Smith held a meeting under a tent in 1902. Here a new generation of members gathers for a portrait. (Courtesy of Josephine and Richard King.)

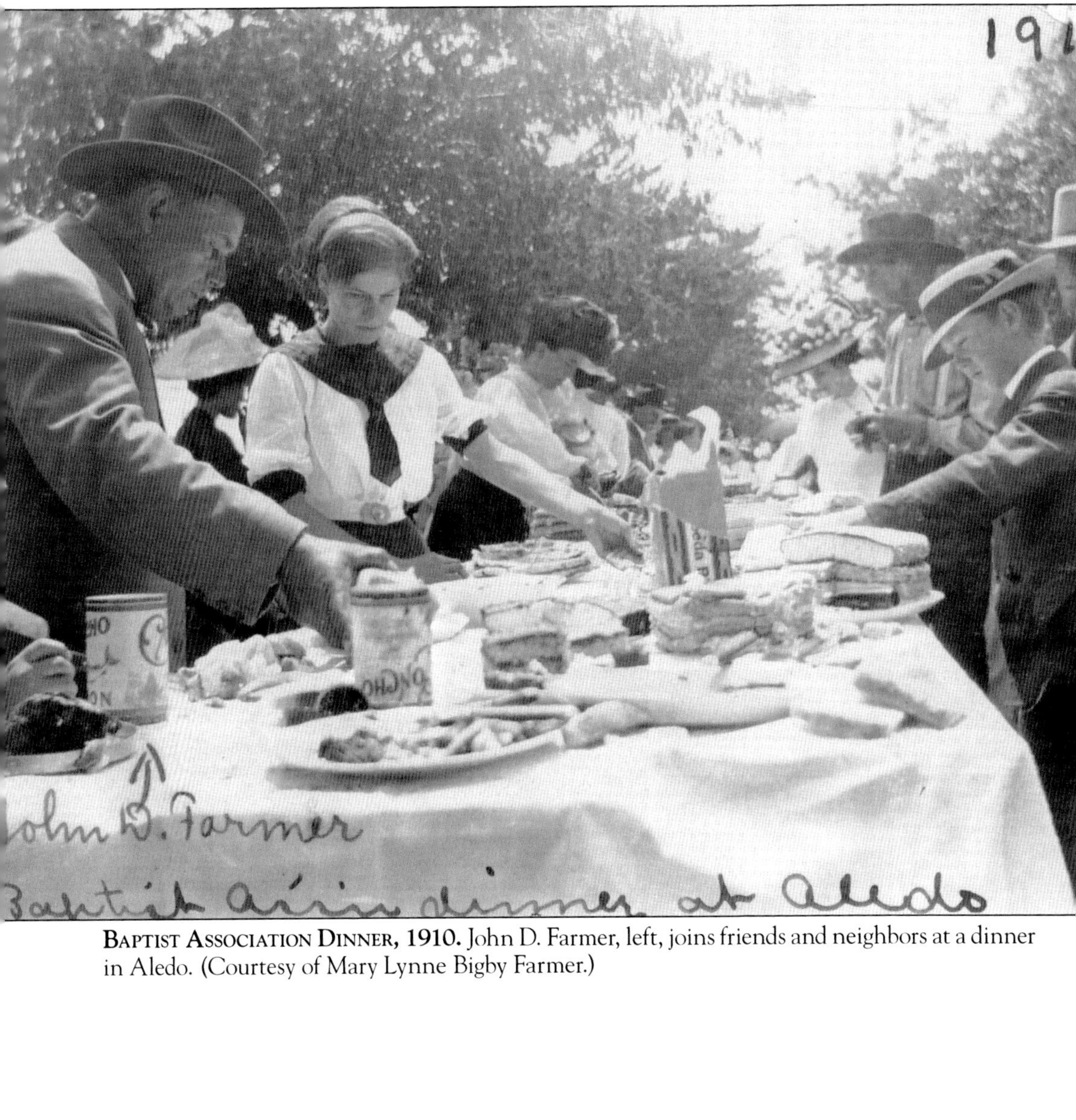

Baptist Association Dinner, 1910. John D. Farmer, left, joins friends and neighbors at a dinner in Aledo. (Courtesy of Mary Lynne Bigby Farmer.)

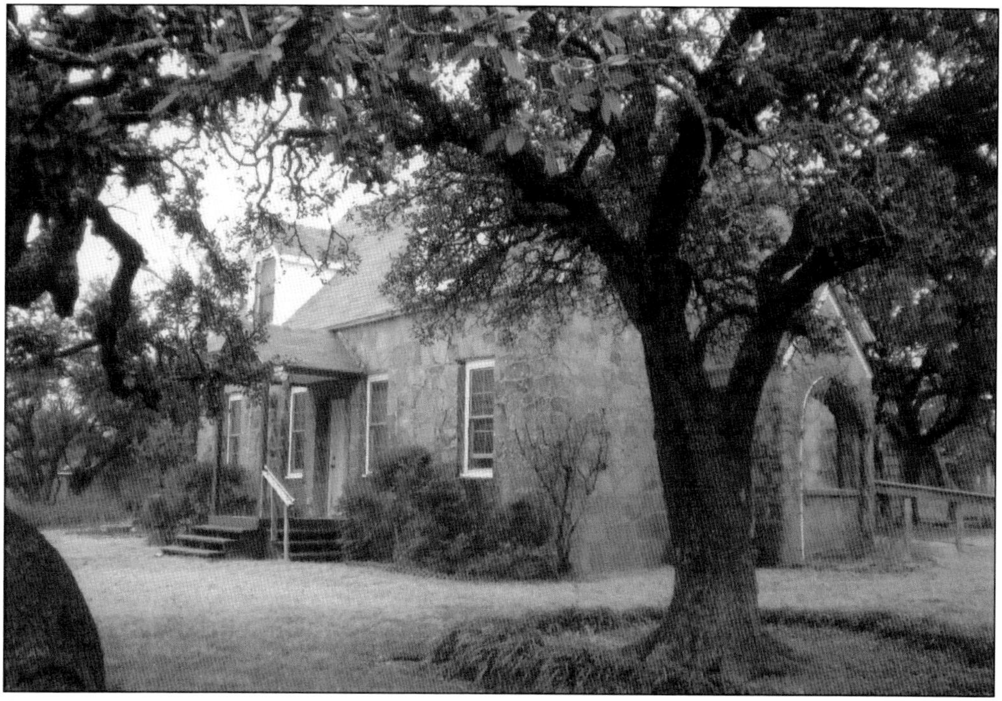

Chapel Hill Church. The Methodist church that served the Mary's Creek and Prairie Hill communities has a plaque by the door honoring E. D. Farmer, a real estate developer and philanthropist who owned a cattle ranch in the area and provided generous funds to the church. The structure is now a private residence. (Photograph by the author.)

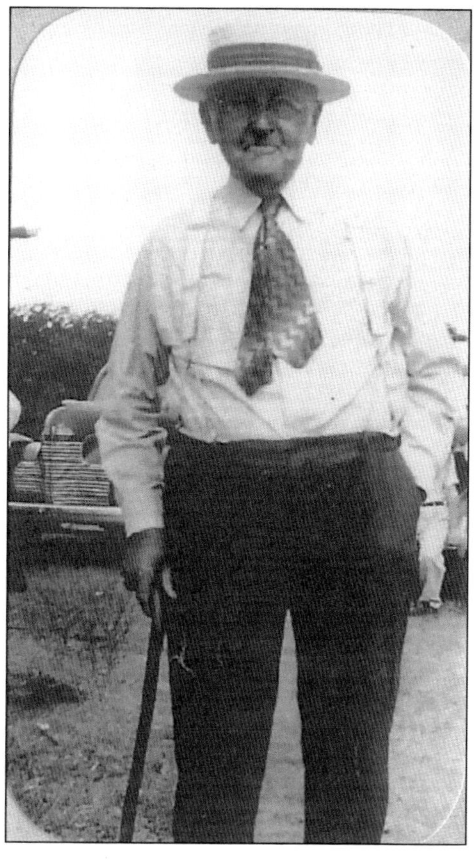

Ben F. Spain. The Spains were an early family in the area. Spain was one of the founding members of the Aledo Church of Christ. (Courtesy of Josephine Ondra King.)

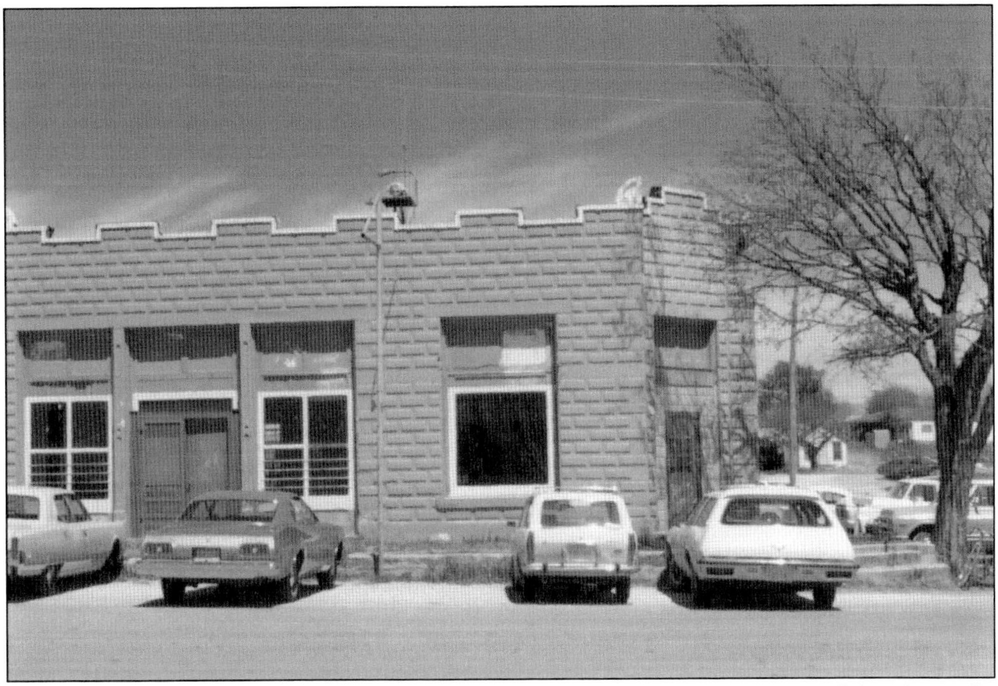

ALEDO CHRISTIAN CENTER, 1974. Pastor Grady Barton and his wife, Rose, opened their home for a weekly Bible study in 1972 before the group organized as Aledo Christian Center, a Pentecostal church, and purchased this building on North Front Street. (Courtesy of Rose Barton.)

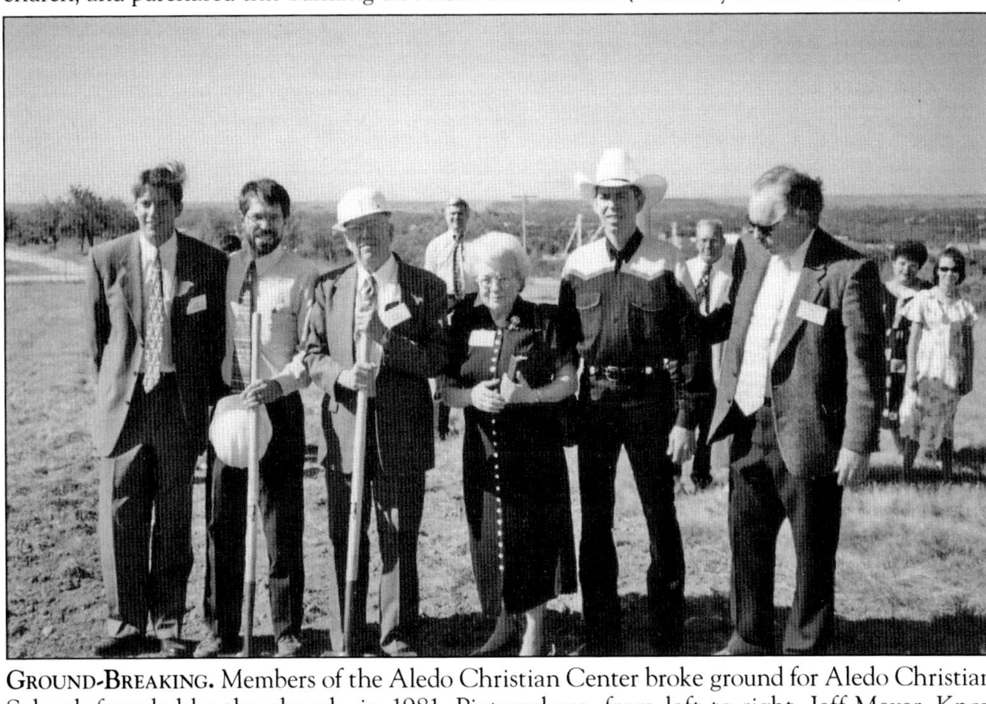

GROUND-BREAKING. Members of the Aledo Christian Center broke ground for Aledo Christian School, founded by the church, in 1981. Pictured are, from left to right, Jeff Meyer, Knox Ross, Pastor Grady Barton, Rose Barton, David Barton, and Bob Lewis. (Courtesy of Aledo Christian School.)

Four

FARMING AND RANCHING

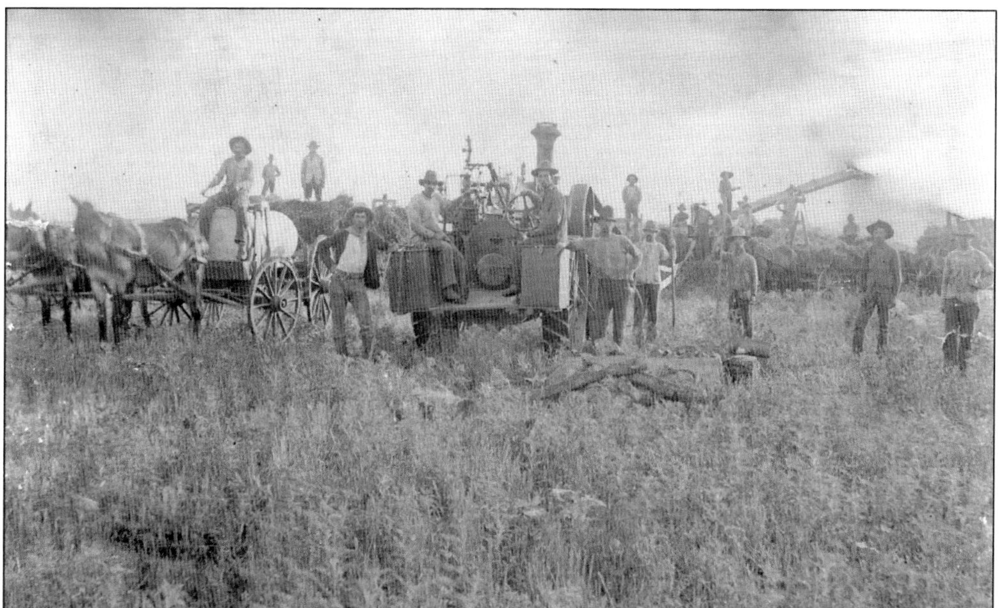

HARVEST, CODER FARM. Farming was the predominant occupation in eastern Parker County until late in the 20th century. Here, J. P. Martin's threshing crew brings in the harvest at the C. F. Coder farm at Mary's Creek around the turn of the century. The stacked wood was used to fuel the machinery. (Courtesy of the Doss Heritage and Cultural Center.)

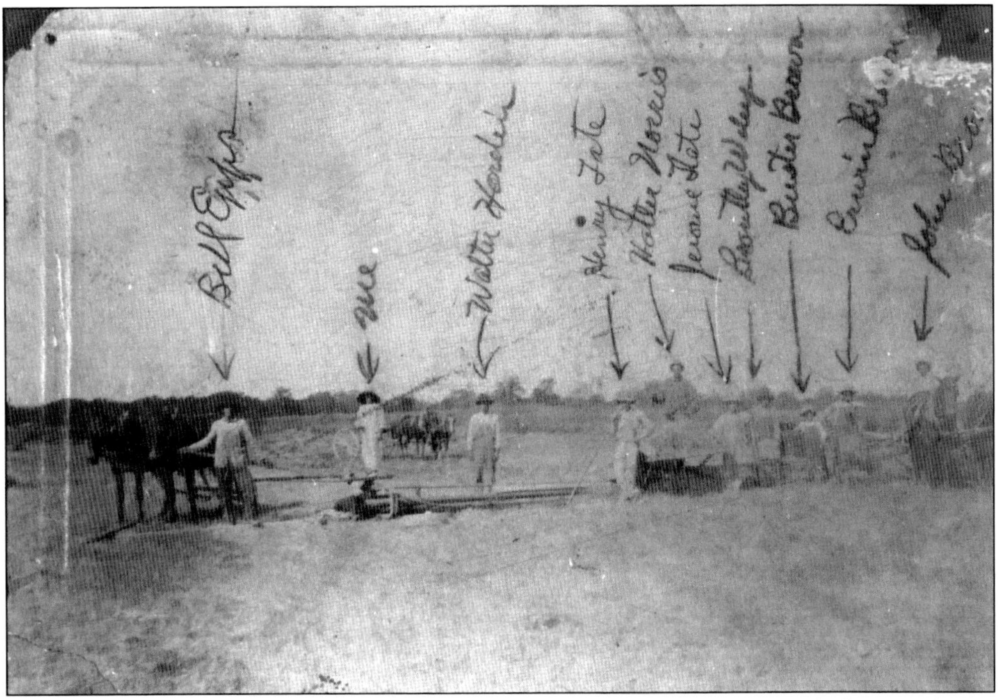

EARLY HARVEST. Horse-drawn harvest equipment brought in early crops of wheat and oats. From left to right are Bill Epps, Henry B. Norris, Walter Hardin, Henry Tate, Hatler Norris, Jerome Tate, Brantley Wiley, Buster Brown, Erwin Brown, and John Brown. (Courtesy of Evlyn Wiley Broumley.)

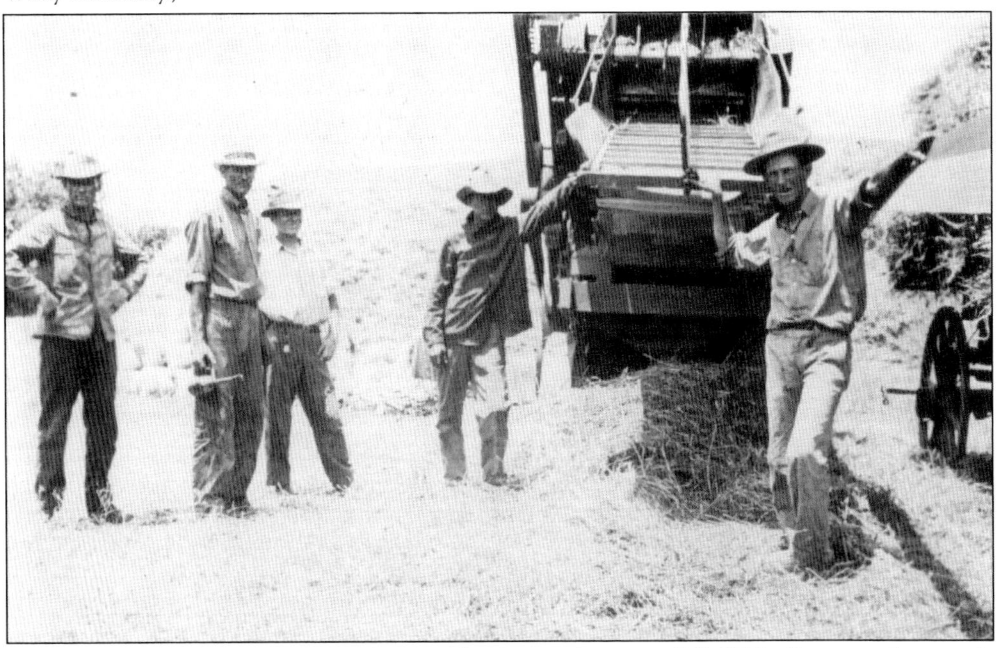

MCGLINCHEY THRESHING CREW. John McGlinchey and stepson Bill O'Neall pose with an early threshing crew, date unknown. John McGlinchey is third from left in a light hat. O'Neall stands at far right. (Courtesy of Don Collins.)

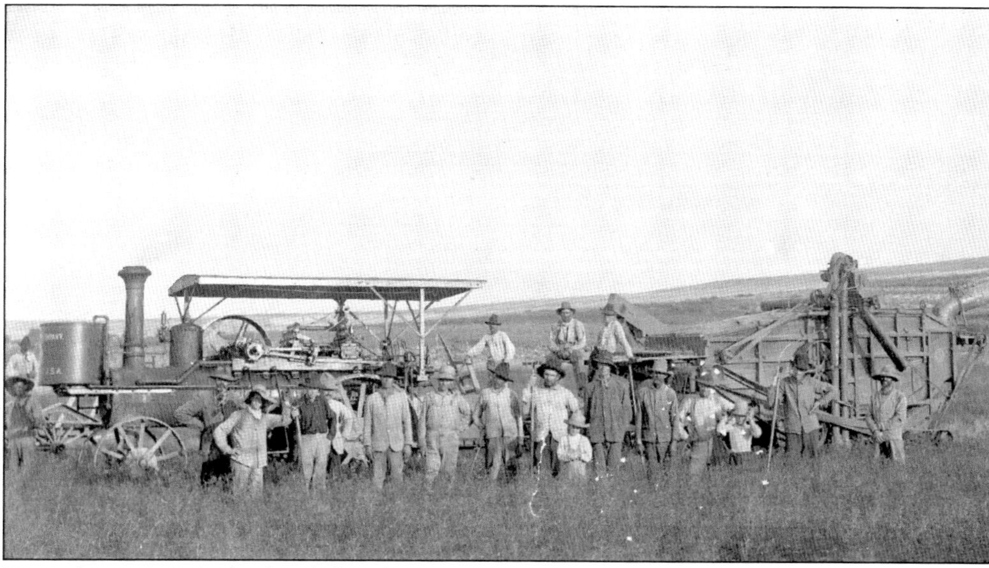

YEARY CREW. C. F. Coder, fourth from left, stands with one of his sons and Dave Yeary's thresher crew on C. F. Coder's farm in 1905 or 1906. (Courtesy of the Doss Heritage and Cultural Center.)

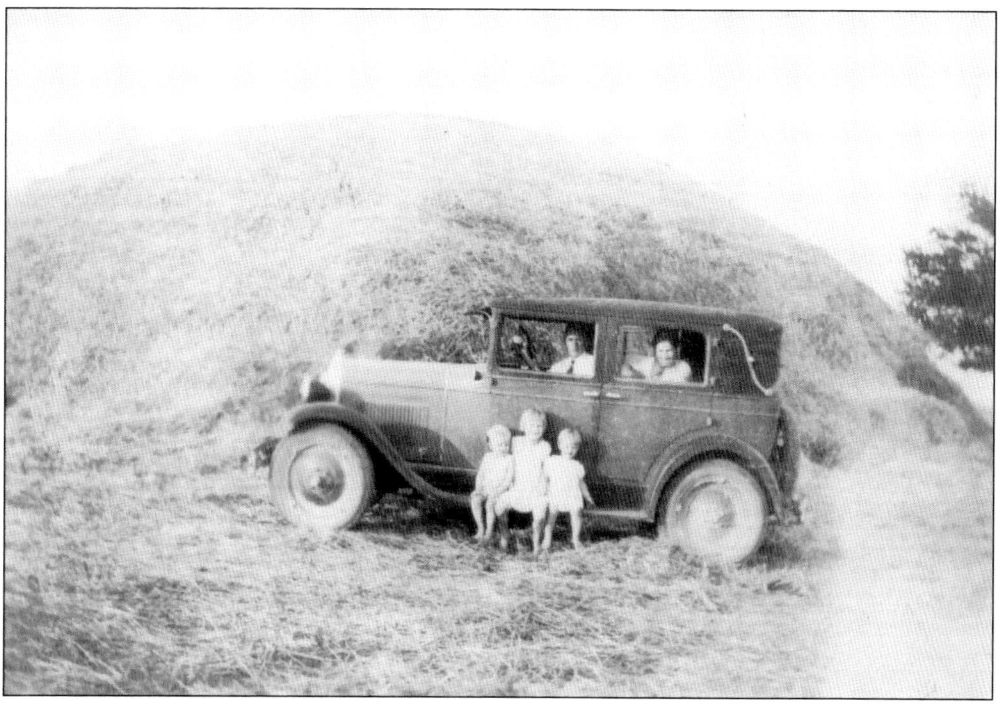

CODER BOUNTY. Burton and Minnie Coder, their 1928 Chevy, and (from left to right) children Jean, Jackie, and Ann, are dwarfed by a stack of hay or straw after the season's threshing. (Courtesy of the Doss Heritage and Cultural Museum.)

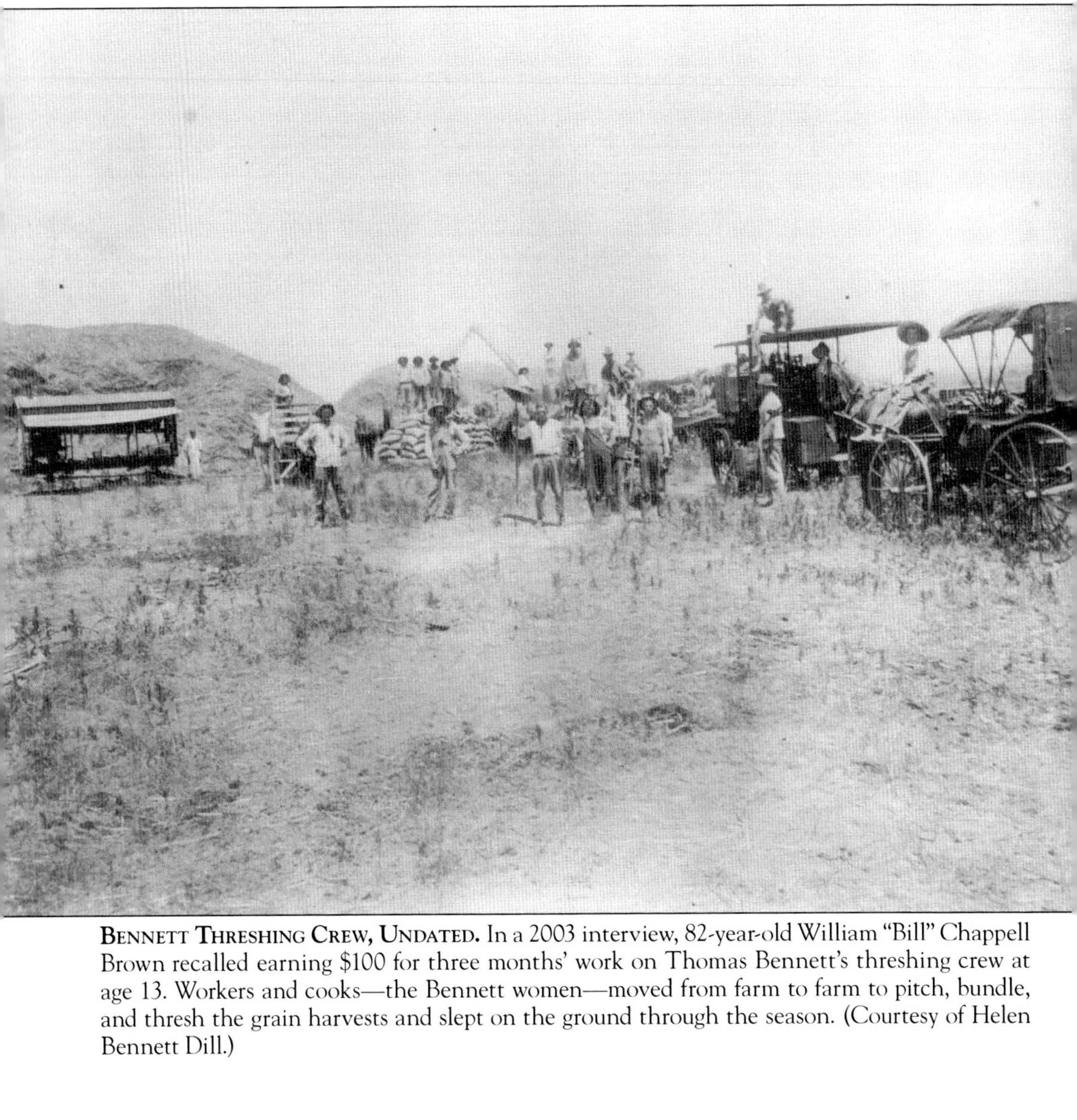

Bennett Threshing Crew, Undated. In a 2003 interview, 82-year-old William "Bill" Chappell Brown recalled earning $100 for three months' work on Thomas Bennett's threshing crew at age 13. Workers and cooks—the Bennett women—moved from farm to farm to pitch, bundle, and thresh the grain harvests and slept on the ground through the season. (Courtesy of Helen Bennett Dill.)

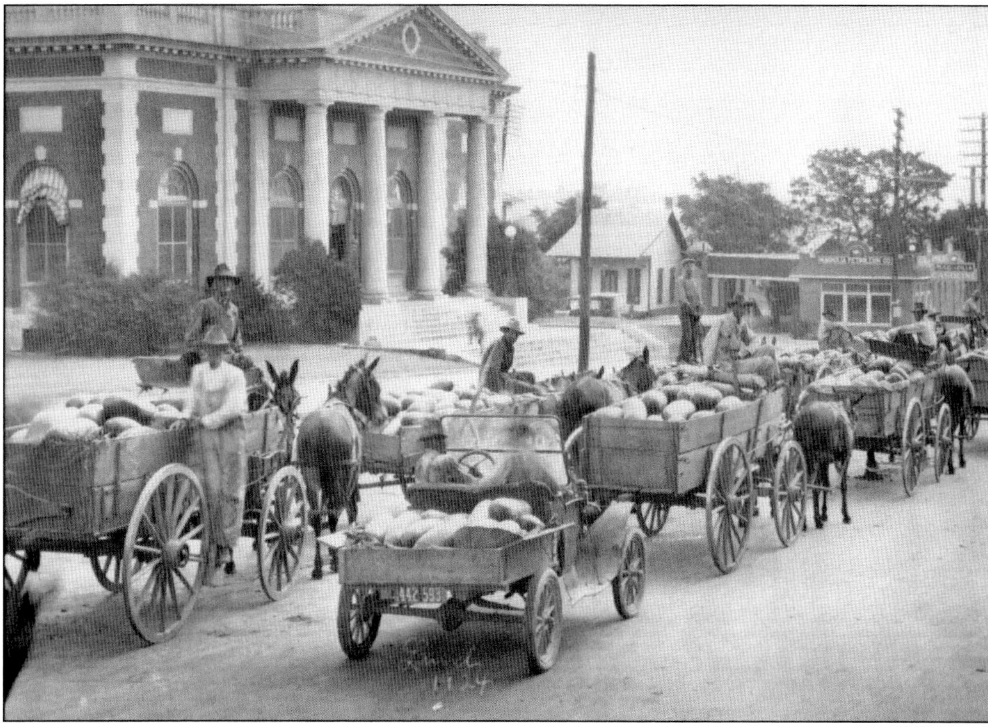

GOING TO MARKET, 1924. Parker County watermelons won the gold medal prize at the 1904 World's Fair and the county seat declared itself the Watermelon Capital of the World. Broadway and film star Mary Martin—mother of *Dallas*'s J. R. Ewing, Larry Hagman—recalled of her hometown that wagons filled with the harvest would line up during the night. The following morning, each farmer would wait his turn to load his goods on trains at Weatherford's depot. (Courtesy of the Doss Heritage and Cultural Center.)

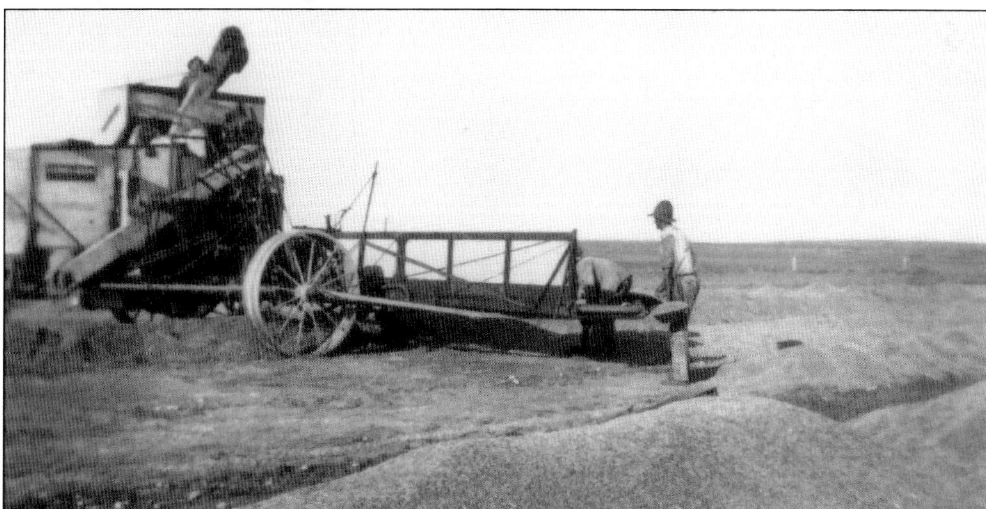

MCFARLAND RANCH HARVEST. Of the 7,000-acre McFarland Ranch, approximately 1,000 acres were farmed. Wheat, oats, and barley were raised; in 1912, workers threshed a bumper crop of more than 36,000 bushels of oats. In 1980, Fred McFarland recalled that hay was baled all summer long, with three hay presses running at once. (Courtesy of Diane McFarland Cornwall.)

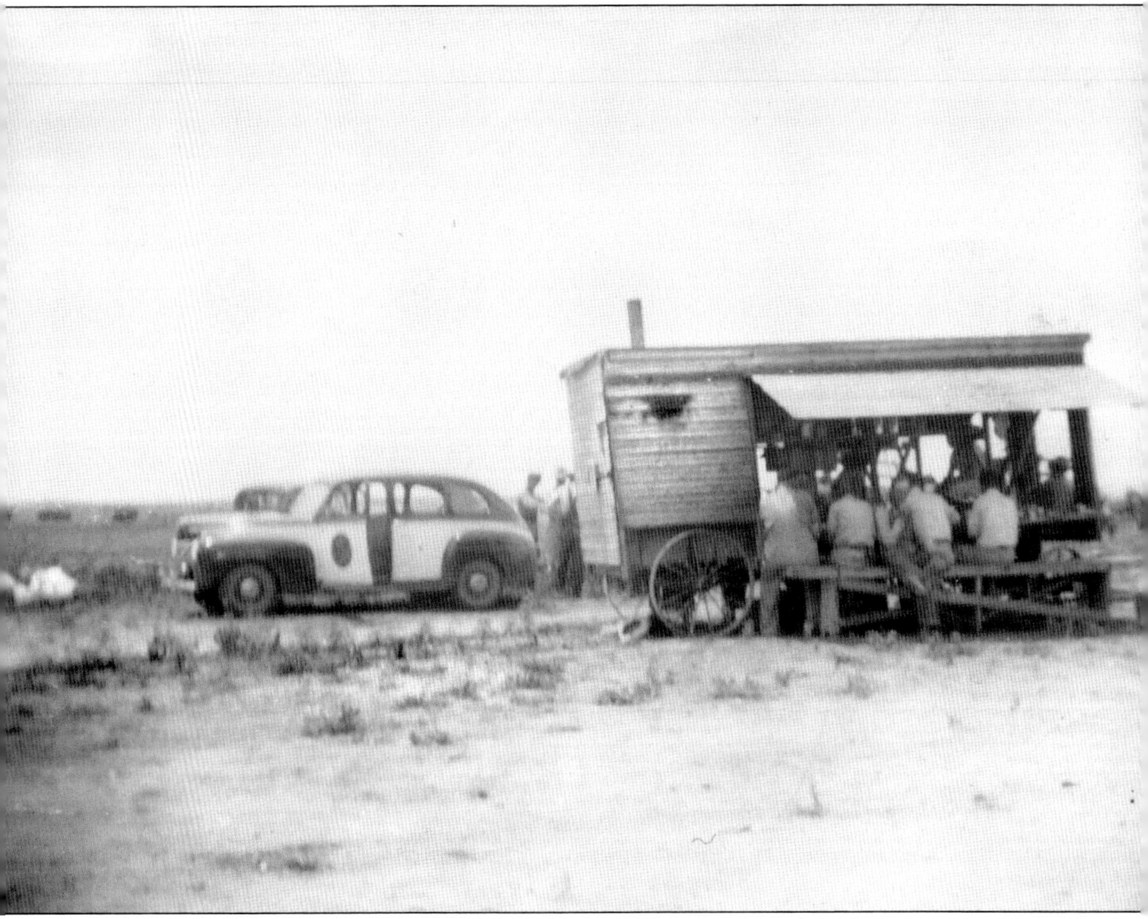

Cook Shack. Decades later, Bill Brown and other old-timers praised the Bennett women's meals, which included fruit cobblers cooked in a wood-fueled oven. "Dessert was stored on a shelf over the cooking area," Bill Eastman told the author. "We'd finish our dinner and ask, 'What have you got upstairs?' " (Courtesy of Mary Lynne Bigby Jones.)

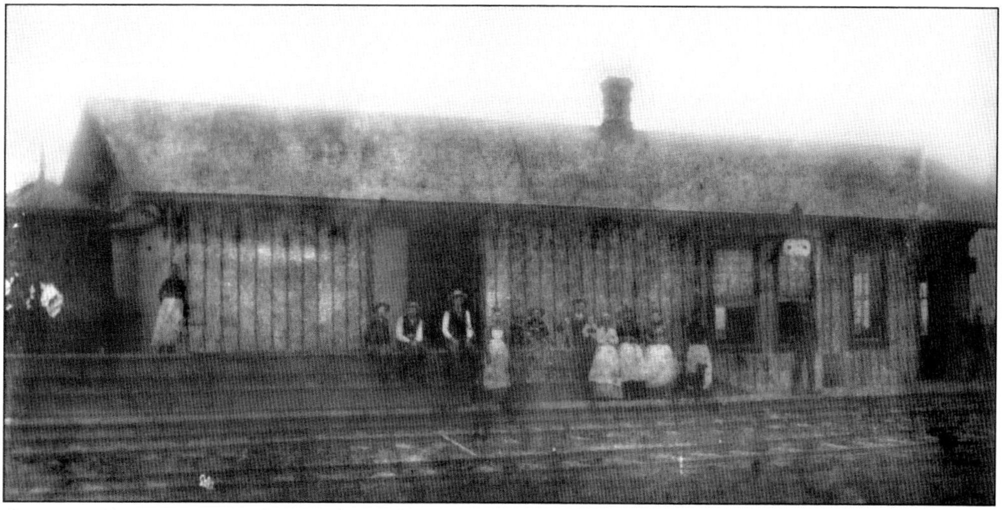

Cresson Depot, 1887. Situated a mile or so east of Cresson, which sits in present-day Parker, Hood, and Johnson Counties, the Cresson depot was the departure point for countless head of cattle from eastern Parker County. A later depot, in operation through at least the late 1950s, sat across Highway 171 and was a stop for "Old Nancy," the Weatherford-to-Cleburne-to-Weatherford train that enabled Cressonians to take the train to either terminus town for 25¢. (Courtesy of Chris Cornwall.)

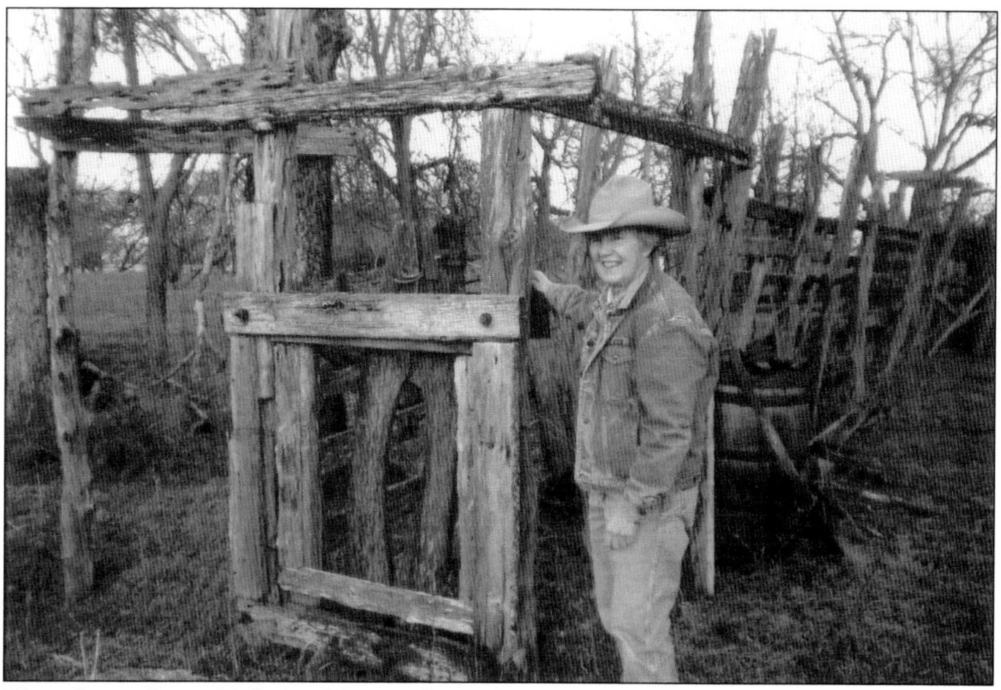

Head Gate. Diane McFarland Cornwall stands near a head gate from the historic McFarland Ranch. Still used to inoculate calves on the D Bar B Ranch owned by Cornwall and her partner, Bev Baetge, the contraption is a rarity on modern ranches. (Photograph by the author.)

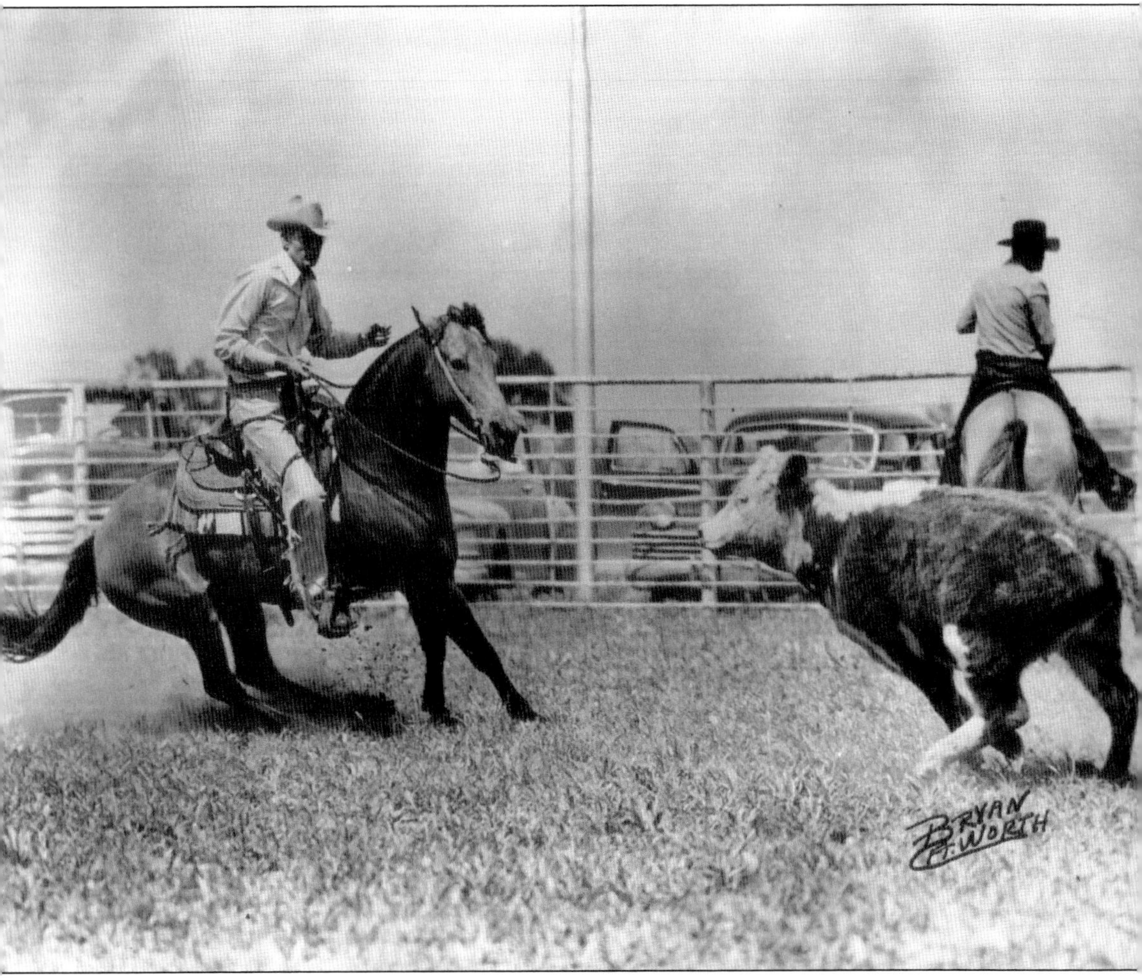

RAY SMYTH, 1948. National Cutting Horse Association (NCHA) cofounder Ray Smyth is shown on Barney, a horse bred by Barney R. Holland by crossing banker Fred Smith's stud with his mare so his son, Barney B. Holland, would have a horse upon his return from Princeton. World War II changed everything, and young Barney became a submarine officer in the Pacific. After epic haggling (Smyth said he was "just a broke cowboy"), Holland sold him the pair. Smyth gelded the colt and trained Barney for ranch work, where he excelled at cutting. NCHA records are incomplete, but Smyth related that Barney was the first NCHA-registered horse—or the first to earn a Certificate of Merit, as it was termed in 1946. (Courtesy of Barney B. Holland Jr.)

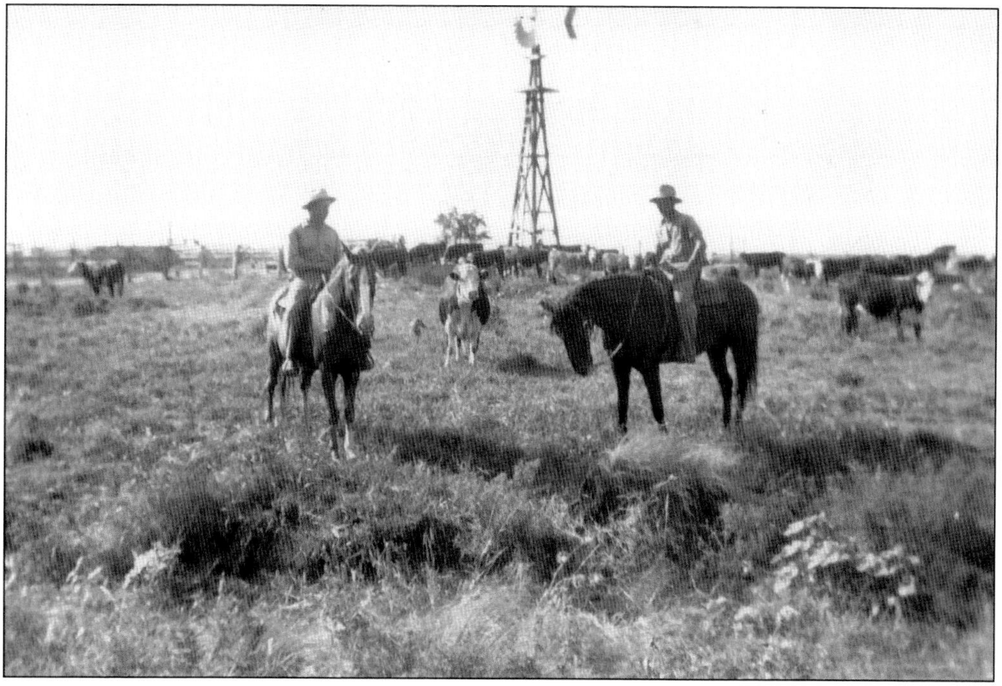

COWBOYS AND CATTLE. The McFarland Ranch has been in the same family for more than 100 years. Charles McFarland suggested the idea for a stock show in 1896, thereby giving birth to the renowned Southwestern Exposition and Livestock Show in Fort Worth. (Courtesy of Diane McFarland Cornwall.)

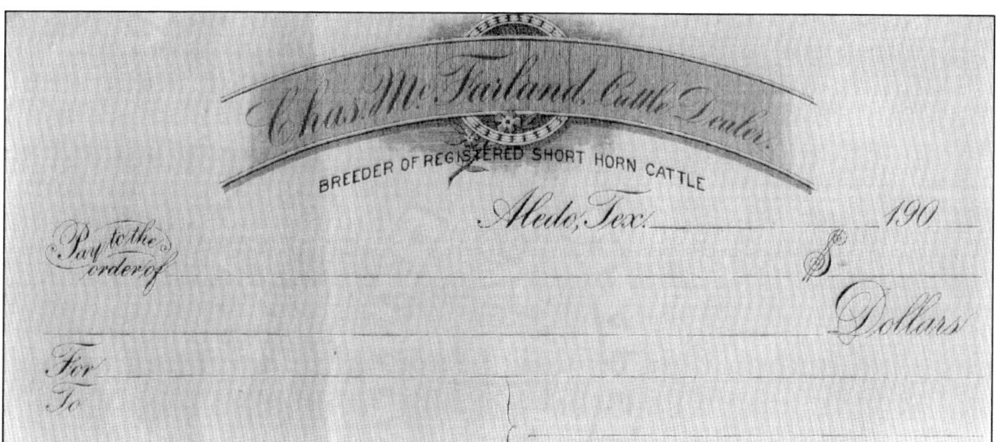

Chas. McFarland, Cattle Dealer.
BREEDER OF REGISTERED SHORT HORN CATTLE
Aledo, Tex. ______ 190__
Pay to the order of ______ $______
______ Dollars
For ______
To ______

CHARLES MCFARLAND CHECKS. The McFarland Ranch patriarch conducted business with style. (Courtesy of Diane McFarland Cornwall.)

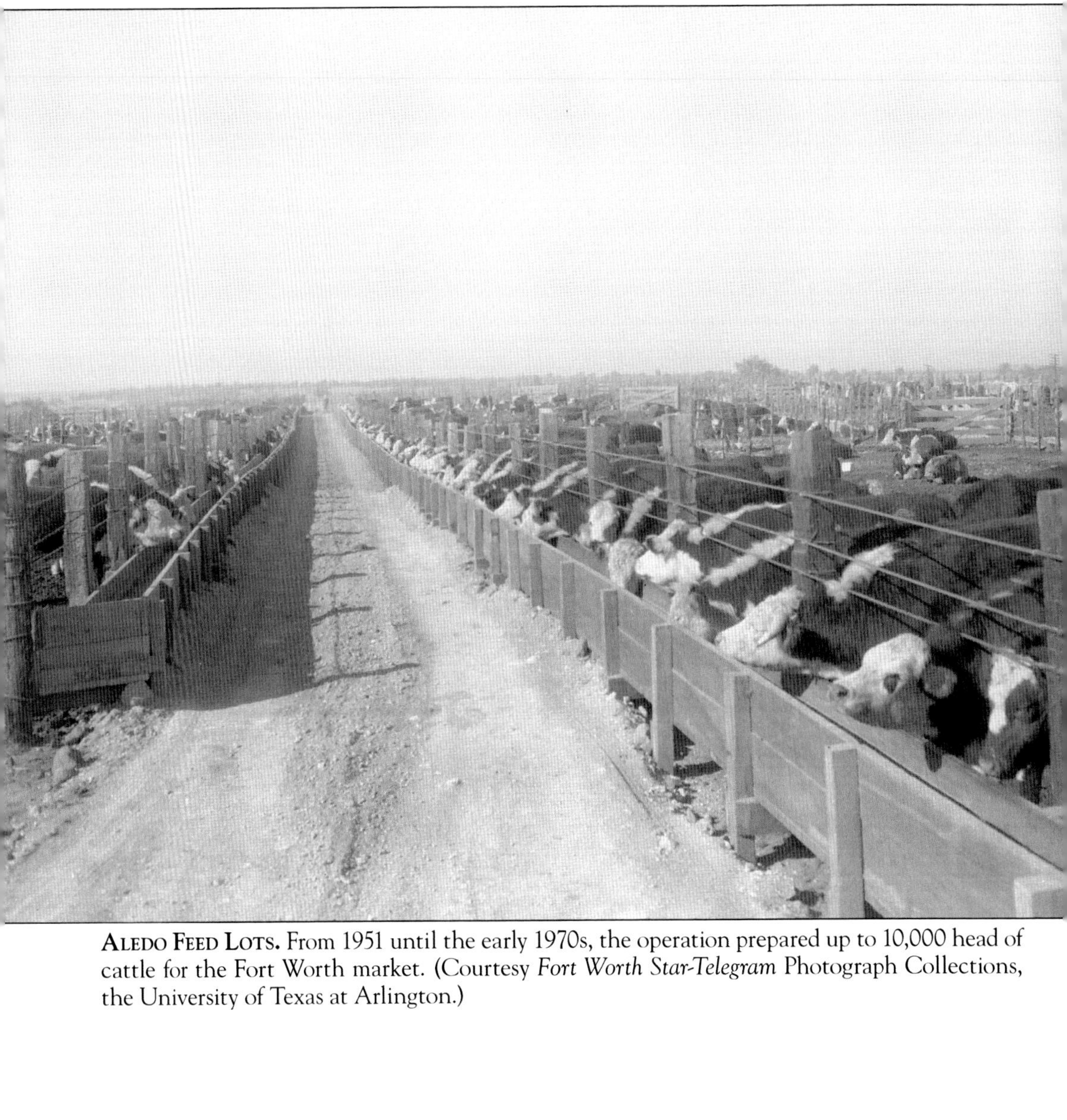

ALEDO FEED LOTS. From 1951 until the early 1970s, the operation prepared up to 10,000 head of cattle for the Fort Worth market. (Courtesy *Fort Worth Star-Telegram* Photograph Collections, the University of Texas at Arlington.)

Keeping Cattle Records. Jack Stewart maintained detailed records regarding the operation. (Courtesy *Fort Worth Star-Telegram* Photograph Collections, the University of Texas at Arlington.)

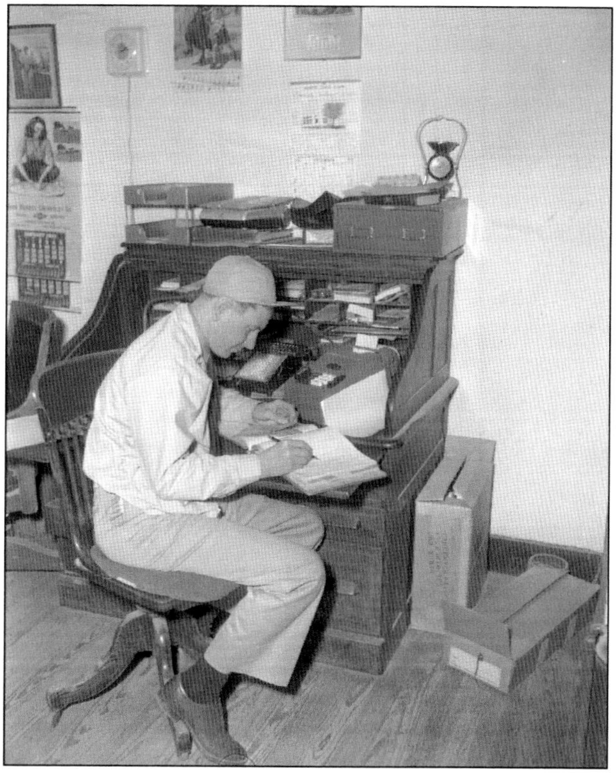

Aledo Cattle Pens. Describing the pens, Aledo cowboy and businessman Ray Smyth once told a reporter, "The old-timers say there were more cattle shipped out and more feed shipped in than at any station in the area." (Courtesy *Fort Worth Star-Telegram* Photograph Collections, the University of Texas at Arlington.)

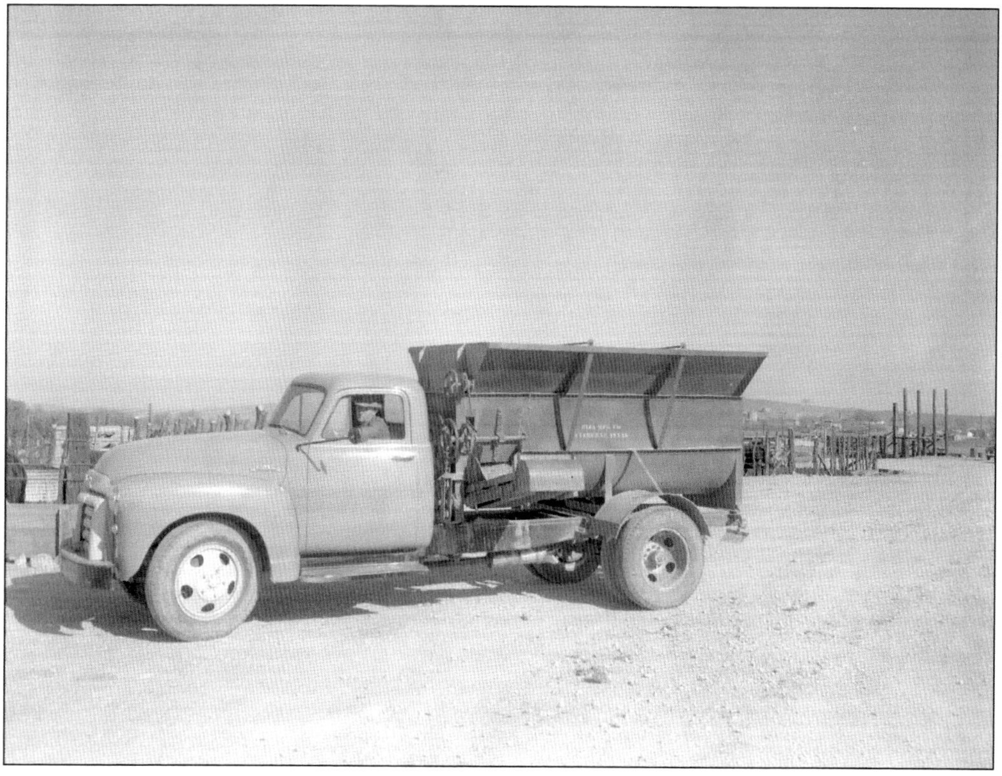

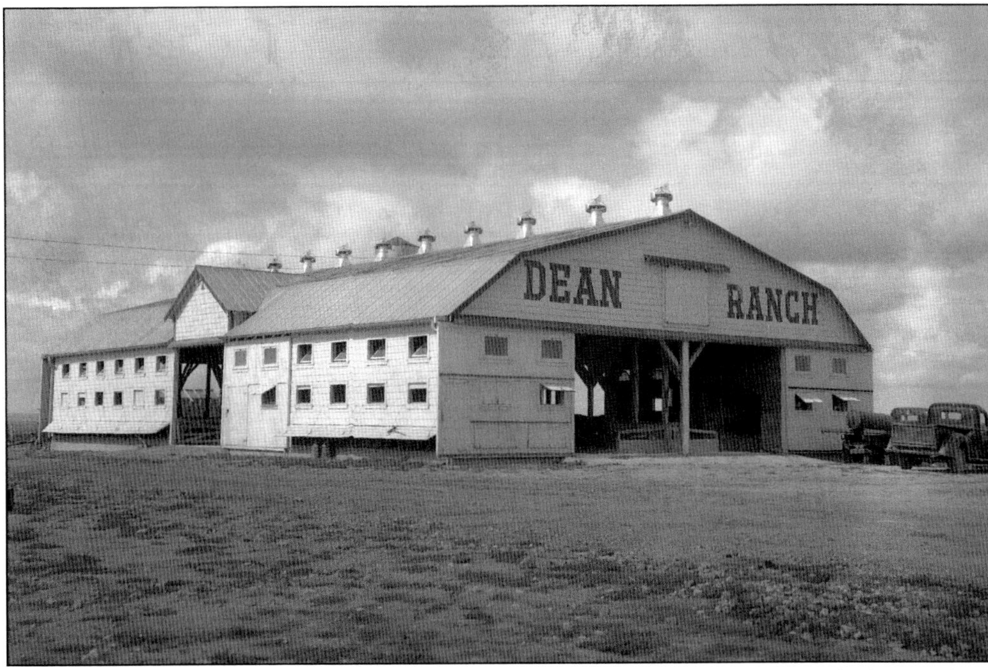

DEAN RANCH BARN. An iconic structure to residents, for decades the barn was the lone sight to welcome those who exited the highway for Aledo. (Photograph by Frank Reeves Sr.; courtesy of *Fort Worth Star-Telegram* Photograph Collections, the University of Texas at Arlington.)

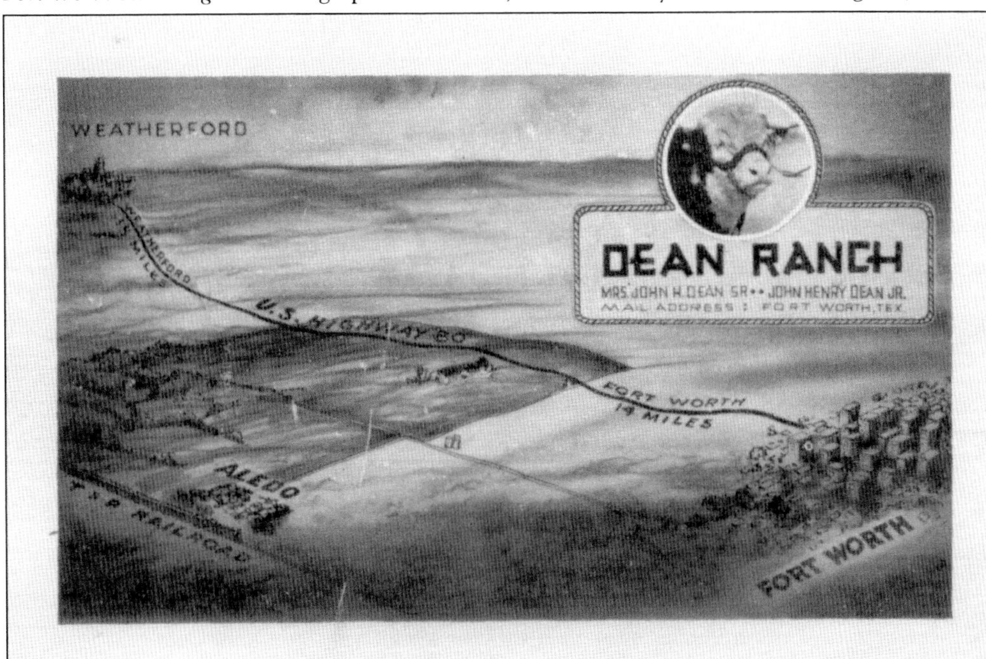

DEAN RANCH. This promotional notepad provided blank pages for notes while touting the bloodlines and cattle at the Dean Ranch of Aledo. Dean Ranch Herefords earned "best 10 head" at the National Hereford Show at the Texas State Fair in 1939, among other honors. (Courtesy of Weldon Turner.)

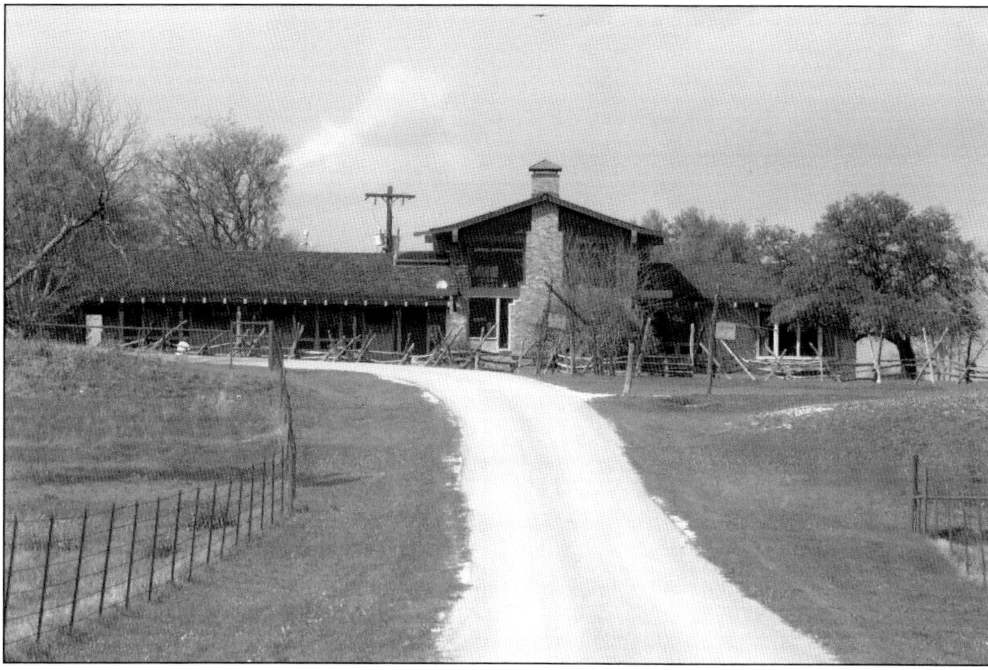

North Star Ranch. In 1947, F. Howard Walsh purchased the North Star Ranch near Mary's Creek; the ranch served as headquarters of the Walsh family ranching operations, which included more than 16,000 acres in Texas and Oklahoma. Under general manager Lewis H. Marshall, the Walsh Ranches managed as many as 7,000 head of cattle and earned a reputation for their Charolais cattle-breeding operation as well as originating and owning one of the largest Charbray herds in North America. The 7,200-acre ranch in Parker County is slated for conversion to a multi-use community. (Photograph by B. J. Lacasse; courtesy of B. J. Lacasse.)

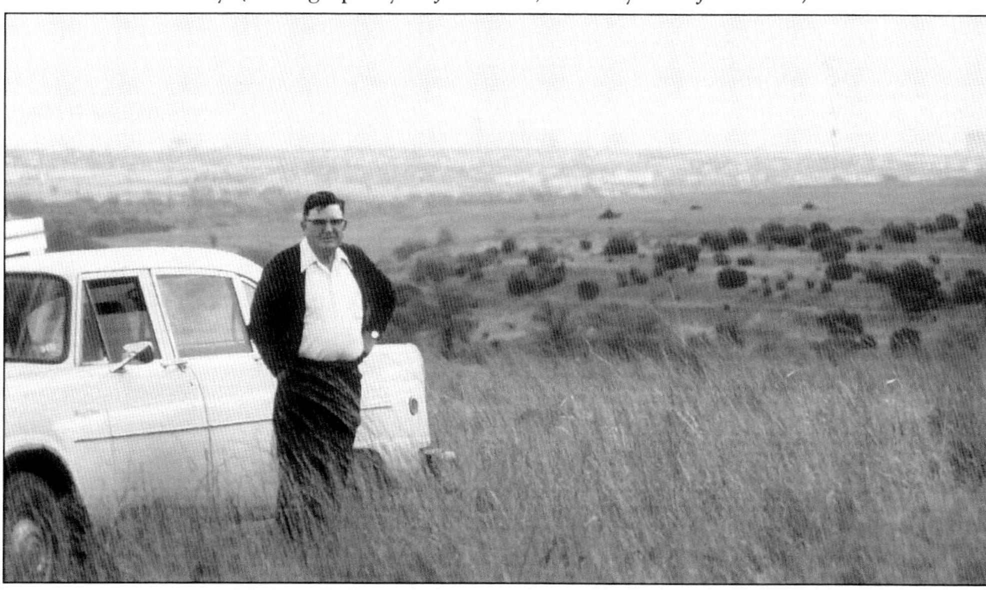

Lewis Marshall. Walsh Ranch foreman Marshall was inducted into the Charolais Association Hall of Fame, the first non–ranch owner to receive such recognition. Marshall and his old taxi cab were a familiar sight to local residents. (Courtesy of the Marshall family.)

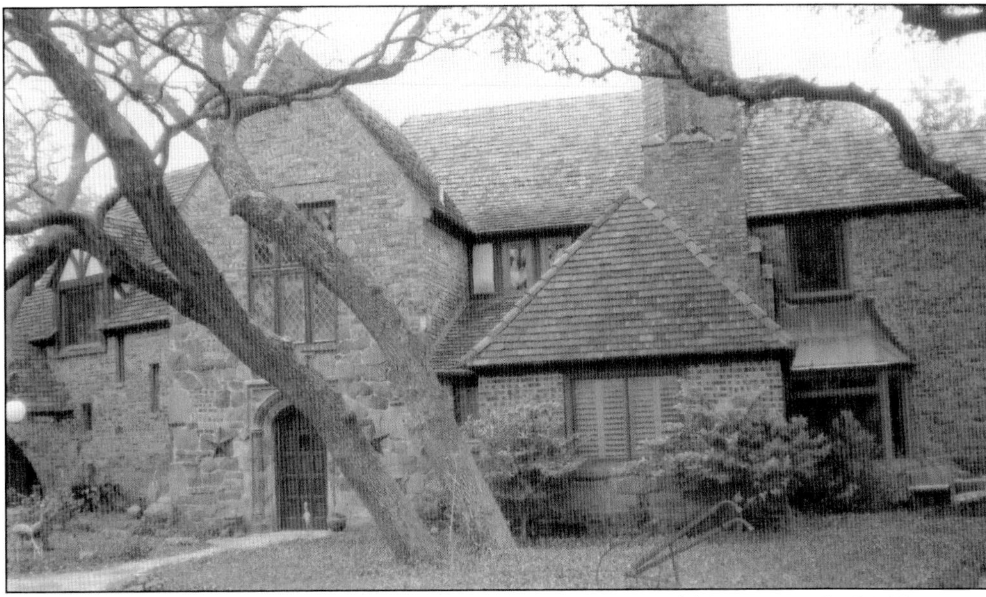

Winston Home, Bear Creek Ranch. In 1933, Joe Winston paid $30 an acre for 3,000 acres in the Bear Creek community in southeastern Parker County. There he and his wife, Dot Kelly, built an English manor-style home. The home and ranch remain in the family. (Photograph by the author.)

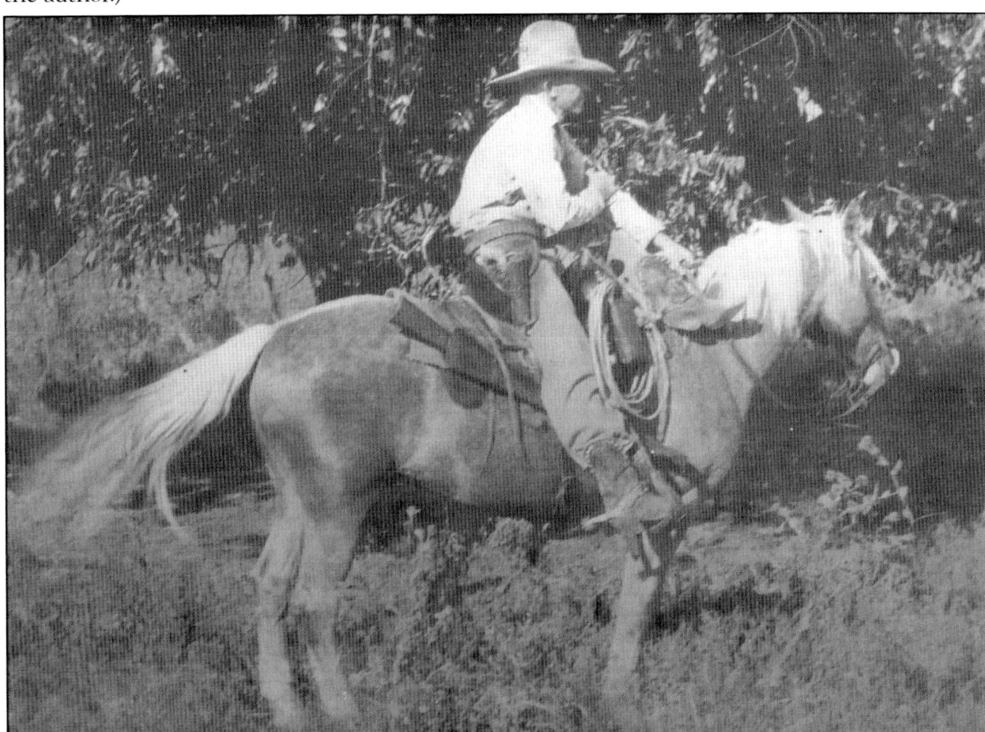

Pete Kelly (1910–1965). Robert Jackson "Pete" Kelly, brother of Dot, lived on the Bear Creek Ranch with his wife, Carrie, and children, and helped run the ranch, which raised Herefords and had more than 500 acres of grain in cultivation. (Courtesy of Jerry Reid.)

Five

Business and Pleasure

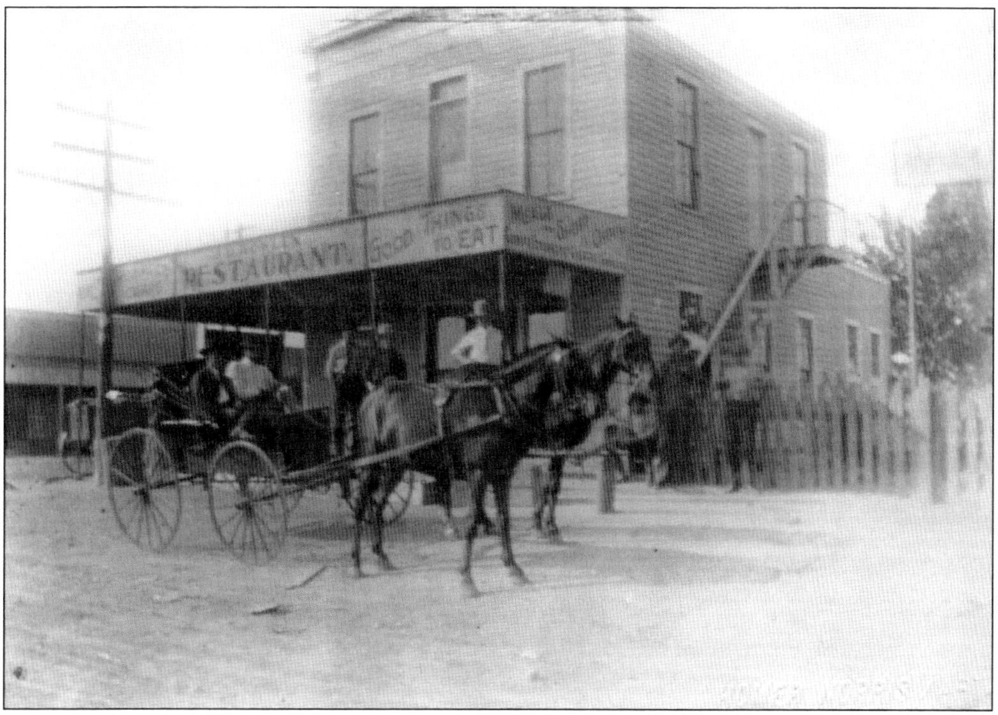

Parker Station. John Bowlen's business on North Front Street was one of the first in the new burg of Parker Station that arose near the Texas and Pacific railroad station. Soon, however, letters intended for the county seat, Weatherford, were mistakenly sent to Parker Station. The postal service requested a name change; a railroad engineer suggested Aledo, after his hometown in Illinois. "My grandmother always called it 'The Station.' I don't know if she ever called it Aledo," Ray Smyth later recalled. (Courtesy of Homer Norris.)

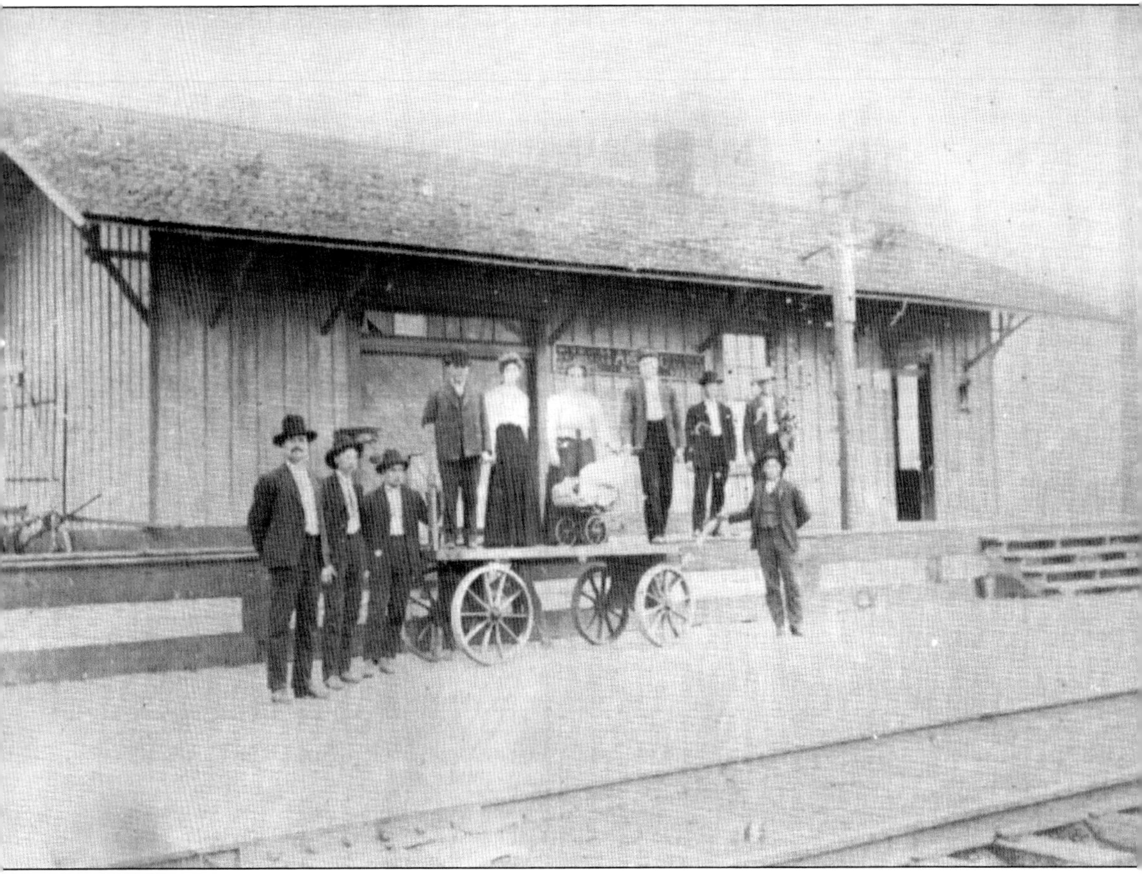

ALEDO STATION, AROUND 1902. A rare photograph of the station during its early days on North Front Street includes T. J. and Mary Elizabeth Collins standing by a carriage that held their infant daughter, Vada. Allie Gill, father of Keith and Jewel Gill White, has his hand on the rail cart at right. T. J. Collins served as the rail agent at the station. (Courtesy of Jon Vandagriff.)

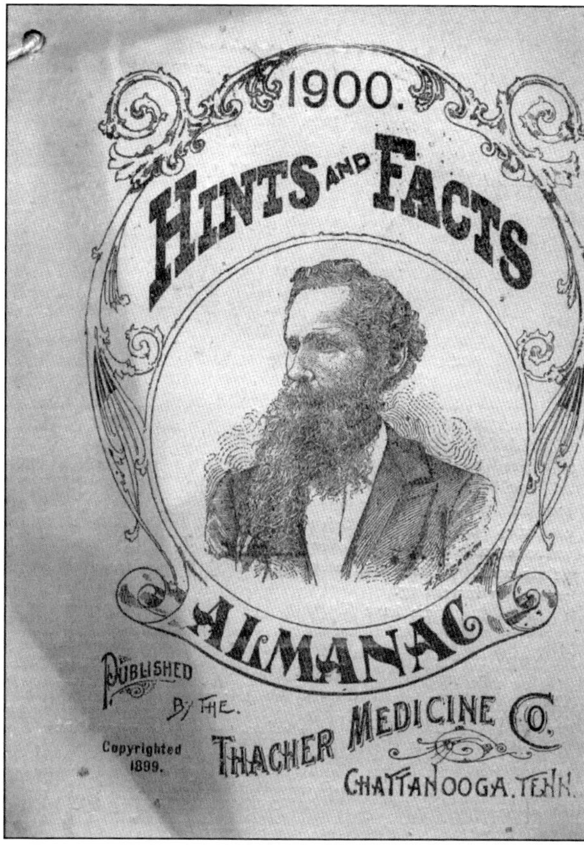

1900 Almanac. In addition to train tickets, the agent at Aledo Station sent telegrams and sold money orders, newspaper subscriptions, and almanacs. The almanac for 1900 promised weather forecasts "prepared by eminent scientist Berlin H. Wright of New York." Advertisements for products of Thacher Medicine Company touted a cholera mixture, worm medicine for children, and a liver and blood syrup, all "offered to a suffering humanity." (Courtesy of City of Aledo.)

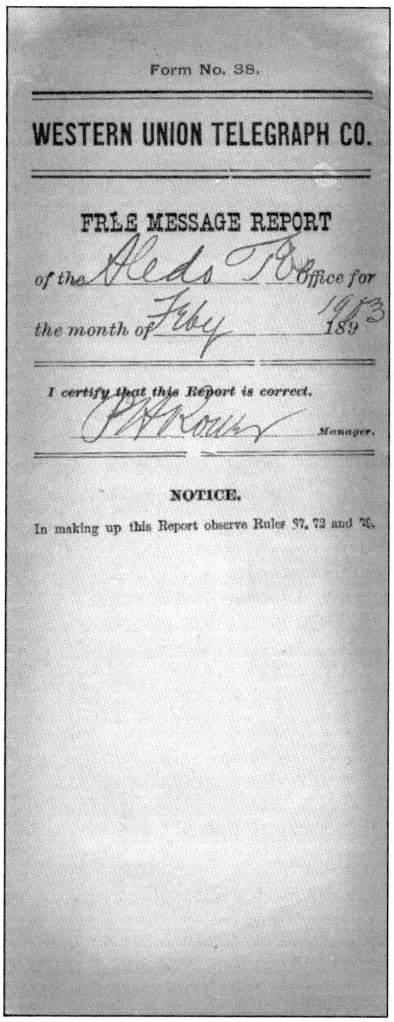

Western Union Form, 1903. The Aledo agent kept detailed records of all transactions at the station. This form summarized activity related to telegrams sent free of charge. (Courtesy of City of Aledo.)

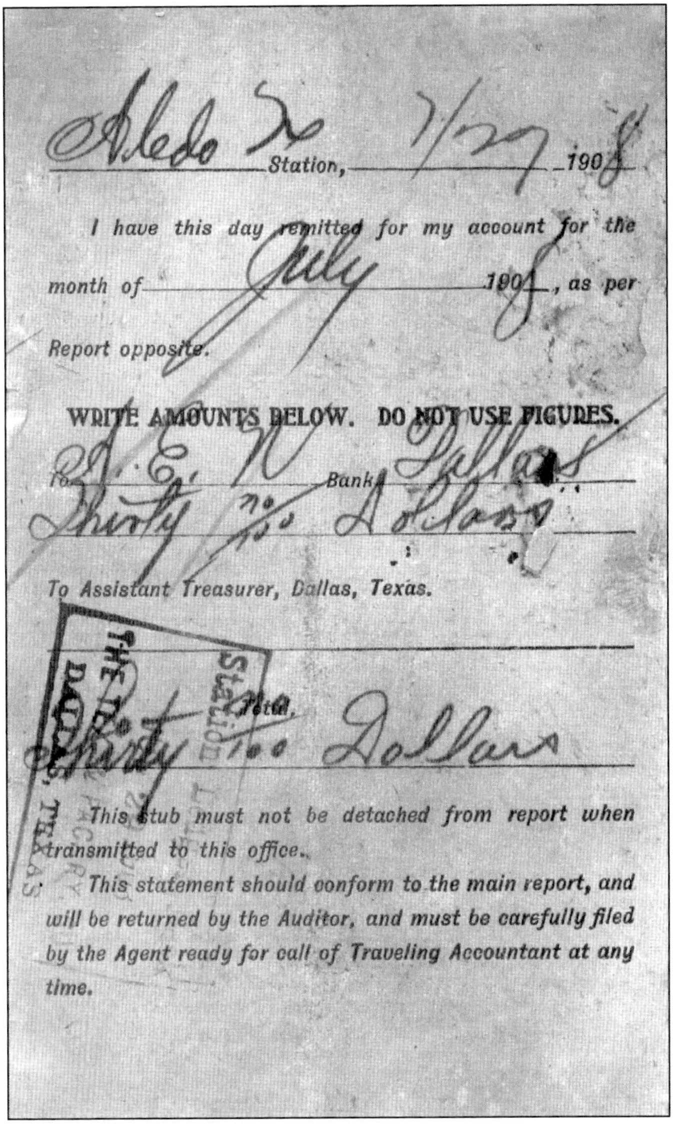

Aledo Tx 7/29 Station, 1908

I have this day remitted for my account for the month of July 1908, as per Report opposite.

WRITE AMOUNTS BELOW. DO NOT USE FIGURES.

To A. E. N. Bank Dallas

Thirty 70/100 Dollars

To Assistant Treasurer, Dallas, Texas.

Total, Thirty 70/100 Dollars

This stub must not be detached from report when transmitted to this office.

This statement should conform to the main report, and will be returned by the Auditor, and must be carefully filed by the Agent ready for call of Traveling Accountant at any time.

Remittance Form, Aledo Station, 1908. This form was submitted to the Texas and Pacific Railroad assistant treasurer by T. J. Collins. (Courtesy of City of Aledo.)

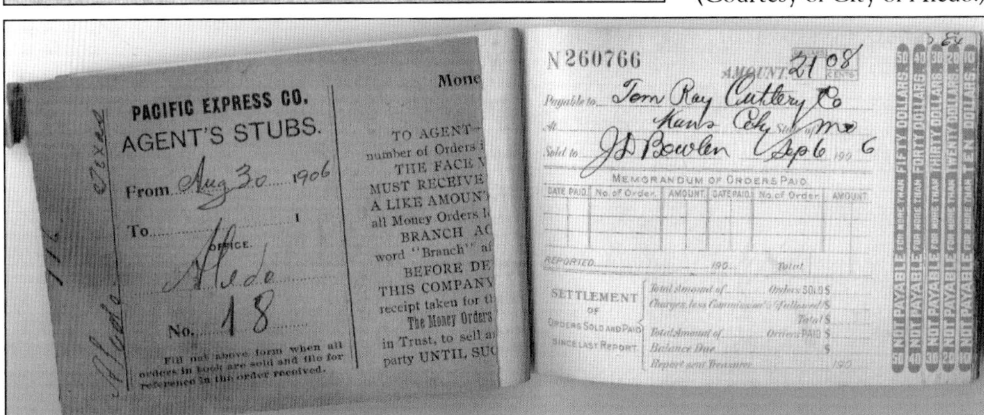

Money Order, 1906. Money orders reveal routine business transactions, like this payment of $21.08 to Tom Ray Cutlery Company by Aledo merchant J. D. "Chink" Bowlen, recorded by the station agent. Telegrams often tell a more personal story, as in the message dated July 15, 1895, from H. A. Thompson to Walter Rosinburg of Decatur, Texas: "My wife died this morning. I will bring her to Decatur for Burial. Please send this to Joe Thompson. For him to have the grave dug at Bethel at the side of our Children's graves. We will come up tomorrow on the 12 o'clock train. Meet us at the Depo [*sic*]. Dig the vault." (Courtesy of City of Aledo.)

J. J. SEARS PLATE. In 1909, J. J. Sears presented this cake plate to Brantley and Mary Wiley upon the birth of their son. The back reads, "From the store that appreciates your trade. J. J. Sears, Aledo, Texas." (Courtesy of Evlyn Wiley Broumley.)

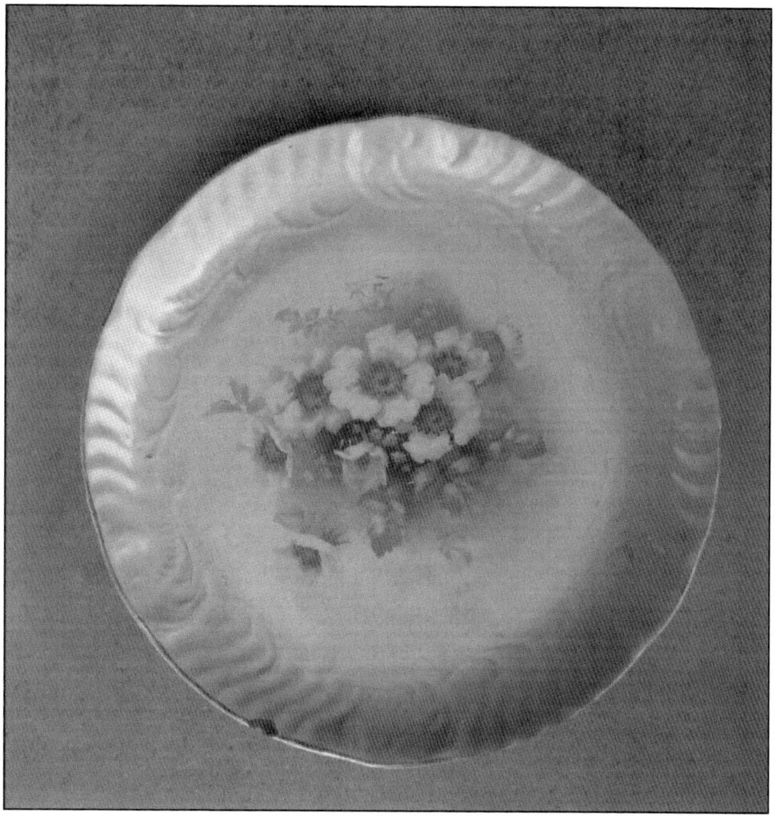

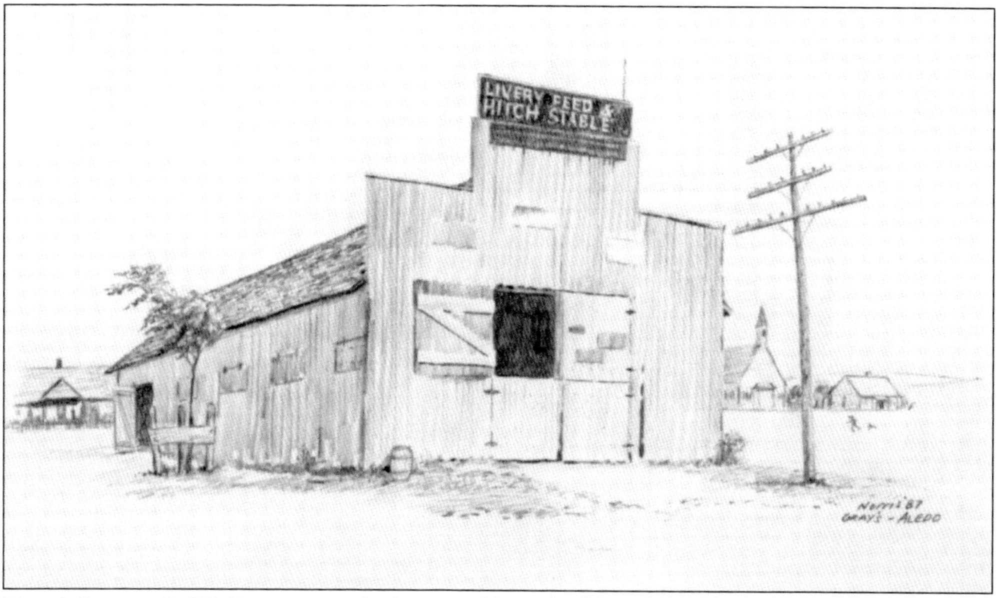

GRAY'S LIVERY. R. W. Gray operated a livery stable and sold pianos and cookstoves. Nearby, Esther Gray ran a millinery shop. Aledo United Methodist Church can bee seen in the background (Sketch by Homer Norris; courtesy of Homer Norris.)

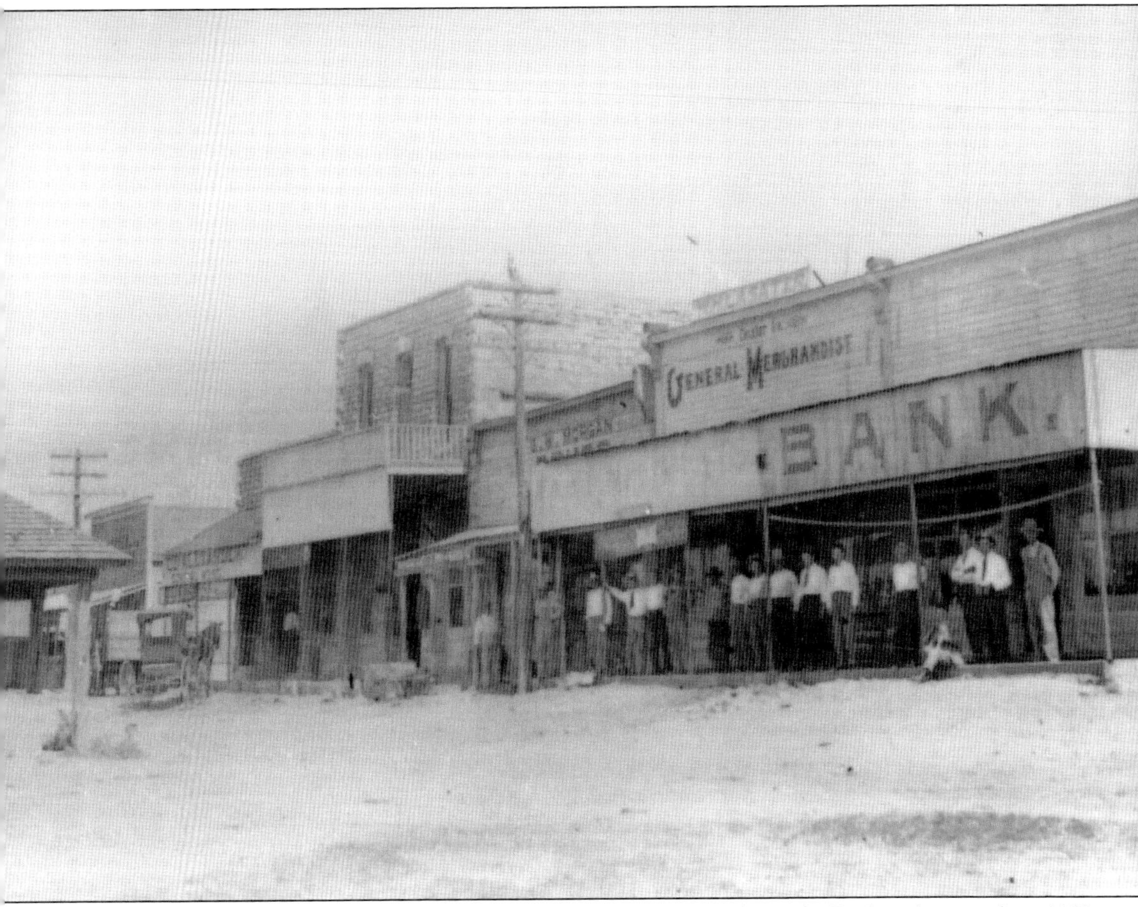

NORTH FRONT STREET, AROUND 1906. After the Texas and Pacific Railroad arrived in 1879, businesses sprang up along North Front Street in Aledo near the train station. A mail office was established in T. J. Overmier's general store; between the store and the tracks, Overmier dug a water well. For a few cents, thirsty passengers could purchase a dipper of cool water. This photograph, and a sketch of the scene by Homer Norris, have become iconic images of Old Aledo. (Photograph restoration by John Chase; courtesy of John Chase.)

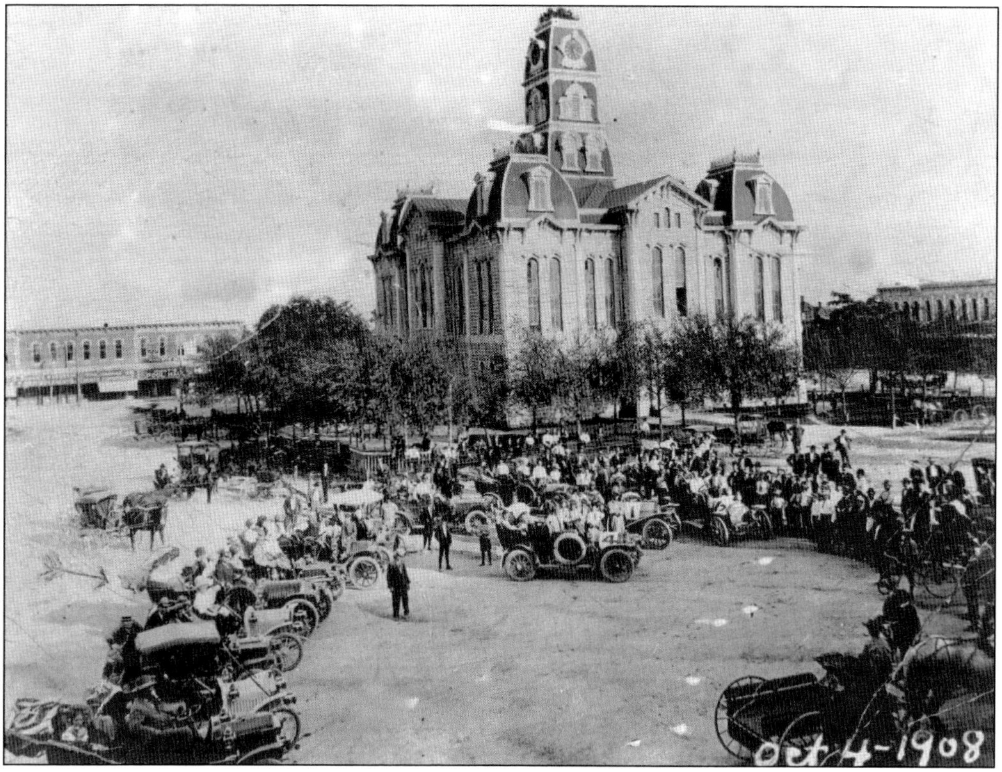

TIN LIZZIES, 1908. The car in front of the arrow drawn on the photograph at left is a seven-passenger Rainier (which cost $5,000 at the time). Charles and Eloise McFarland are in the front seat; Fred McFarland and J. P. McFarland are seated on the jump seats, and the McFarland girls are in the back seat. The cars with numbers in the center of the photograph were participants in an automobile endurance race. (Courtesy of Diane McFarland Cornwall.)

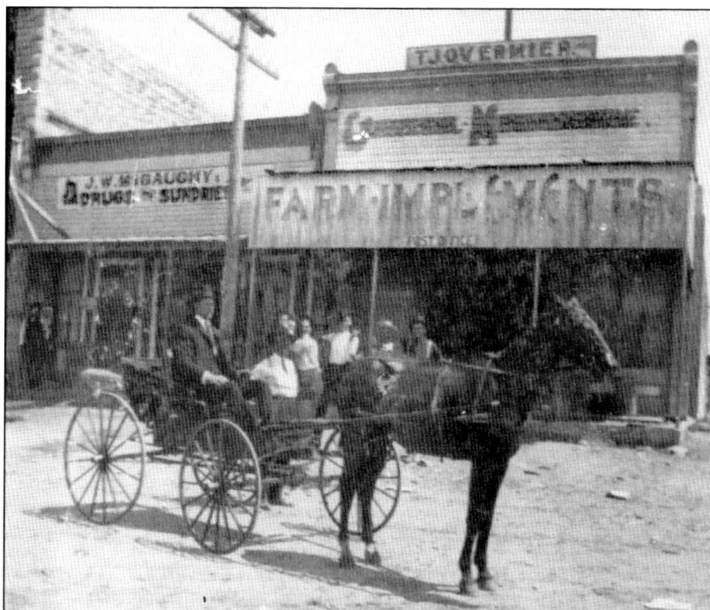

HAMPTON MEDFORD, ABOUT 1909. Medford had a windmill business and was a familiar face around town. He suffered a serious head injury after he fell off a windmill, and the resulting impairment remained for the rest of his life. Medford lived in a stone house on a bluff overlooking the Clear Fork Valley south of Aledo. Locals called the scenic point Hamp Medford Hill. (Courtesy of Homer Norris.)

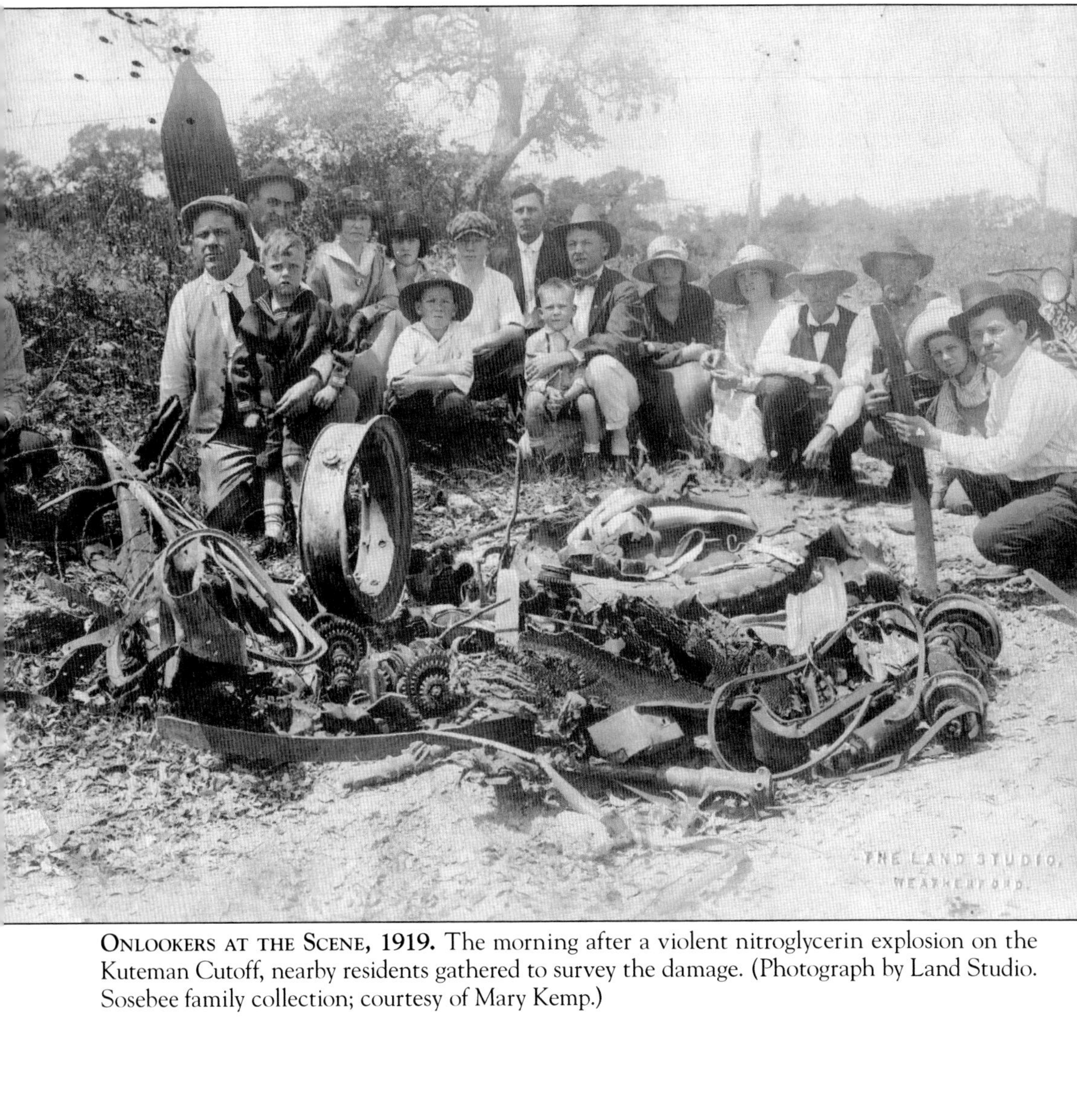

ONLOOKERS AT THE SCENE, 1919. The morning after a violent nitroglycerin explosion on the Kuteman Cutoff, nearby residents gathered to survey the damage. (Photograph by Land Studio. Sosebee family collection; courtesy of Mary Kemp.)

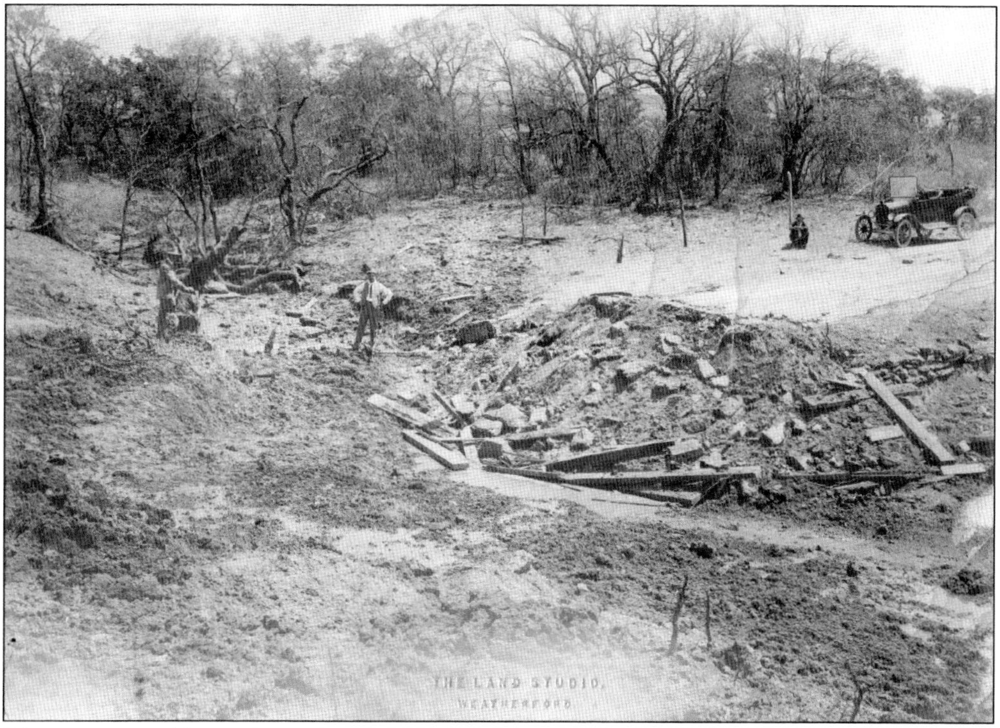

Nitroglycerin Explosion, 1919. During the oil boom of the early 20th century, nitroglycerin was used to shoot the wells. William Lindsey, a 23-year-old employee of Eastern Torpedo Company, and fellow employee John G. Evans were transporting 600 quarts of the combustible liquid when their truck hit a rough spot in the road on Kuteman Cutoff near present-day Bankhead Highway, west of Ranch House Road. The resulting explosion jarred people and broke dishes half a mile away and created a depression that was 20 feet across and 6 feet deep. Jack Borden was miles away, plowing a field in Dicey behind a team of mules; his alarmed animals escaped for several hours. (Photograph by Land Studio. Sosebee family collection; courtesy of Mary Kemp.)

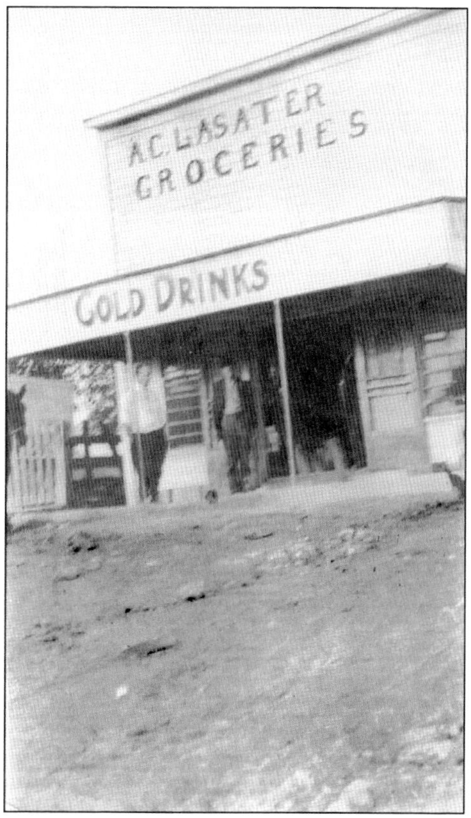

A. C. Lasater Groceries, North Front Street. Proprietor Claude Lasater, left, and an unidentified man stand in front of the longtime business in this undated photograph taken in the early 20th century. (Courtesy of Homer Norris.)

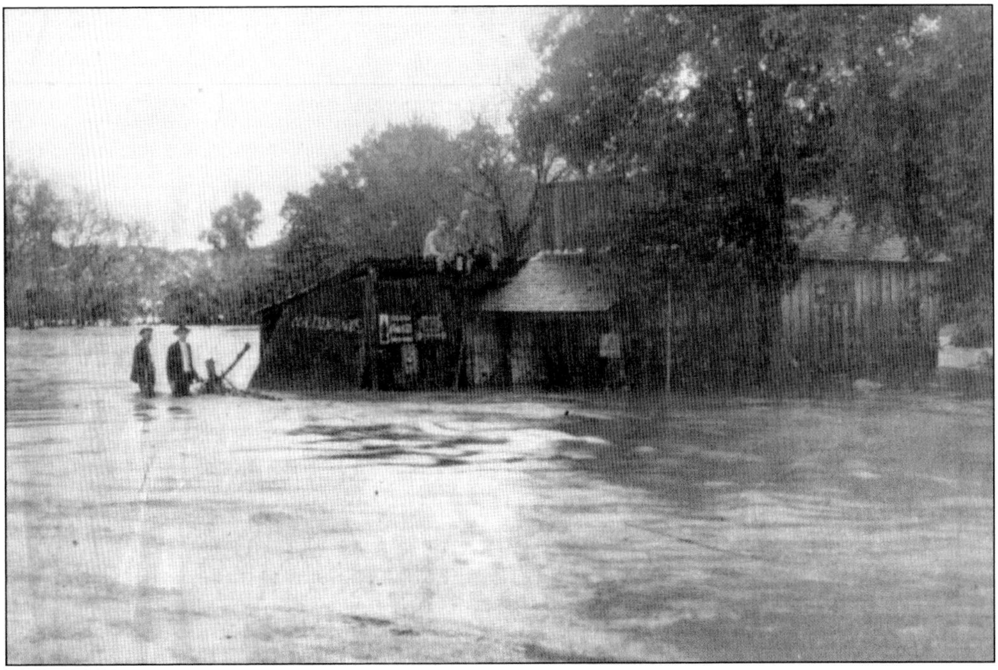

Clear Fork Flood, 1921. Tinsley's Store was literally under water when the Clear Fork rose out of its banks after torrential rains. On the roof are Everett Carnes and Roy Acres. The two men standing in the water are not identified. (Courtesy of Evlyn Wiley Broumley.)

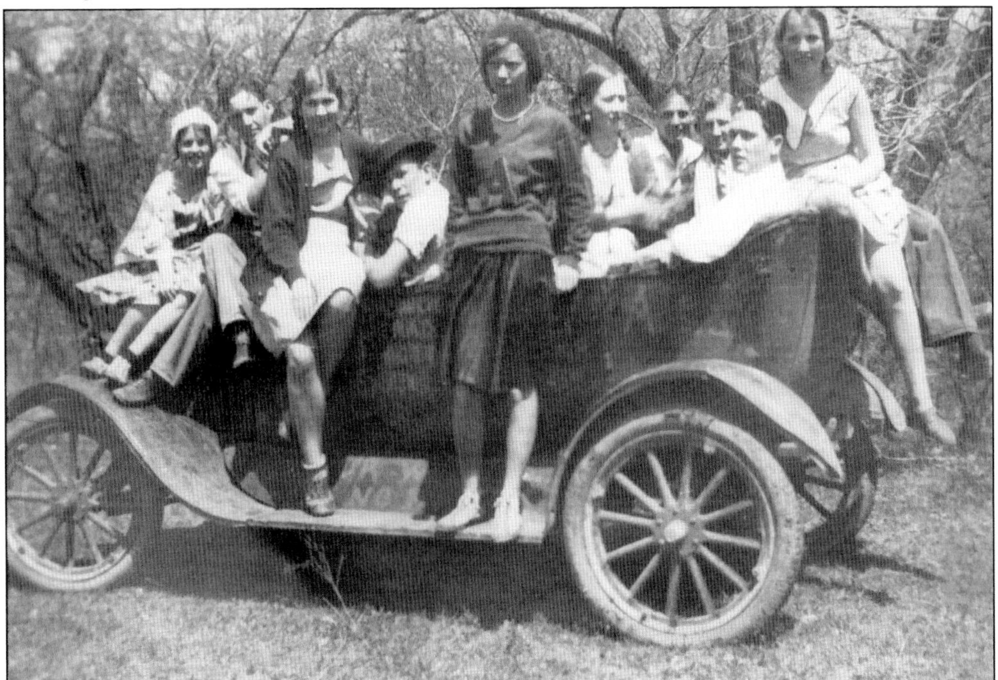

Loads of Fun. The Great Depression forced everyone to work harder, people recall, but the times sweetened friendships as well. Thomas Marvin Bennett, third from right, is pictured with his friends in this undated photograph. (Courtesy of Helen Bennett Dill.)

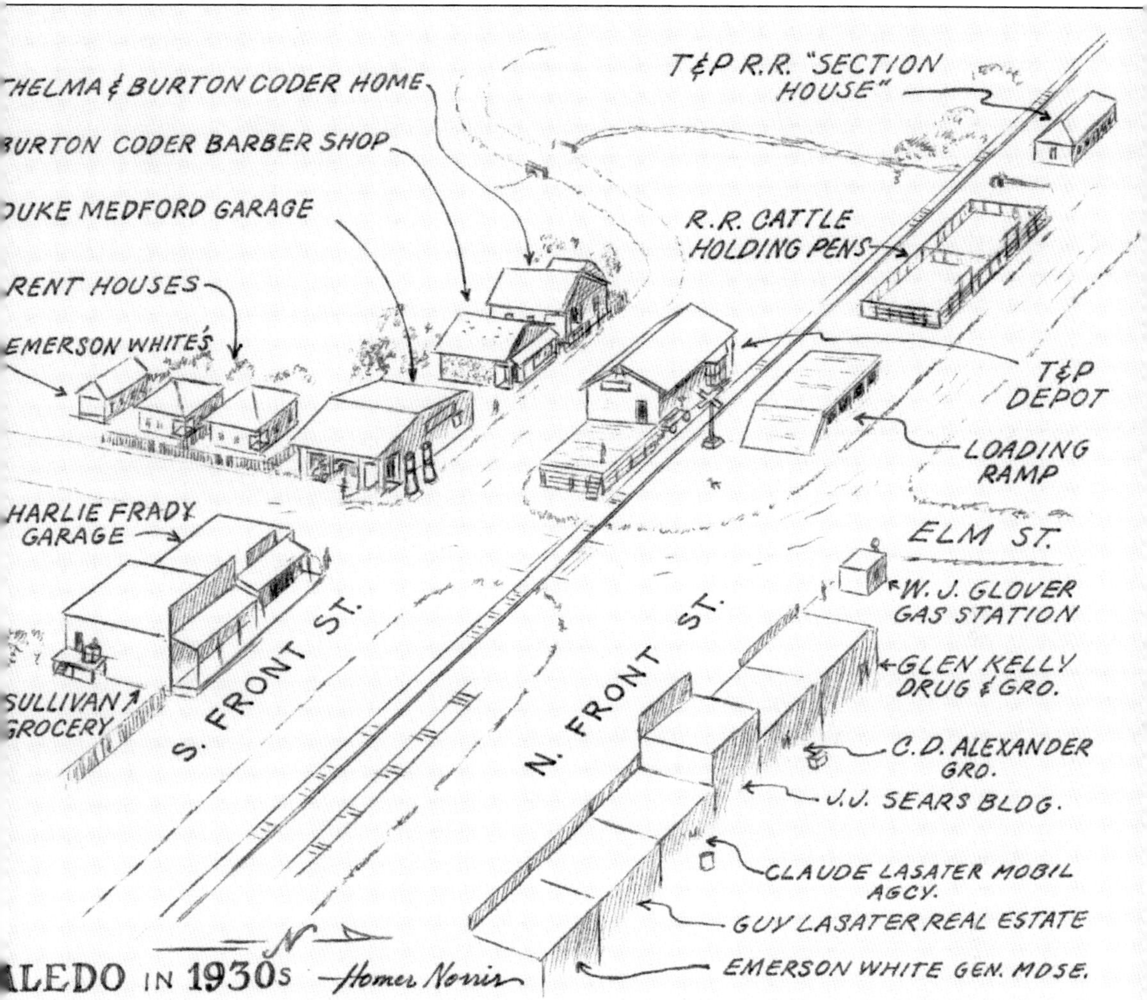

ALEDO IN THE 1930S. For much of the 20th century, Aledo served as a shipping station for cattle raised on nearby ranches. Holding pens and a loading ramp were situated near the tracks, along with a section house that provided a residence for the Texas and Pacific section foreman. FM1187, today a main thoroughfare through the town, was formerly a gravel street called Aledo Road. (Sketch by Homer Norris; courtesy of Homer Norris.)

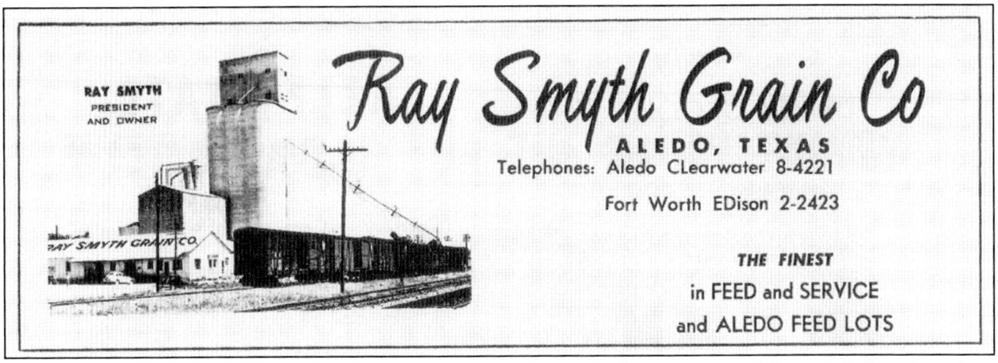

SMYTH GRAIN COMPANY, ALEDO. Depression days were tough for many of the area's families. Ray Smyth built a grain mill west of the Methodist church, pictured in this advertisement, and later expanded it to North Front Street. At times, Smyth employed 100 men; many thanked him in later years for the jobs. In a 1982 interview, he recalled, "The grain business was the only payroll Aledo had at one time." (Courtesy of Vickie Ballow Slagle.)

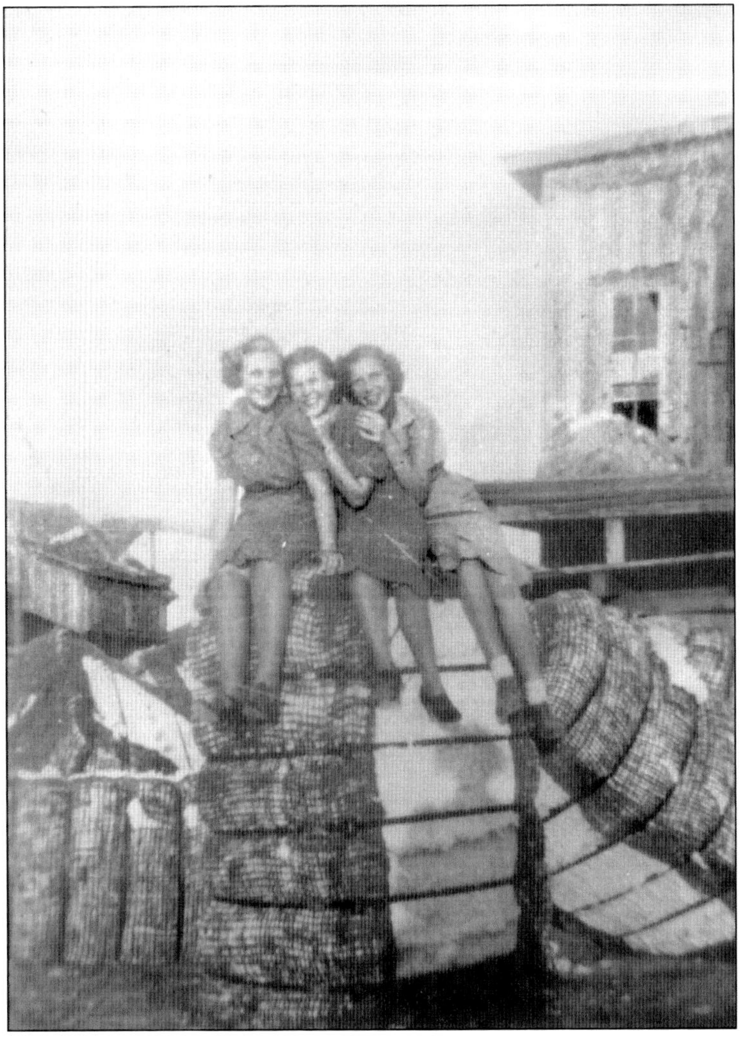

HIGH COTTON. Lenora Brown (left), Gracie Lee Barnwell (center), and Katherine Savage are pictured atop cotton bales at Tom Bennett's cotton gin in this undated photograph. (Courtesy of Helen Bennett Dill.)

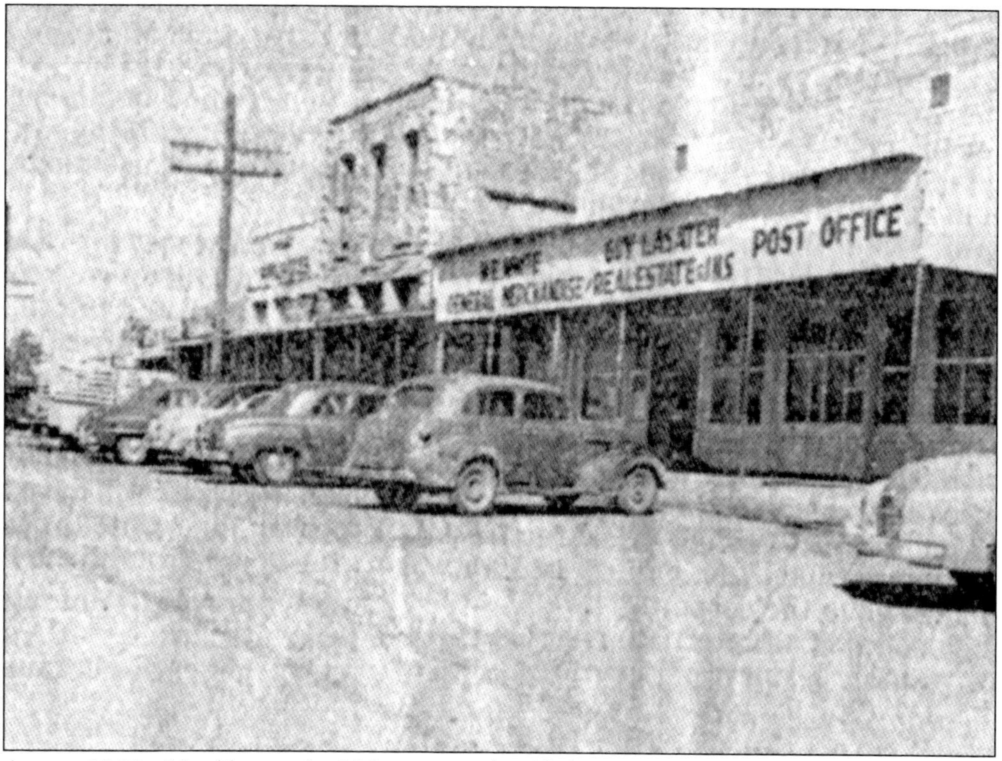

ALEDO, 1940s. Until late in the 20th century, the Aledo Post Office was located on North Front Street. (Courtesy of Nelda McGlinchey.)

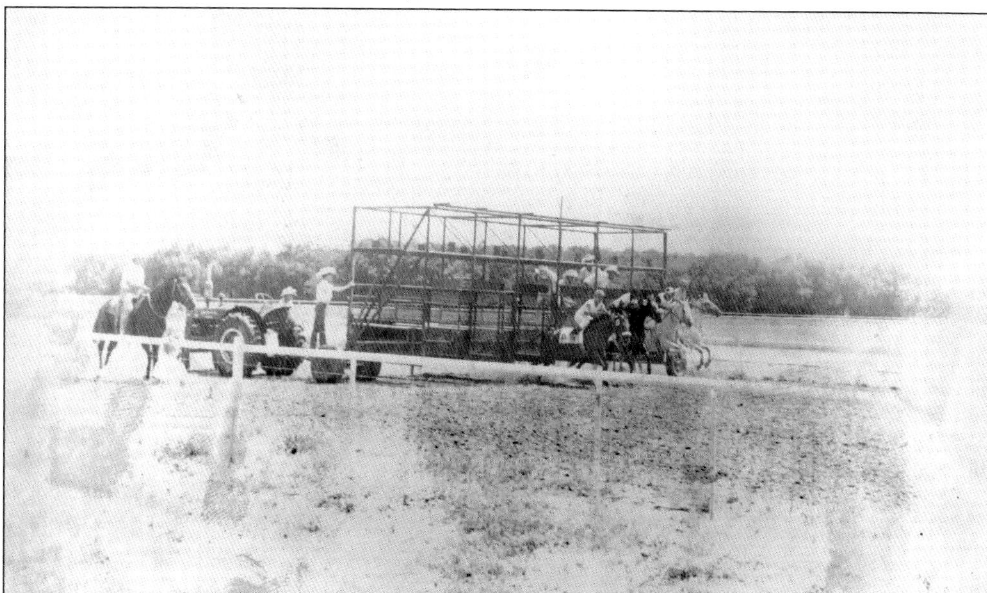

CLEAR FORK DOWNS. Horses have either trained or raced at the track near Willow Park since the 1940s. First called Clear Fork Downs, then Squaw Creek Downs during a attempt in the 1990s to create a venue for pari-mutuel racing, the facility is now a racehorse training center called Trinity Meadows. (Courtesy of Jon Vandagriff.)

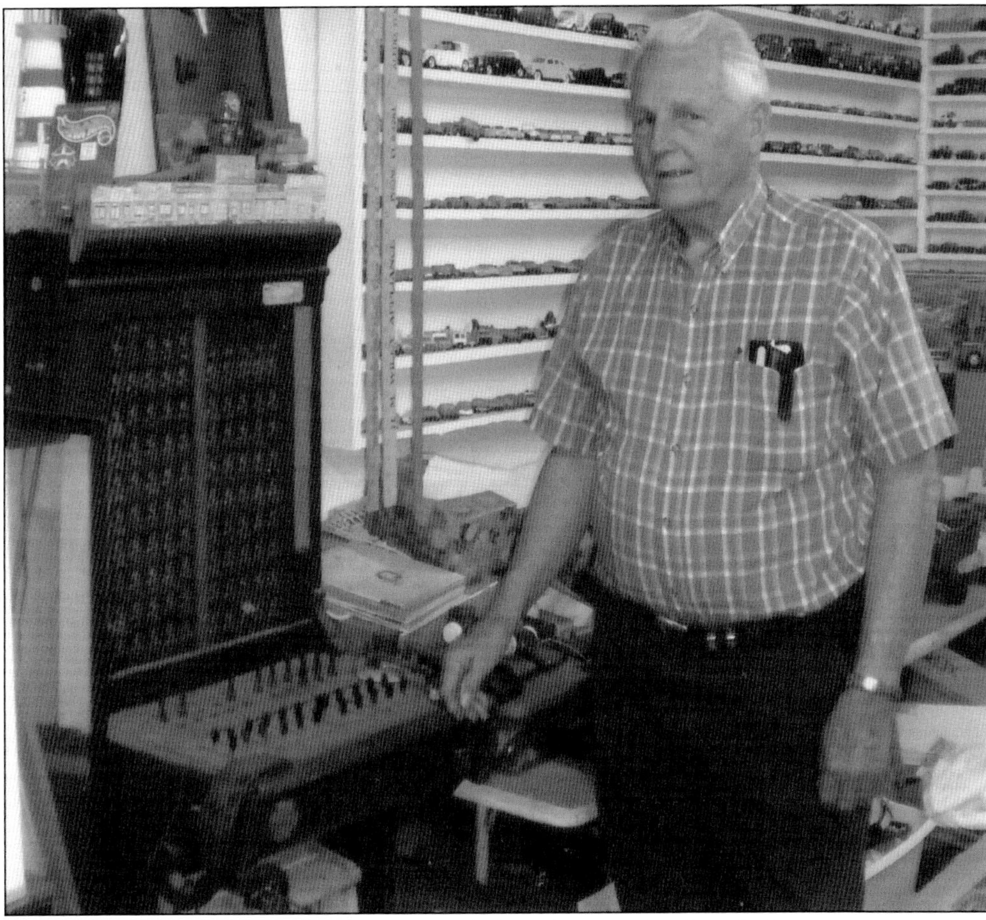

The Party Line. Freddy Detherage once worked as a lineman for the telephone company owned by Duke Medford in Aledo. Today he owns the old switchboard. (Photograph by the author.)

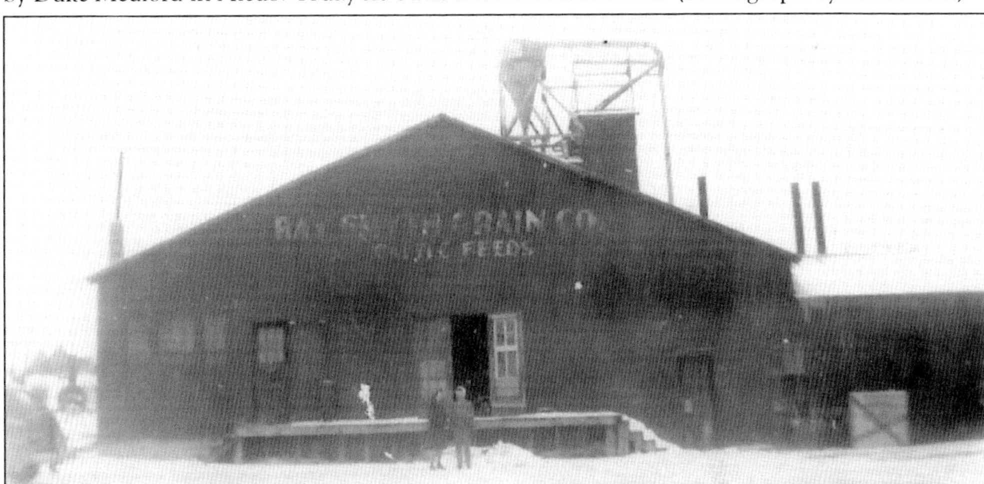

Ray Smyth Grain Company, around 1952. Reflective of its rural roots, Aledo has long had a grain or feed facility at the east end of North Front Street. (Courtesy of Loweda Wood.)

FIRST FIRE TRUCK. Members of the Aledo Volunteer Fire Department stand by the 35-gallon-per-minute booster. Pictured from left to right are Carl Robbins, Jerry Kelly, and Alvin Bennett, the first fire chief. (Courtesy of Homer Norris.)

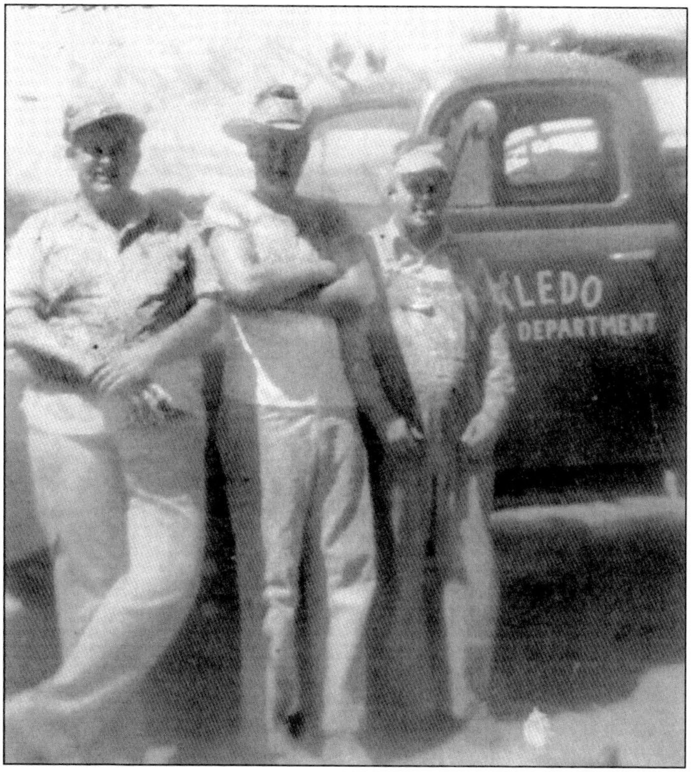

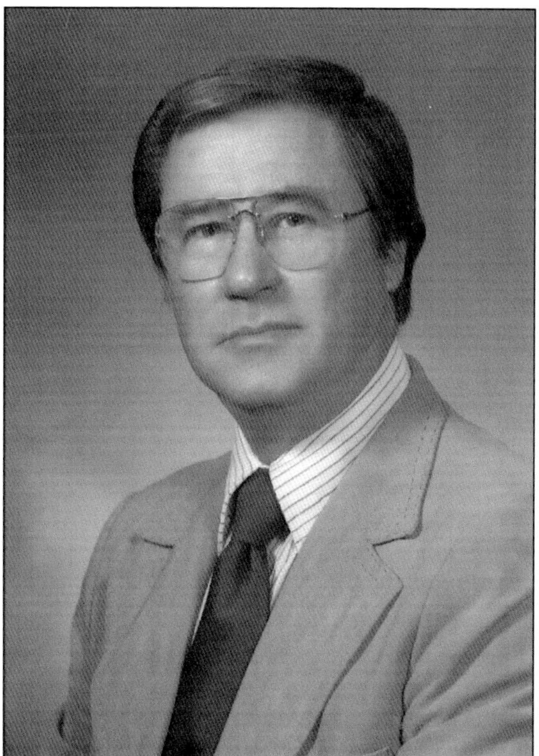

FIRST MAYOR. In 1963, Aledo incorporated. The first mayor, Robert Daugherty, served from 1963 to 1968. (Courtesy of the City of Aledo.)

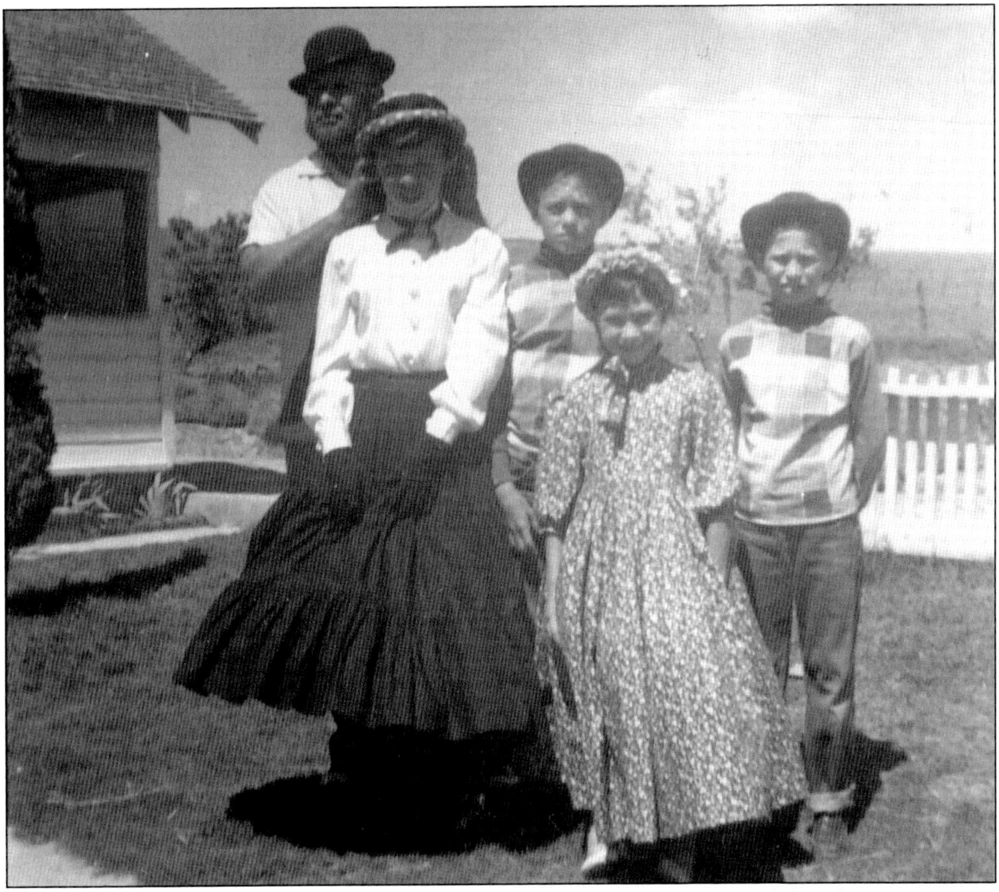

CENTENNIAL CELEBRATION. Tom Scott and his children, (from left to right) Judy, Terry, Mary, and Mike, prepare to participate in the Parker County Centennial Parade in 1956. (Courtesy of Reubene Gressett Scott.)

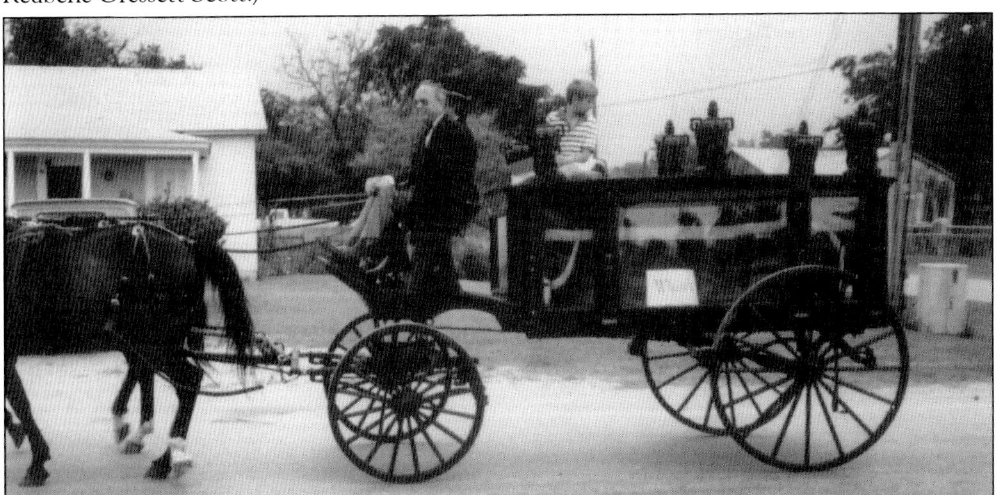

ALEDO CENTENNIAL PARADE. M. L. White led an early hearse through the streets of Aledo as the city celebrated its first 100 years. (Courtesy of Vickie Ballow Slagle.)

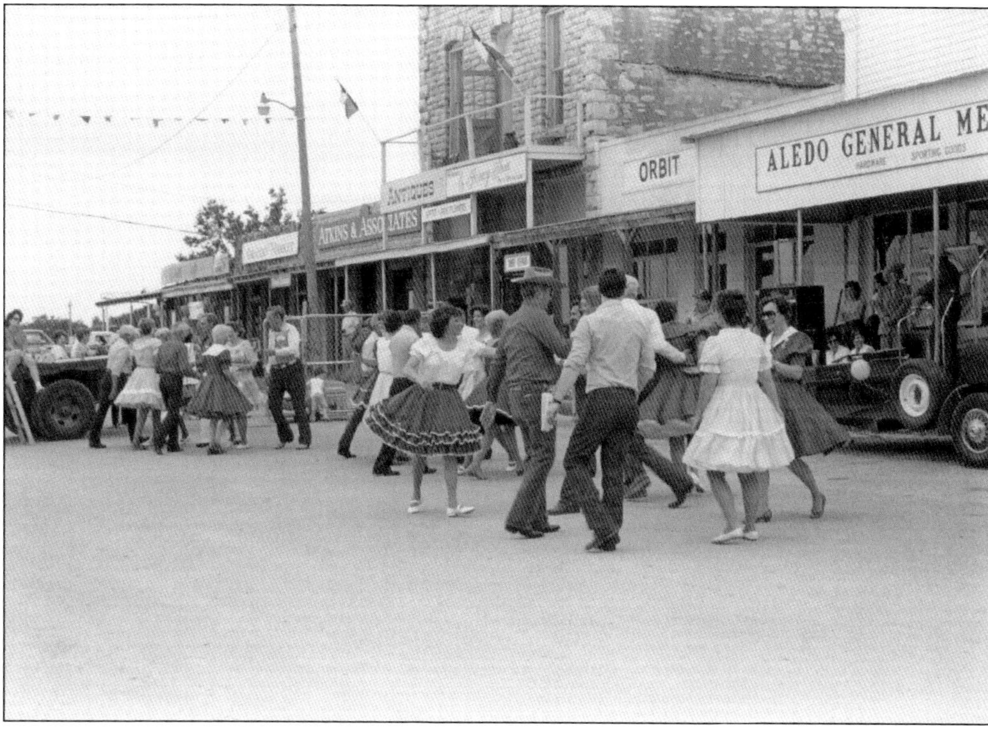

CENTENNIAL STREET DANCE. Aledo residents celebrated the city centennial with a parade, games, and a dance on North Front Street. (Courtesy of John Chase.)

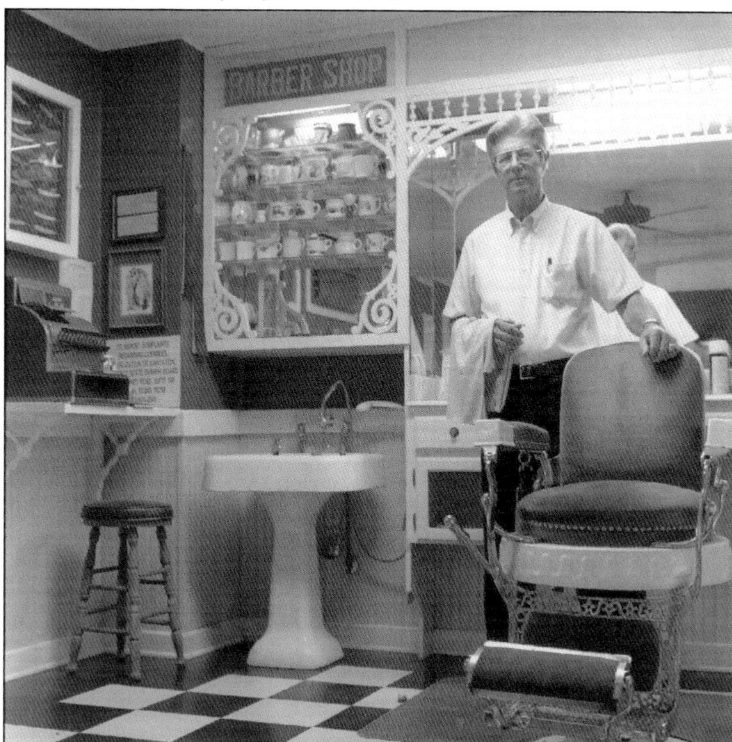

G. L. LOWE, BARBER. The barbershop at Maverick and Old Annetta Road served many an Aledo resident during the late 20th and early 21st centuries. (Courtesy of John Chase.)

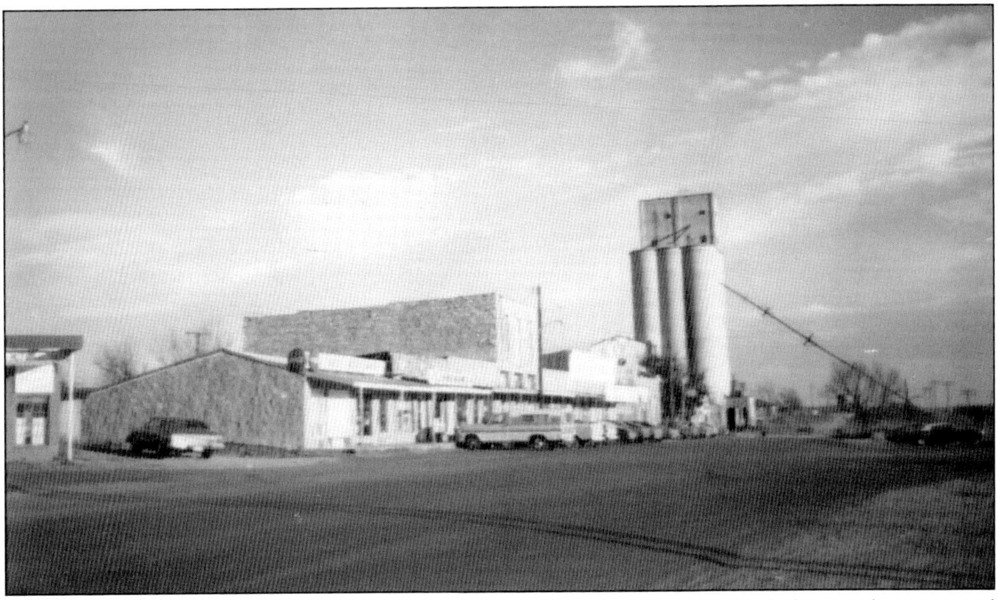

North Front Street in the 1950s and in the 1970s. Devotees of Aledo history have strived to preserve North Front Street, as seen here in the similarities between the photograph above of the street in the 1950s and the 1970s image below. (Above, courtesy of Homer Norris; below, courtesy of John Chase.)

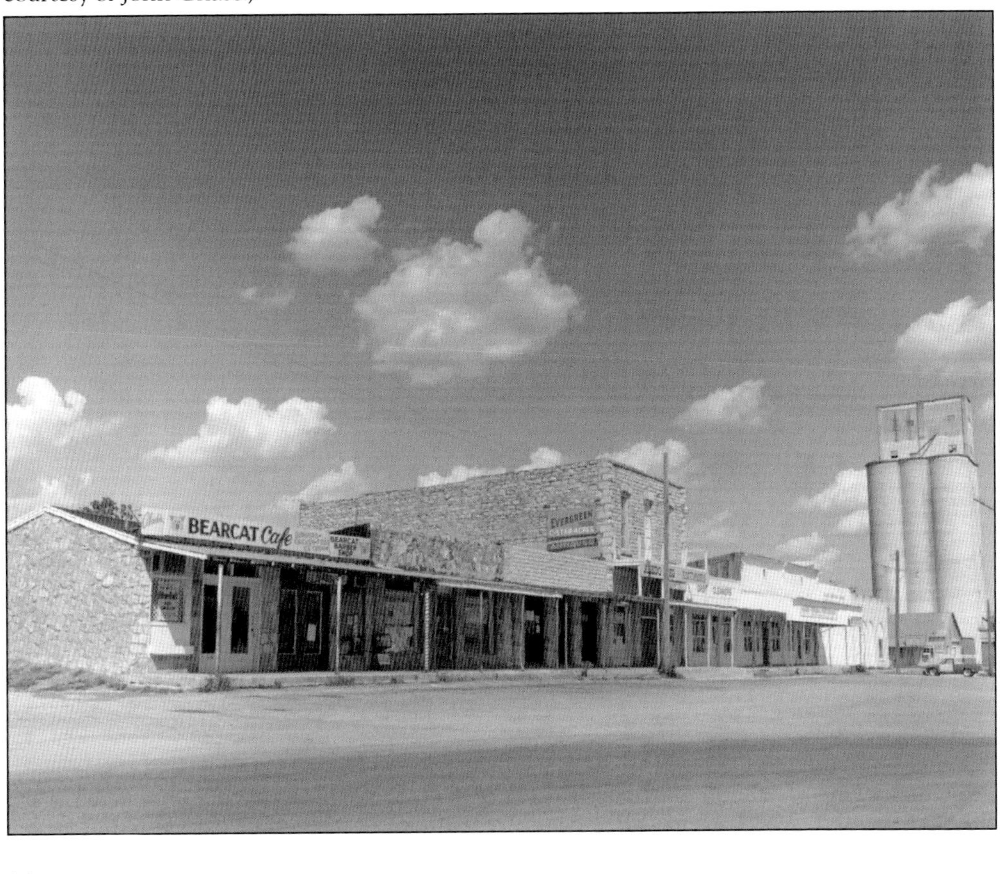

Six

HOME AND HEARTH

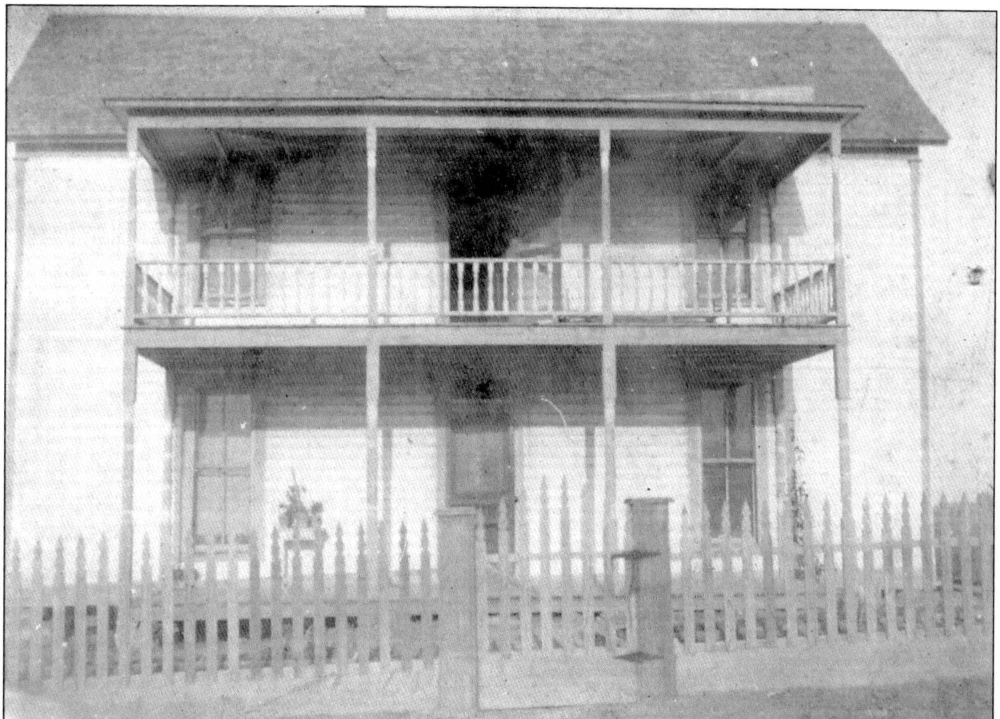

PERRY HOTEL. One of the earliest structures in Aledo, this folk Victorian dwelling on Walnut Street was built in 1863 of pine shipped by rail from Georgia. The Perry family arrived from Alabama in 1869 and purchased the home. No information regarding the original owner survives; brothers and Confederate soldiers William and Jerome Perry rounded up Civil War deserters. The local landmark once served as a rooming house and remained in the family until 2006, when a restorer bought the structure, dismantled it, and placed it in storage. (Courtesy of Randy Keck/ *Community News*.)

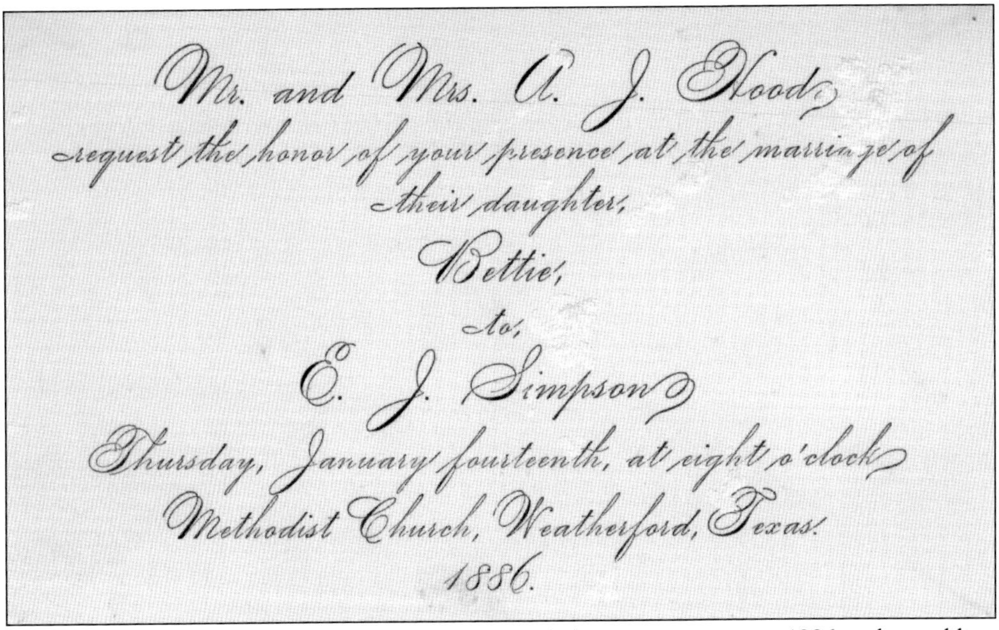

Mr. and Mrs. A. J. Hood
request the honor of your presence at the marriage of
their daughter,
Bettie,
to,
E. J. Simpson
Thursday, January fourteenth, at eight o'clock
Methodist Church, Weatherford, Texas.
1886.

WEDDING INVITATION, 1886. Judge A. J. Hood issued elegant invitations in 1886 to the wedding of his daughter, Bettie, to E. J. Simpson. (Courtesy of Jackie McLennan.)

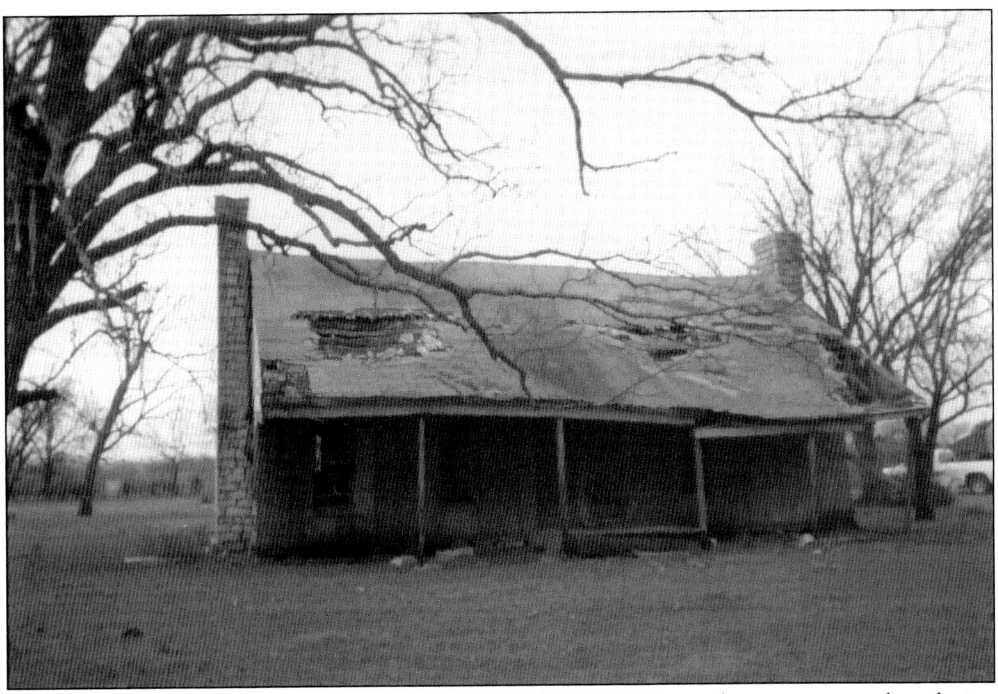

EASTMAN HOME. "May 13, 1873 A.D." was chiseled on an exterior chimney stone, thus dating the two-story home built by A. W. Eastman, an early farmer in the area. The photograph itself is undated. (Courtesy of Bill and Leta Johnson Eastman.)

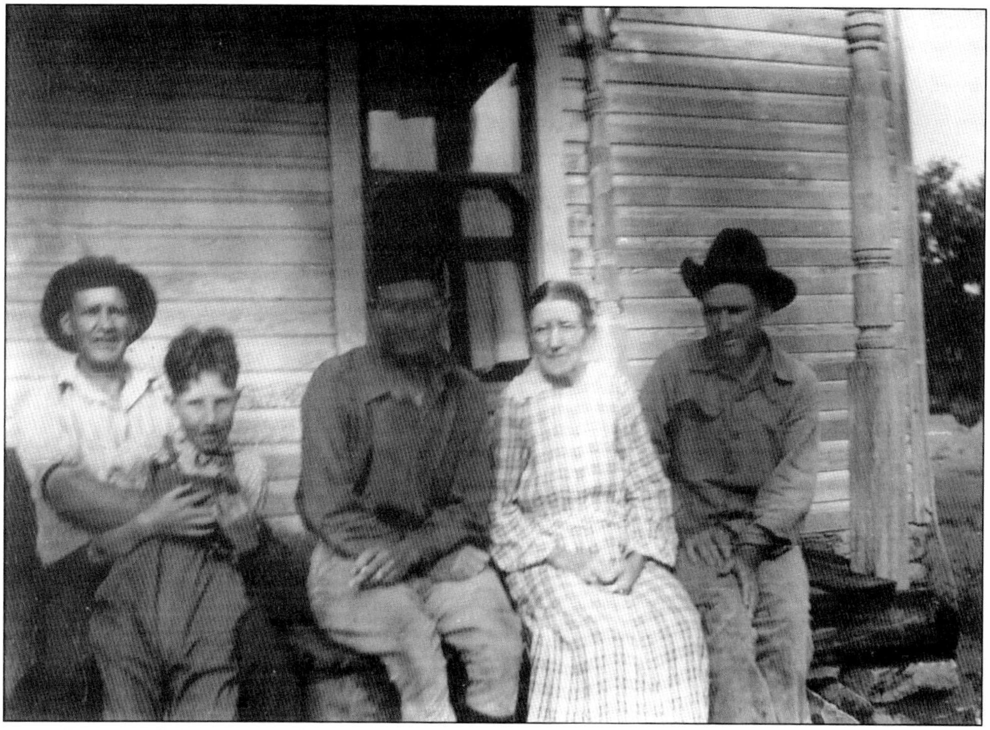

ELLA BROWN O'NEALL MCGLINCHEY AND FAMILY. Born in 1855 in New York, Ella O'Neall was widowed after her arrival in Parker County. She was remarried to Irishman John Joseph McGlinchey. Pictured here at the McGlinchey homestead near Center are, from left to right, Bill O'Neall with an unidentified boy, Finley McGlinchey, Ella Brown O'Neall McGlinchey, and John McGlinchey. (Courtesy of Nelda McGlinchey.)

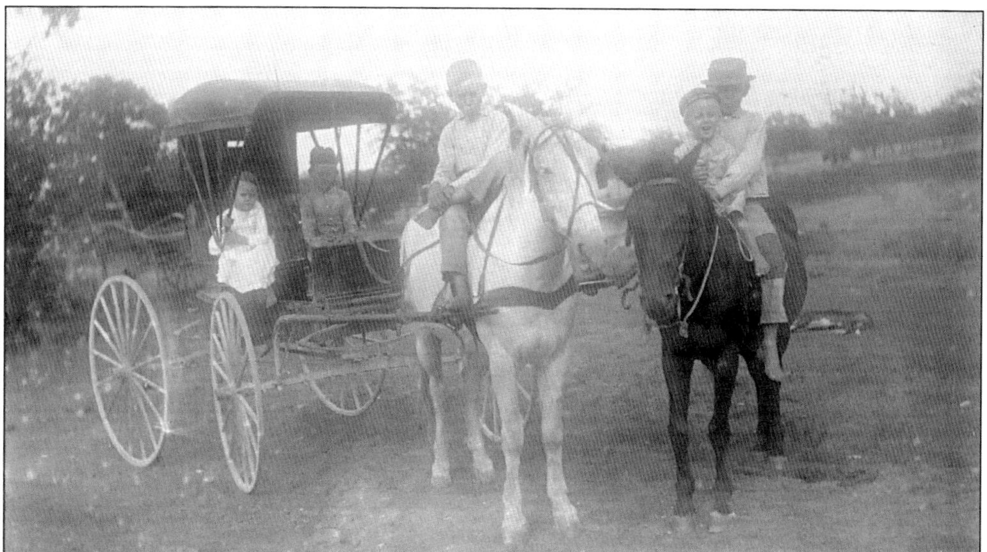

JOHN D. FARMER CHILDREN, 1907. Buggies and horse were the favored mode of transportation for many families until the 1920s. Pictured here from left to right are Linnie, Ralph, Tom, Maurice, and Louie Farmer. (Courtesy of Mary Lynn Bigby Jones.)

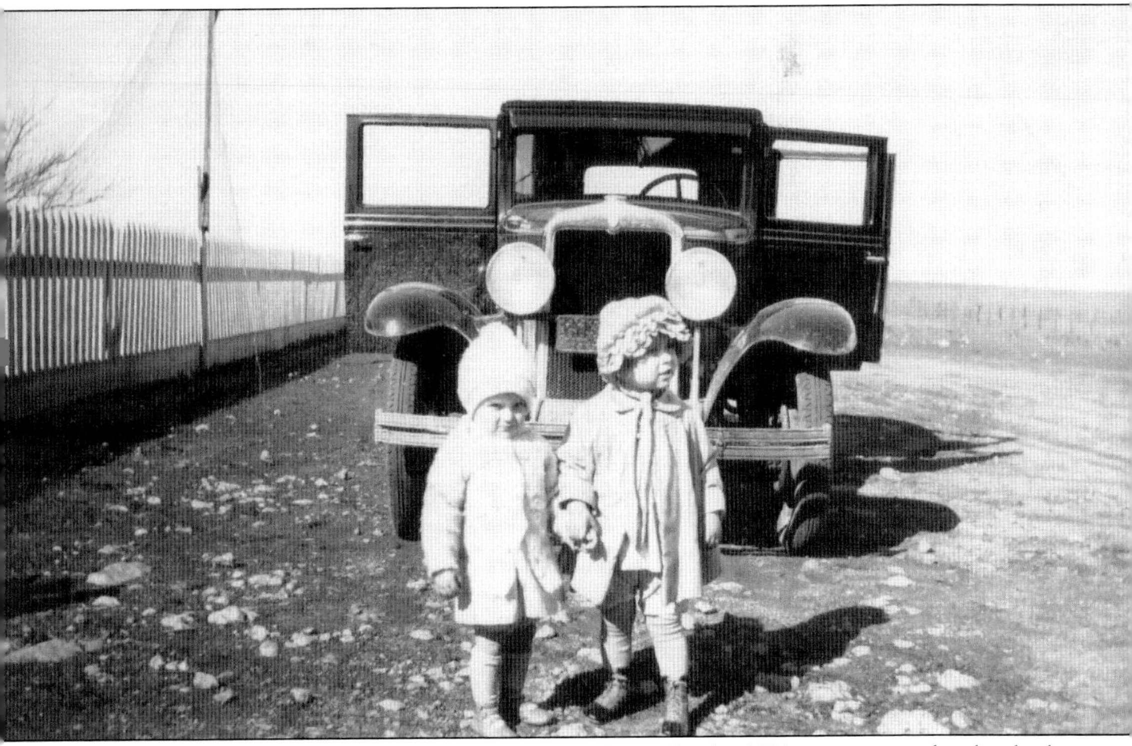

MAURICE CLIFFORD FARMER AND MARY LYNNE BIGBY. By the 1920s, many area families had an automobile—and a horse or two. (Courtesy of Mary Lynn Bigby Jones.)

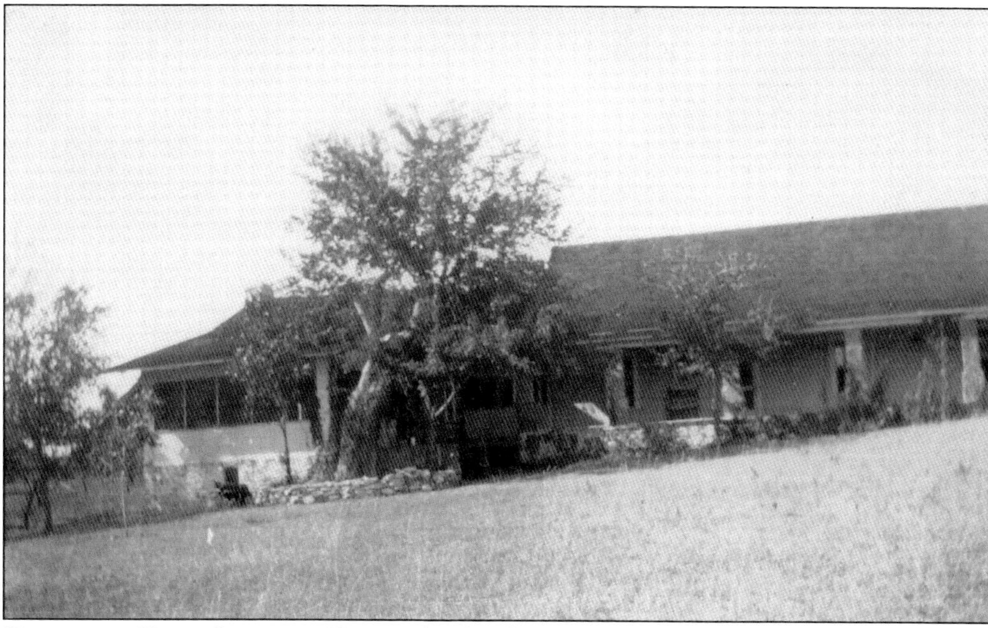

Courtenay Hood Chatham Home. The daughter of early settler A. J. Hood built her home around 1910 near the original Hood cabin and lived in the home until 1950 or so. She often regaled youngsters with stories about the Comanches who roamed the land when the Hoods first arrived in Parker County. Today the home is privately owned, with the historic Hood cabin semi-attached, and the irises that Chatham planted still bloom in the spring. (Courtesy of Jan Orr-Harter.)

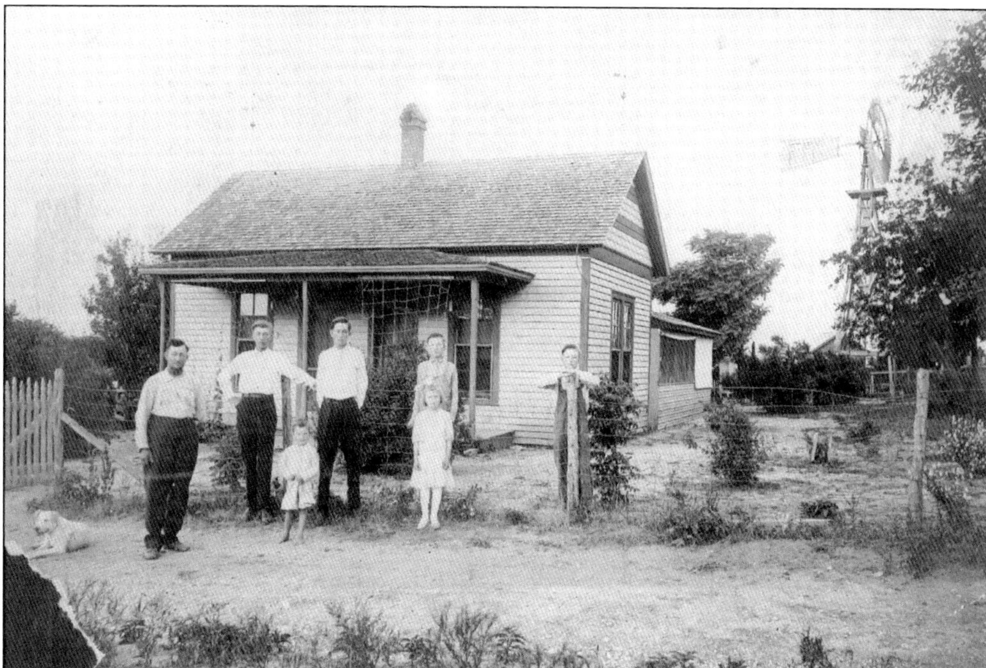

The Coder Family. Early settler C. F. Coder poses at home with six of his eight children, including March, Guy, Burton, Harry, and Kathryn, around 1913. (Courtesy of the Doss Heritage and Cultural Center.)

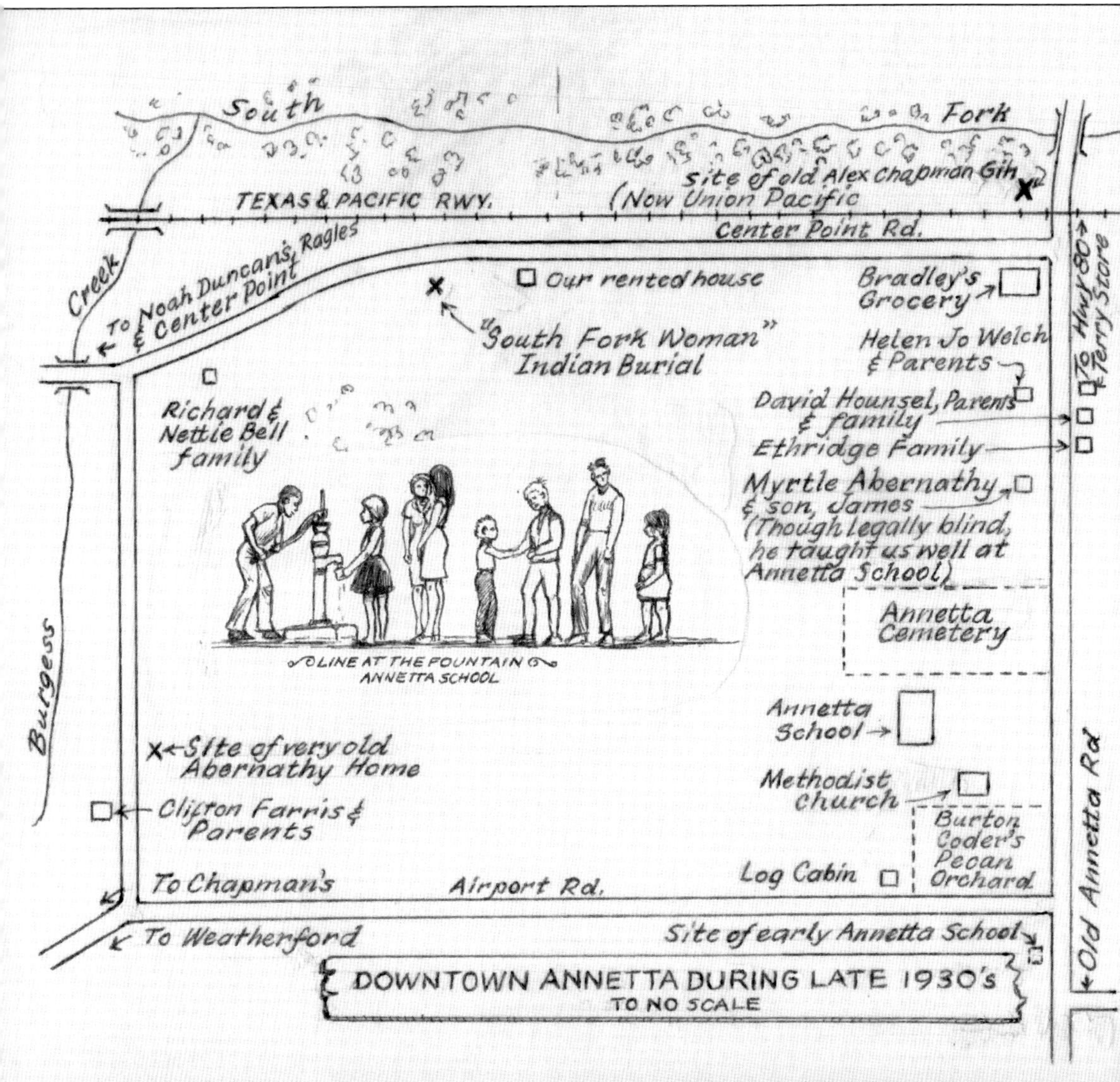

DOWNTOWN ANNETTA, LATE 1930S. The small settlement was established soon after the Texas and Pacific Railroad purchased the right-of-way from S. A. Winslow. A. B. Fraser built a post office and general store and named the new town after his daughter Anneta. By the late 1930s, a small grocery, school and Methodist church served the residents of the burg. In 1979, the area was incorporated as three cities, Annetta, Annetta South, and Annetta North, and the spelling "Annetta" had replaced the original name. (Sketch by Homer Norris; courtesy of Homer Norris.)

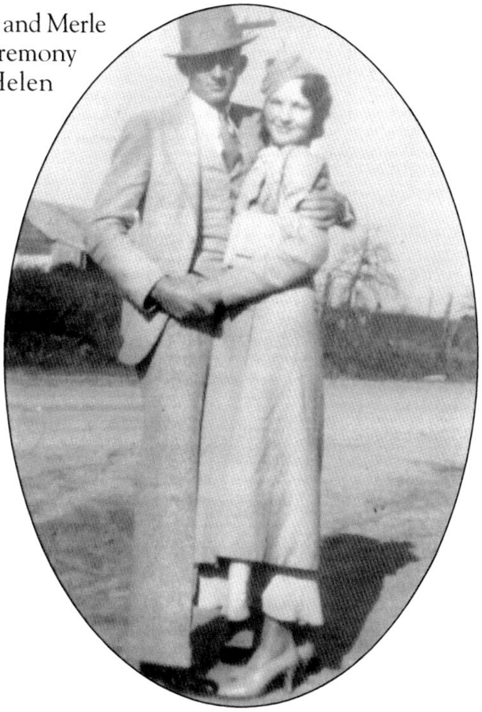

WEDDING DAY, 1932. Newlyweds Thomas Marvin and Merle Bennett posed on the day of their marriage ceremony to create a family keepsake. (Courtesy of Helen Bennett Dill.)

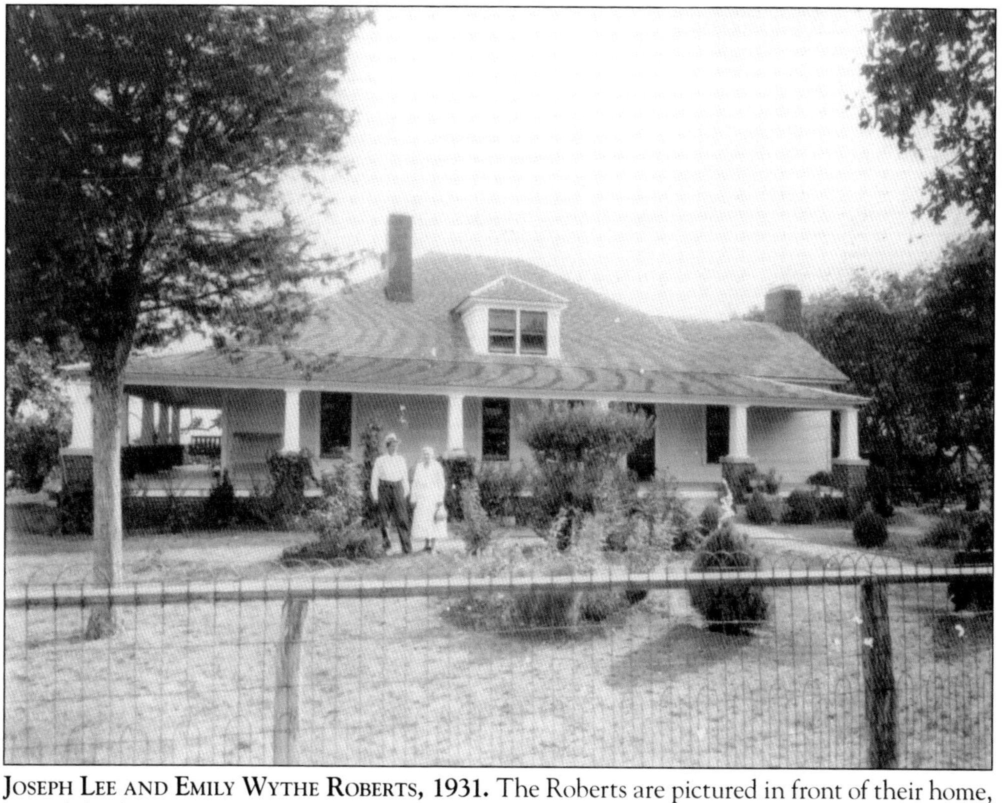

JOSEPH LEE AND EMILY WYTHE ROBERTS, 1931. The Roberts are pictured in front of their home, one of the first in Dicey. (Courtesy of Mary Roberts.)

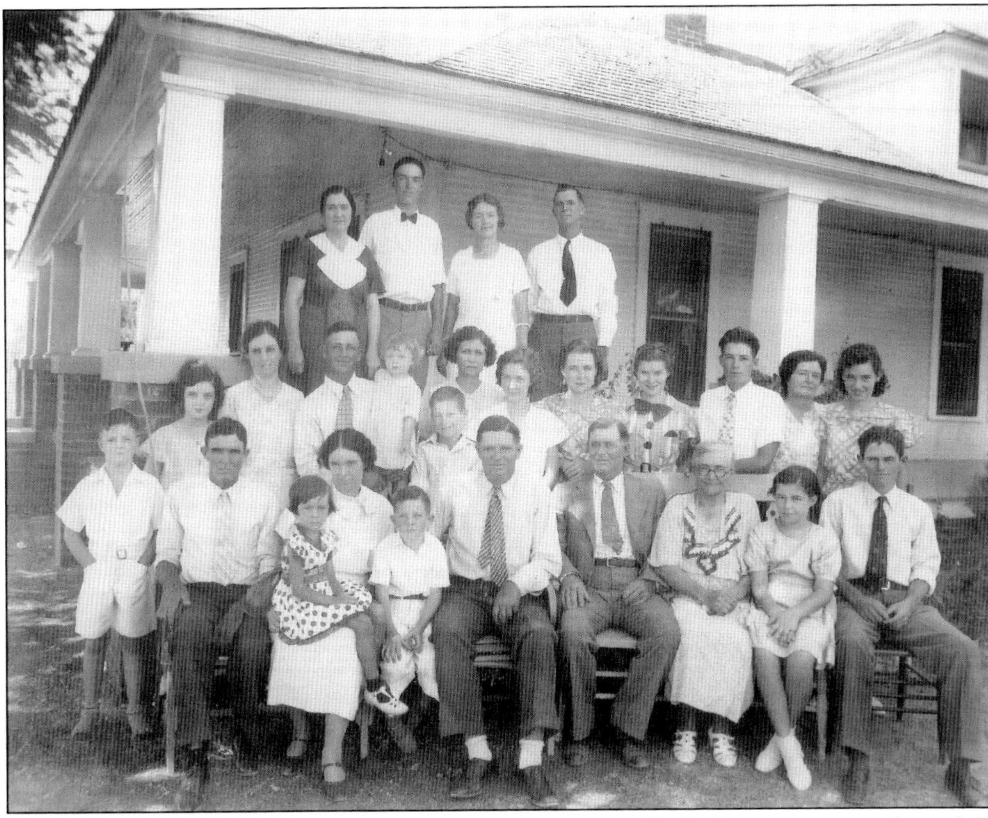

Joseph Lee and Emily Wythe Roberts, 50th Anniversary. The Roberts were integral members of the Dicey community near present-day Lake Weatherford. The extended family gathered to celebrate the couple's golden anniversary on August 13, 1934. From left to right are (first row) Bill and Wythe Roberts, Malvern Pearson, Julia Roberts Pearson, Wyman Pearson, Hubert Roberts, J. Lee and Emily Roberts, Emma Jo Small, and Dan Ballinger; (second row) Anne Beth, Lois Roberts, Austin (holding Patsy), James Pearson, Eunice Roberts, Dorothy Low, Margery and LeFreda Small, Bobby, Mary, and Floy Ballinger; (third row) Augusta Small, Z. E. Roberts, Ruth Roberts, and Zone Roberts. (Courtesy of Mary Roberts.)

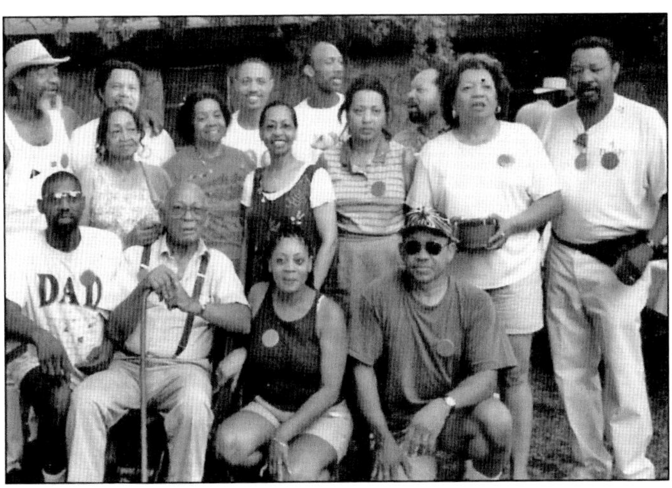

Gratts Family Reunions. The Gratts family was one of Annetta's founding families. Since 1945, family members have gathered each August; up to 200 relatives attend the annual reunion. Here, in 1998, Lawson Gratts III (with cane) poses with 13 of his 15 children. (Courtesy of Josef Gratts.)

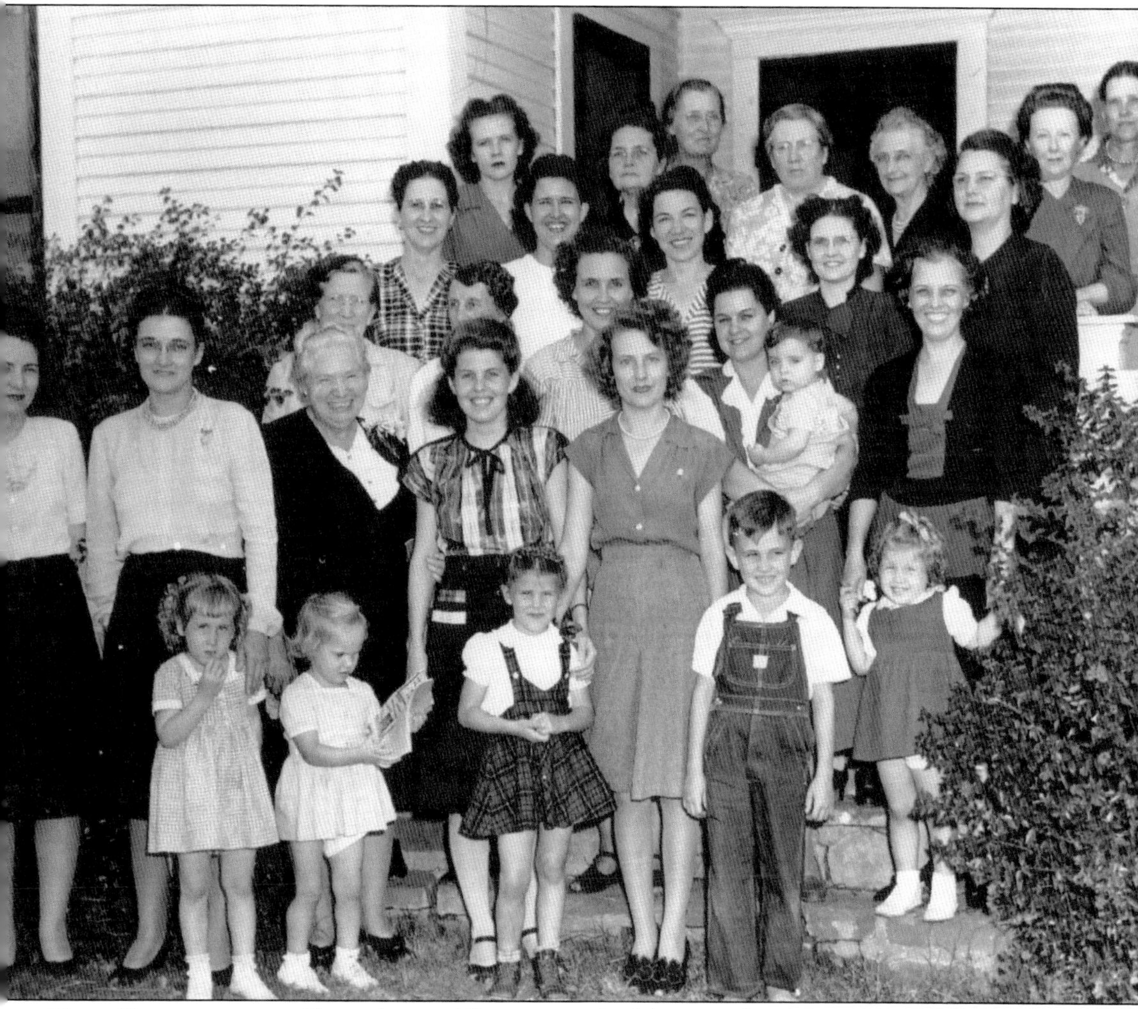

HOME DEMONSTRATION CLUB, ALEDO. These women's clubs earned popularity during the Great Depression, when local agents taught homemakers about relief gardens, food conservation, and clothing construction. By 1950, home demonstration clubs began health and community improvement drives, and agents were helping members with financial planning and preparation of wills. This undated photograph includes the matriarchs of many Aledo area families. (Courtesy of Nelda McGlinchey.)

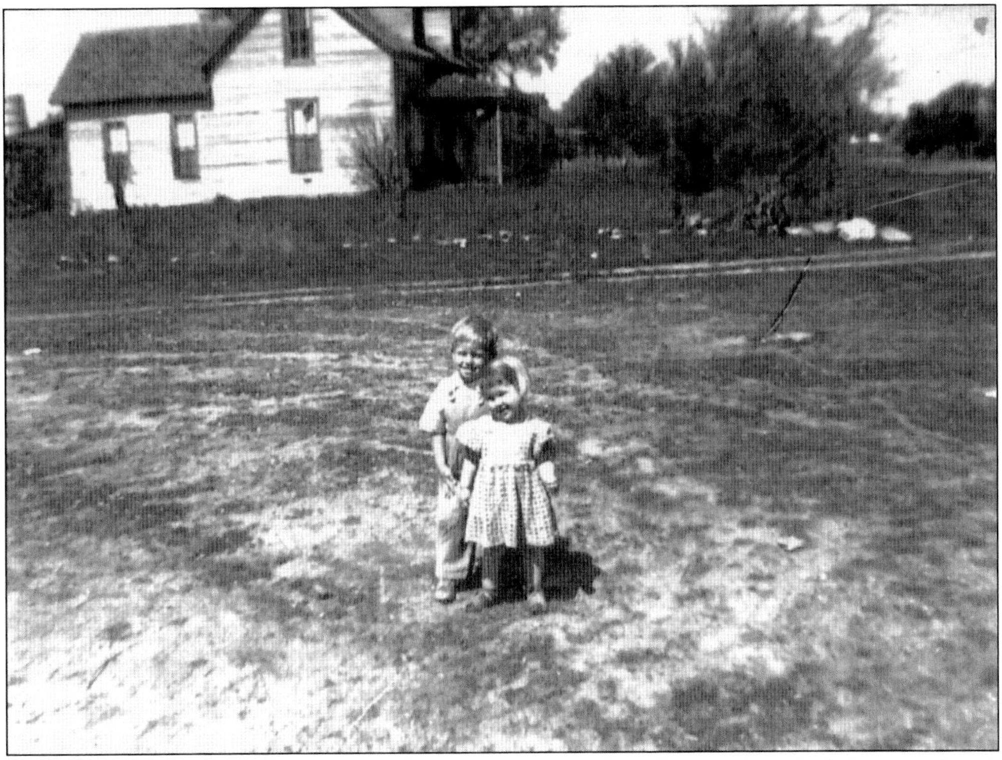

Shirley and Jimmy Norris, 1930s. The youngsters stand in their yard on Old Annetta Road. In the background is a house where one of the few murders in Aledo history took place in 1939, when Charlie Warner shot Buck Whitmire. The Aledo Community Center stands on the site today. (Courtesy of Homer Norris.)

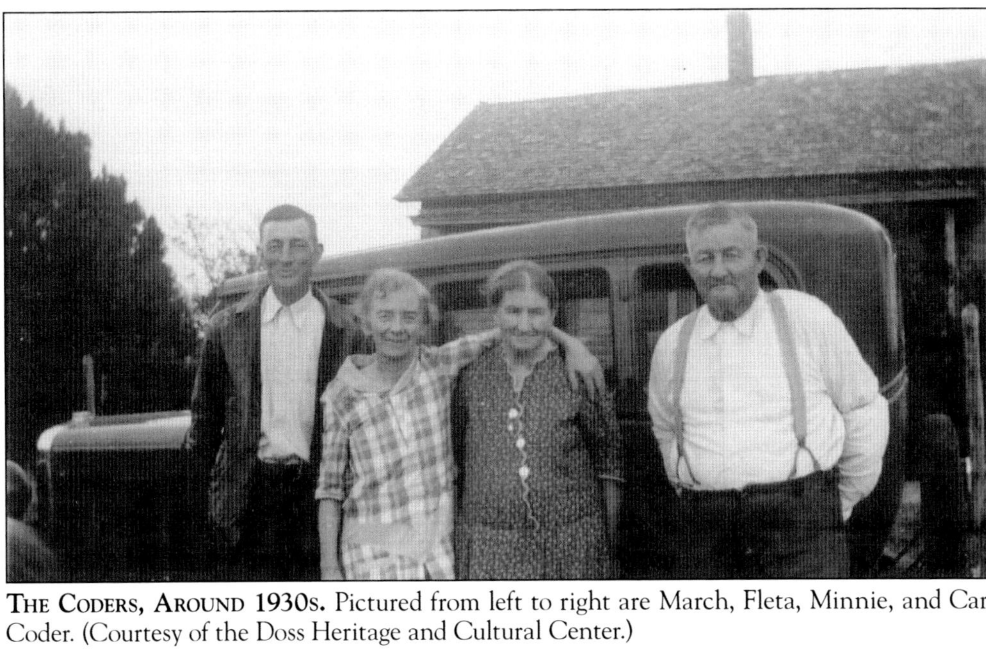

The Coders, Around 1930s. Pictured from left to right are March, Fleta, Minnie, and Carl Coder. (Courtesy of the Doss Heritage and Cultural Center.)

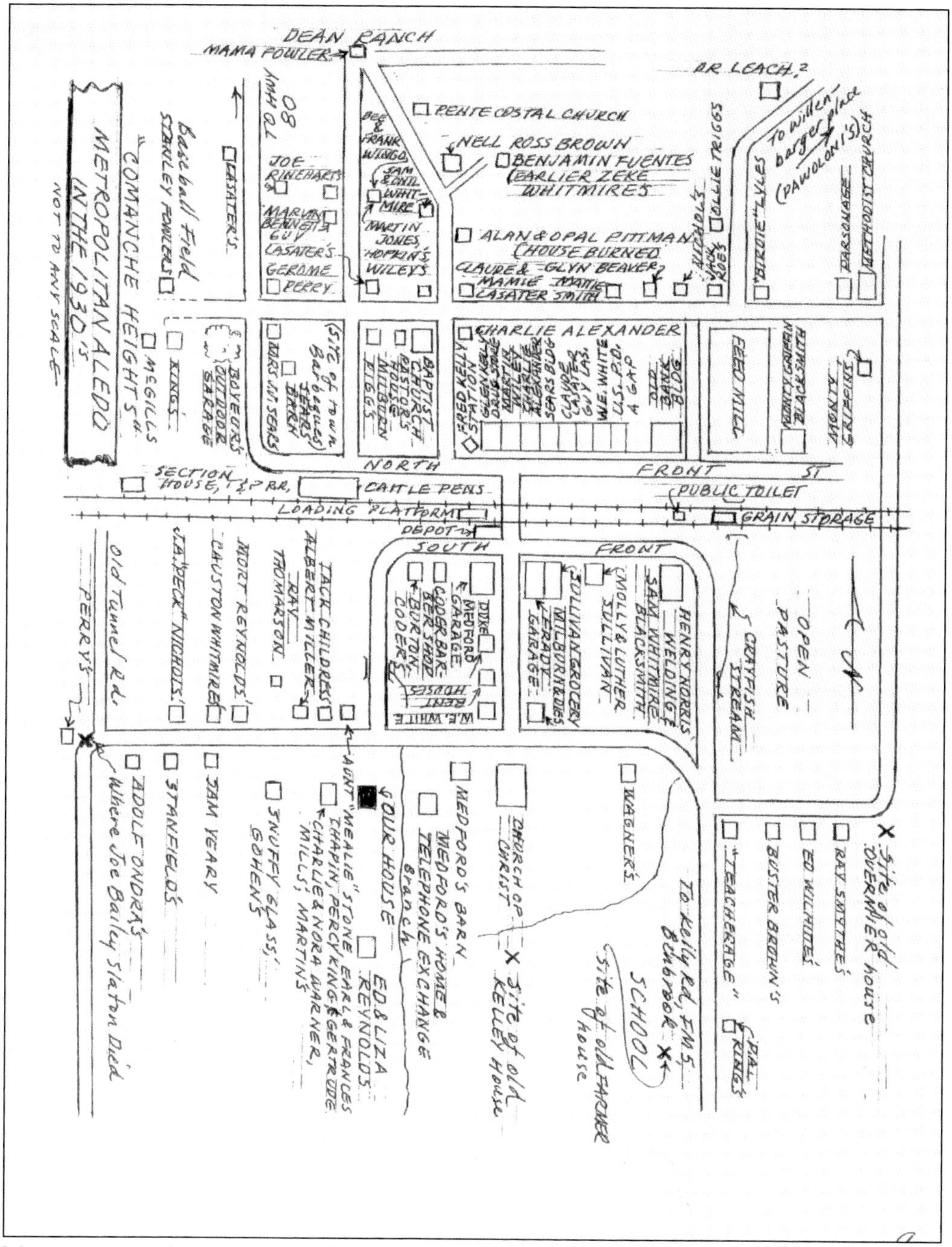

METROPOLITAN ALEDO IN THE 1930s. Artist Homer Norris recalls when a person could name every family in town. (Sketch by Homer Norris; courtesy of Homer Norris.)

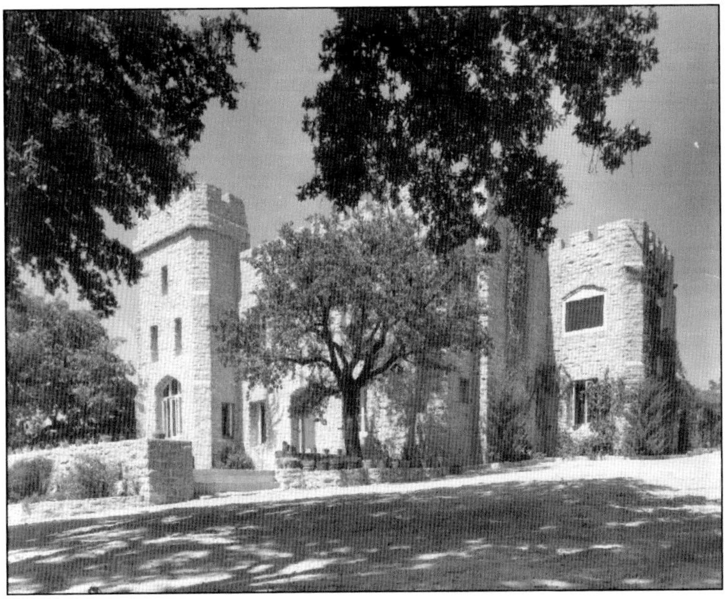

THE BARNEY HOLLAND "CASTLE," 1937. Businessman Barney R. Holland and his wife, Ellen Bowie Holland, began work on their house in Annetta in July 1934. Fourteen-year-old Barney B. Holland worked with the construction crew and was paid $1.50 a day. Young Holland paid for his meals at the carpenters' mess and contributed the occasional rabbit or squirrel to the stew pot. (Courtesy of Barney B. Holland Jr.)

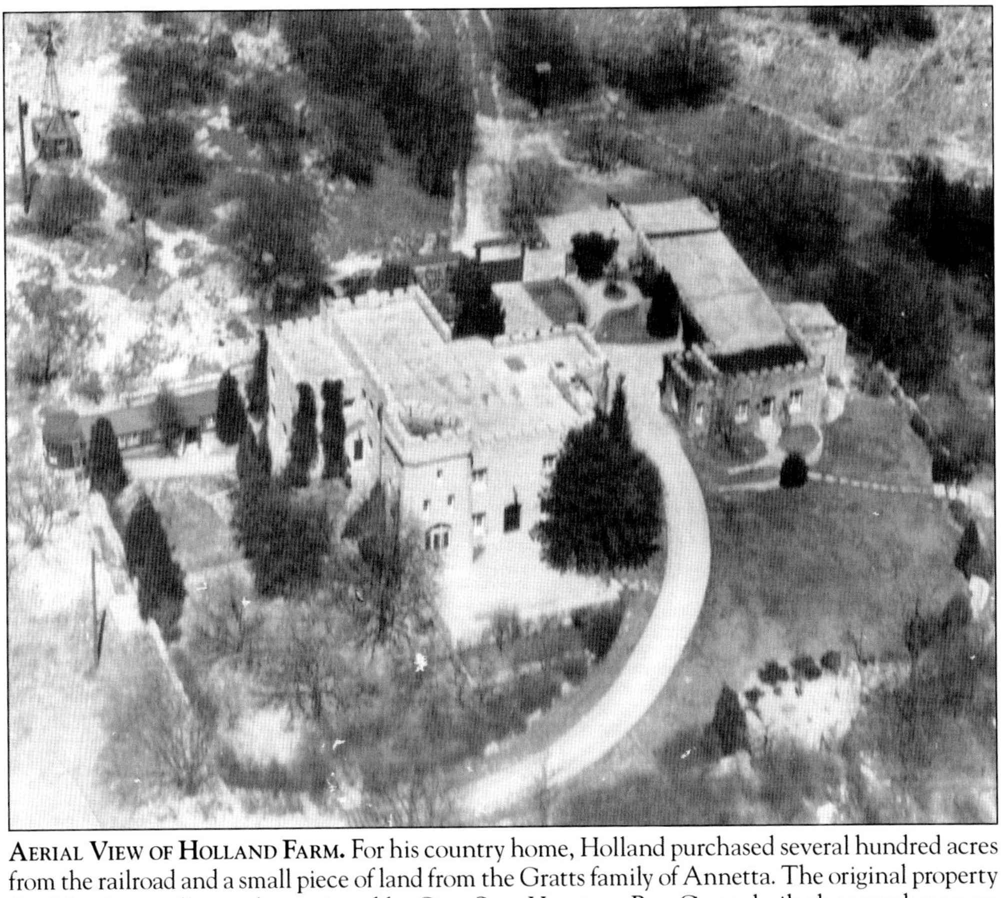

AERIAL VIEW OF HOLLAND FARM. For his country home, Holland purchased several hundred acres from the railroad and a small piece of land from the Gratts family of Annetta. The original property deed for the small parcel was signed by Gov. Sam Houston. Roy Gratts built the guesthouse on the property. (Courtesy of Barney B. Holland Jr.)

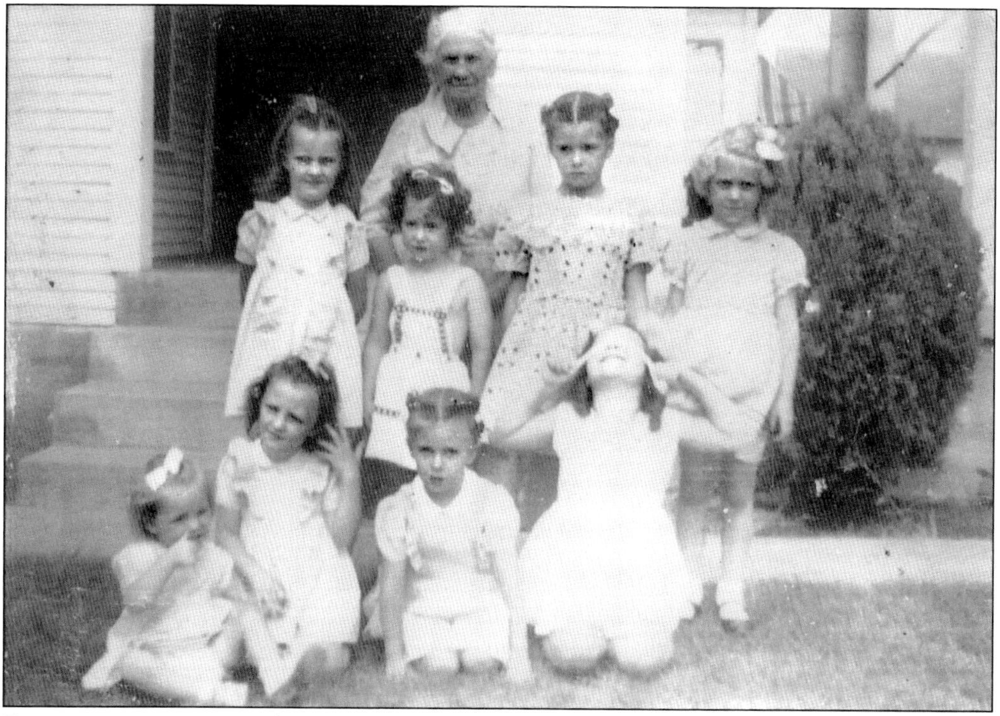

EASTER, AROUND 1945. The Brown family hosted a group of youngsters for an Easter egg hunt, including, from left to right, (first row) Shirley Bennett, Jerry Jo Jelly, Sharon Hildreth, and unidentified; (second row) Judy Bennett, Helen Bennett, Linda Hildreth, and unidentified; (third row) an unidentified Brown family grandmother. (Courtesy of Jerry Reid.)

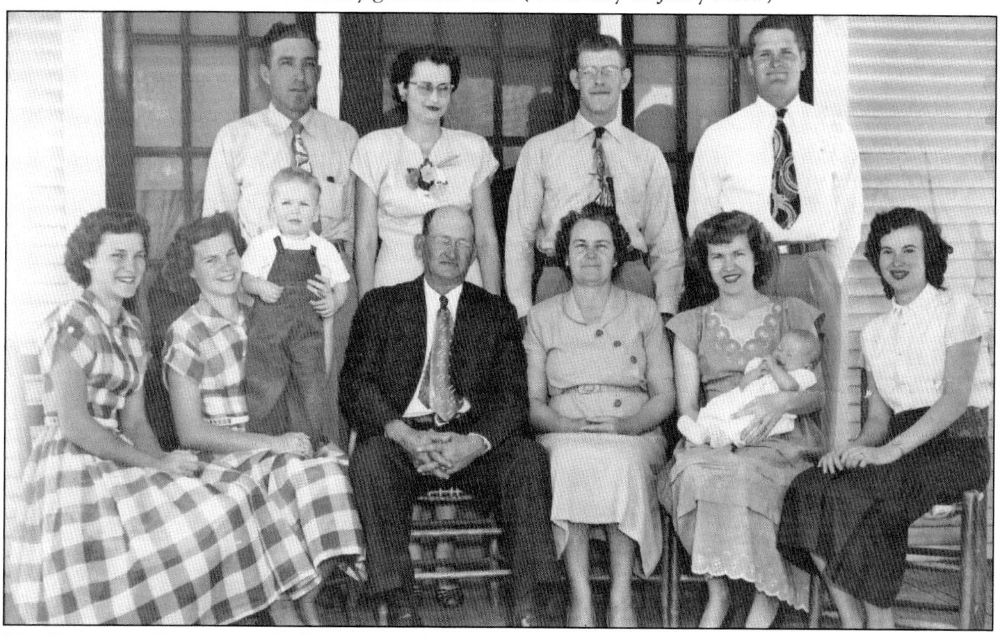

THE JOHNSON FAMILY, 1951. Roy Lee and Fannie McKinzie Johnson gathered with the family for a portrait. Near-identical twins Lula and Leta, left, often confused friends and teachers. (Courtesy of Leta and Bill Eastman.)

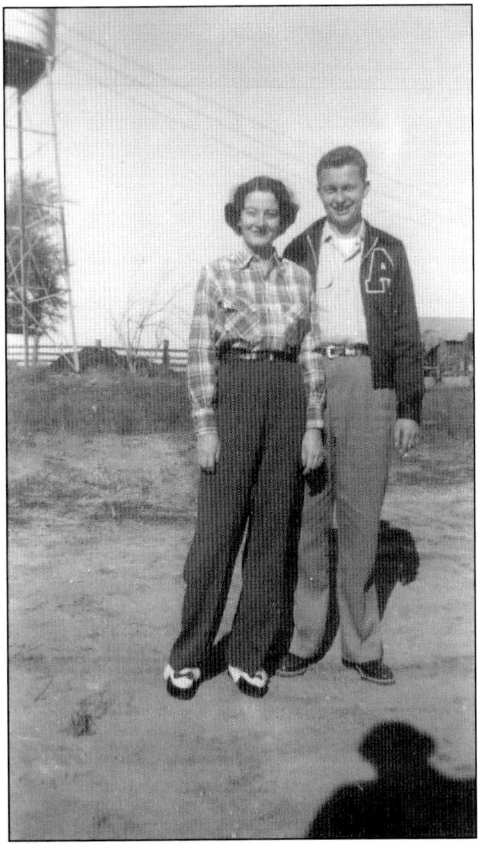

Evlyn and Scotty Broumley. Longtime residents of the area, the Broumleys were photographed soon after their wedding in the early 1950s. Evlyn Wiley Broumley is an expert genealogist and authority regarding Parker County history. (Courtesy of Reubene Gressett Scott.)

Family Gathering, 1969. This family group included longtime residents of the Aledo area. Pictured from left to right are (first row) Scott Munro, Lynn Munro, Barbara Ames Munro, Faye Ames Barnwell, Vada Ames Gilliland, Chawn Gilliland, Edgar Ames, Mildred Ames, E. H. Ames, Loweda Ames Wood, and infant Jim Wood Jr.; (second row) Melvin Munro, Cindy Barnwell, Clyde Barnwell, J. C. Gilliland, Earl Fletcher, Charlotte Wood, Cathy Ames, Cheryl Ames, Harrelene Ames, Luther Wood, Renna Mixson Wood, and Jim Wood. (Courtesy of Jim and Renna Wood.)

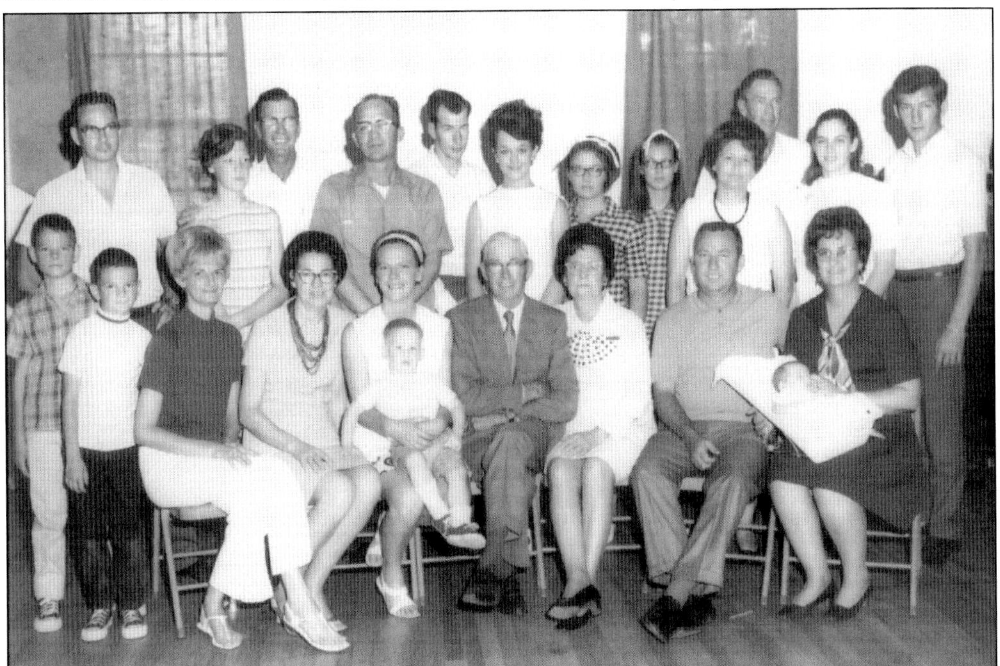

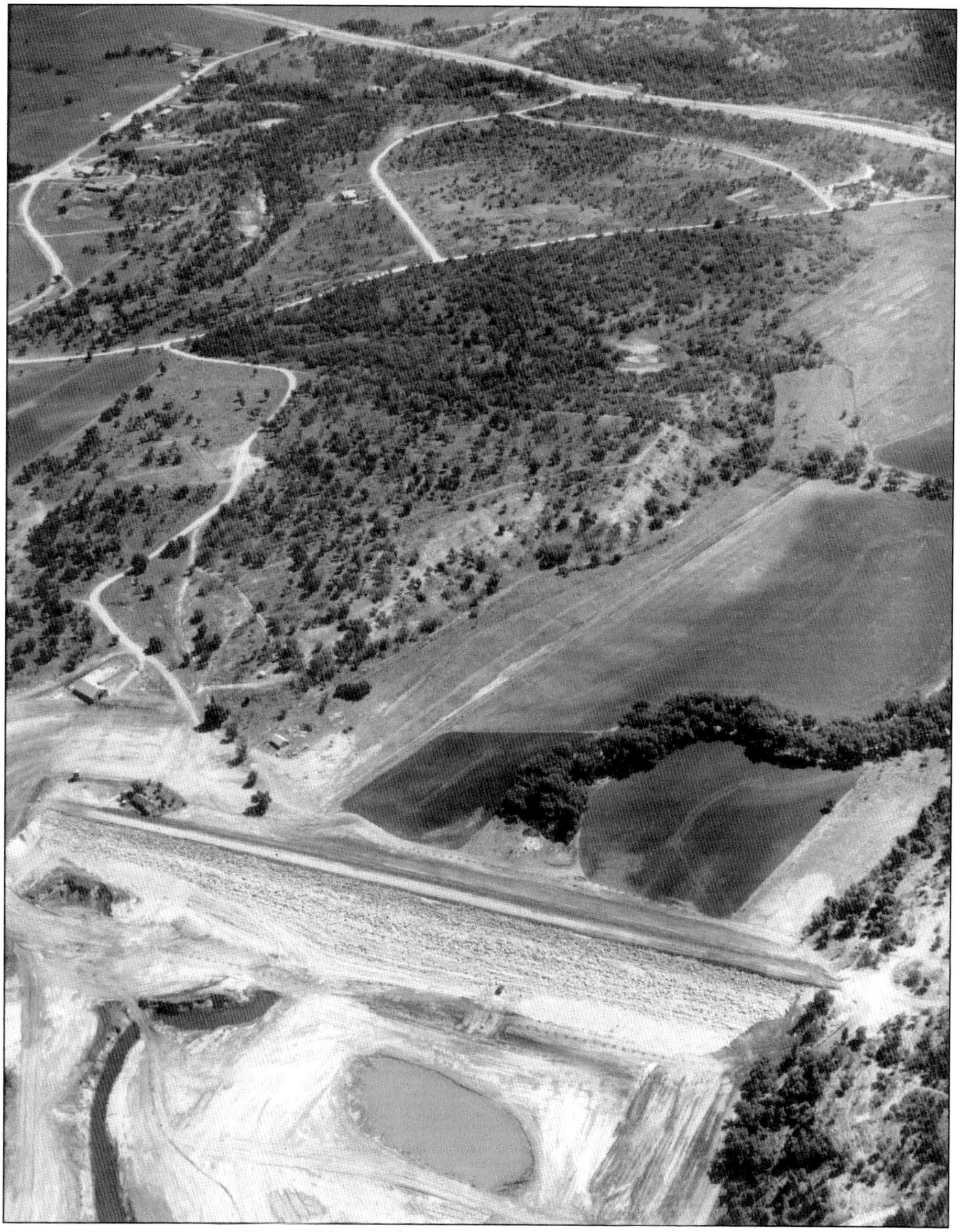

Aerial Shot, Willow Park. This 1957 aerial view, looking south, shows the fledgling Lake Weatherford nearing its completion. (Courtesy Vickie Slagle/EPCGHS.)

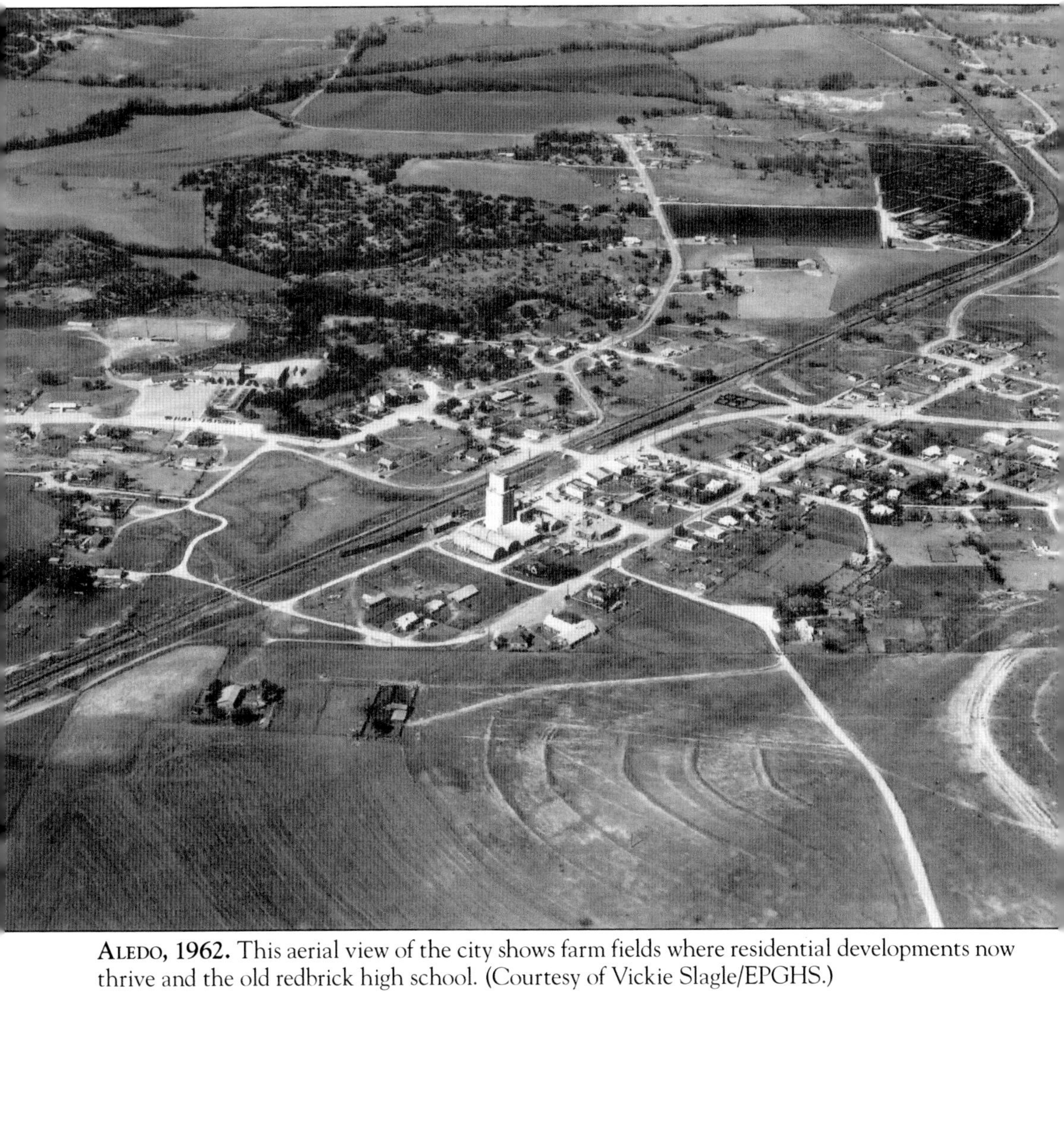

ALEDO, 1962. This aerial view of the city shows farm fields where residential developments now thrive and the old redbrick high school. (Courtesy of Vickie Slagle/EPGHS.)

Seven

LANDMARKS

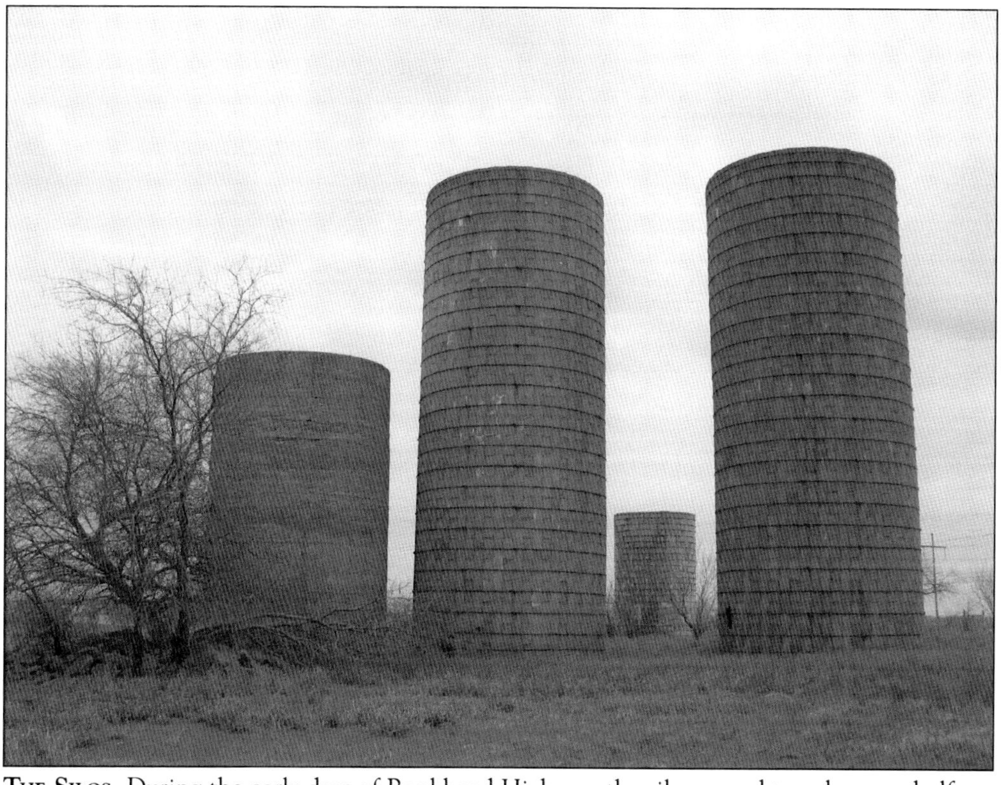

THE SILOS. During the early days of Bankhead Highway, the silos served travelers as a halfway marker between Weatherford, the county seat, and Fort Worth. Today the nearly 100-year-old structures are an Aledo icon and a welcome sight to work-weary commuters at the end of a day. (Photograph by Kit Marshall, courtesy of Kit Marshall.)

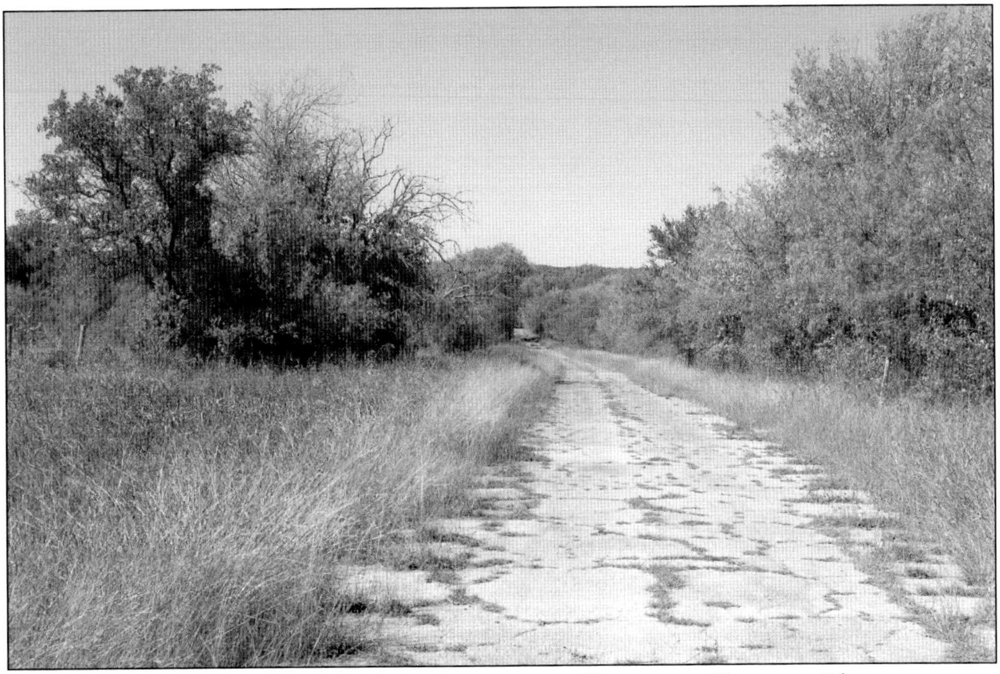

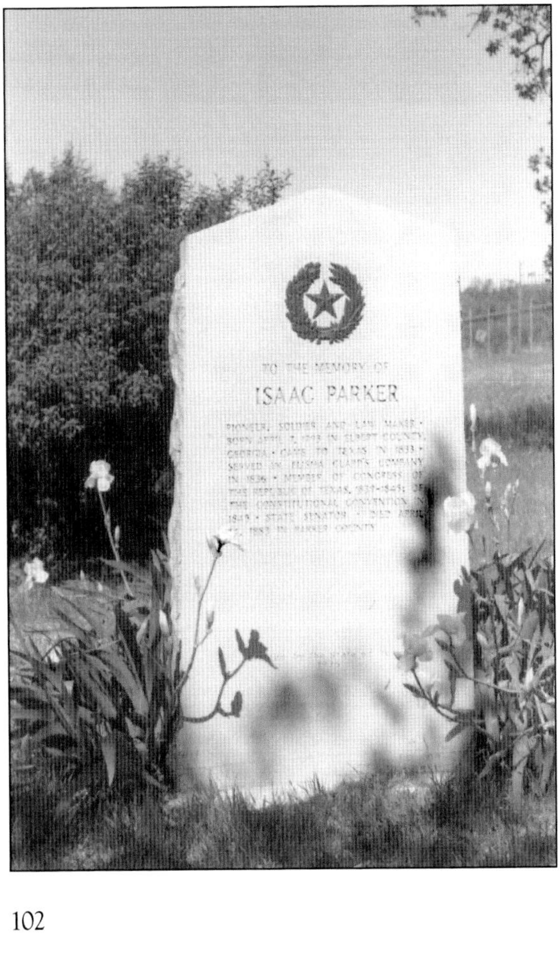

BANKHEAD HIGHWAY. The eastern Parker County section of the first all-weather paved transcontinental road in the nation was completed in 1925. Generally, it covered the 1913 route of Kuteman Cutoff, named for H. W. Kuteman, a Weatherford banker and lawyer who was fond of automobiles and spearheaded the building of a faster route between Weatherford and Fort Worth. Eventually, Highway 80 replaced sections of Bankhead Highway like the one shown here. (Courtesy of Dan L. Smith.)

ISAAC PARKER. Located north of Lake Weatherford, the monument marks the home site of pioneer Isaac Parker. Born in April 1793 in Georgia, he came to Texas in 1833 and fought in the Texas Revolution. A member of Congress of the Republic of Texas, 1839–1845, the Constitutional Convention in 1845, and a state senator, in the 1850s, Parker introduced the bill that created the county, which was named in his honor. Parker died on April 14, 1883, in Parker County. (Courtesy of Jon Vandagriff.)

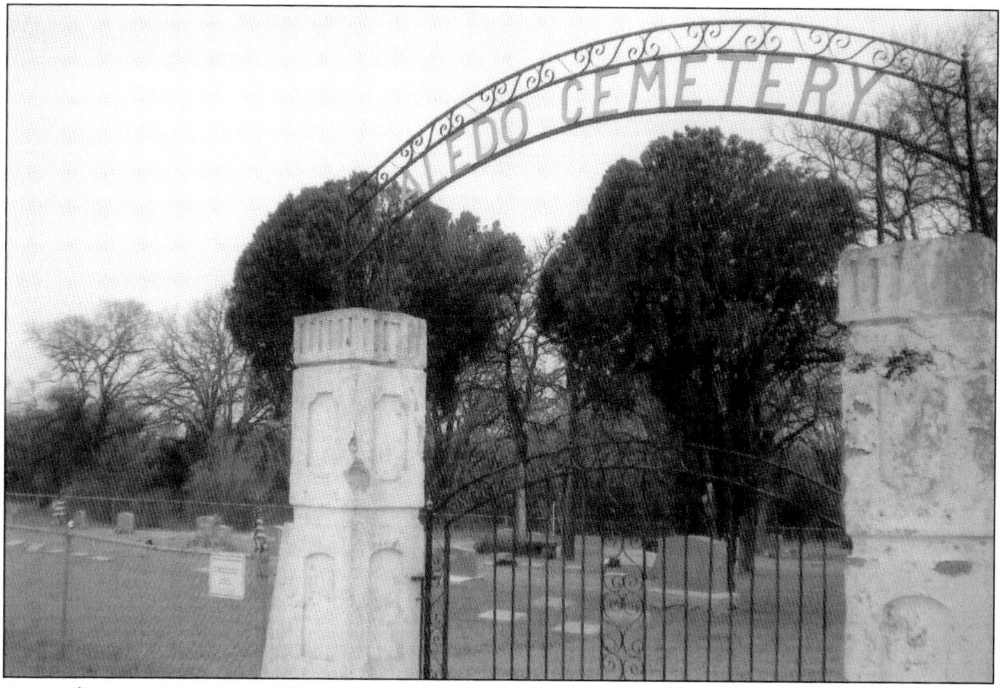

Aledo/Brown Cemetery. The sign may say Aledo Cemetery, but longtime residents call it Brown Cemetery to honor the Thomas Brown family, which donated the land for the cemetery in 1858. (Photograph by the author.)

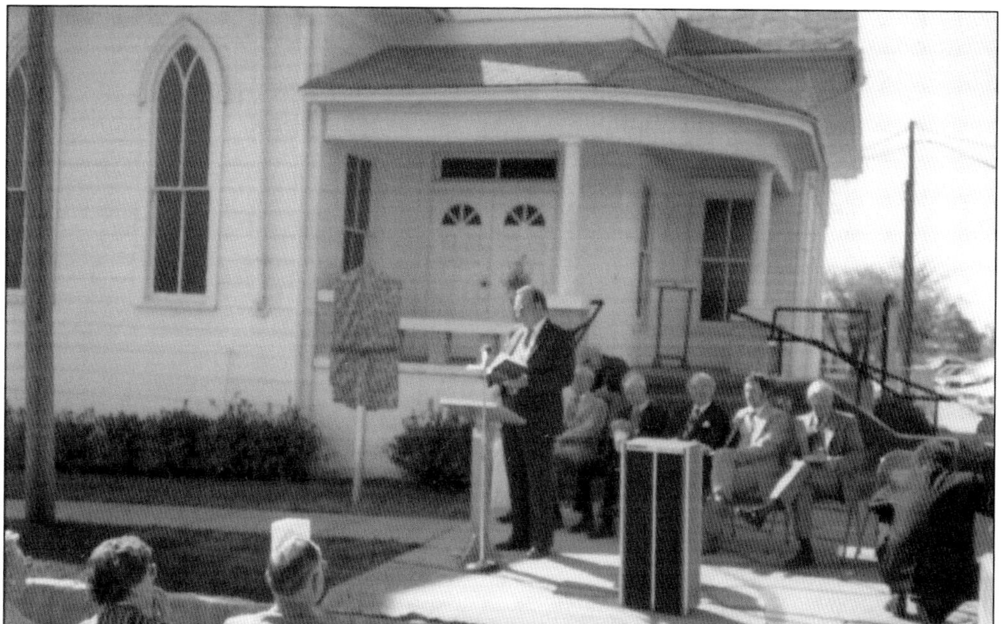

First Baptist Church of Aledo. A Texas Historical Commission Marker was placed at the site in 1983 acknowledging the historic role of the church in the community. Church members Mattie Glover and Reubene Scott compiled the commission application. (Courtesy of Reubene Gressett Scott.)

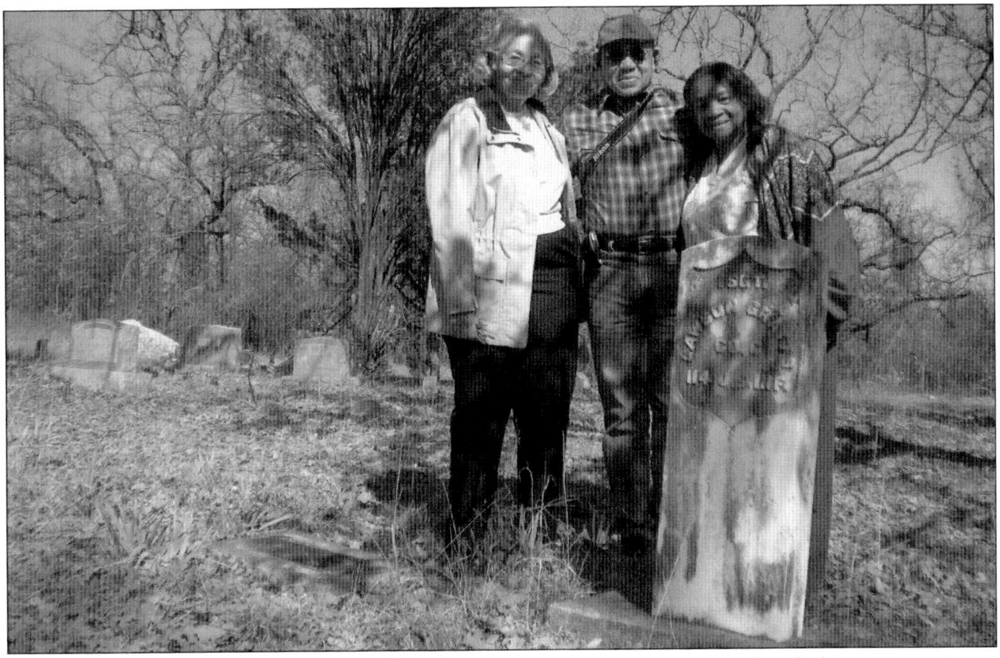

WILLOW SPRINGS CEMETERY. Two Willow Springs cemeteries exist, one that belongs to a private group and one that was donated to the African American families of Annetta by T. K. Yeary during the days of segregation. The latter cemetery was once called the Willow Springs Colored Cemetery or the Gratts Cemetery. Descendants of former slaves and an Annetta founding family, the Gratts, stand at the monument of ancestor Lawson D. Gratts, a Buffalo Soldier. Pictured from left to right are Helen Eldridge, Josef Gratts, and Evelyn Lourdés. (Photograph by the author.)

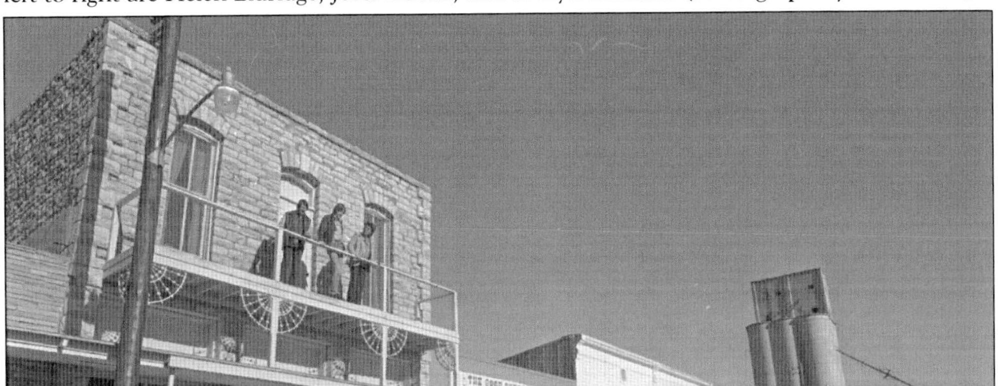

SEARS BUILDING, NORTH FRONT STREET. Built of limestone in 1893 by Aledo businessman J. J. Sears, the building shown in this 1978 photograph first served as a general store. A Masonic lodge met upstairs. Sears owned Citizens' Bank of Aledo, which failed after a bank officer absconded with funds. He sold everything he owned, including his automobile, to satisfy his debts to his customers. His integrity is an enduring chapter in the city history. (Courtesy *Fort Worth Star-Telegram* Photograph Collections, the University of Texas at Arlington.)

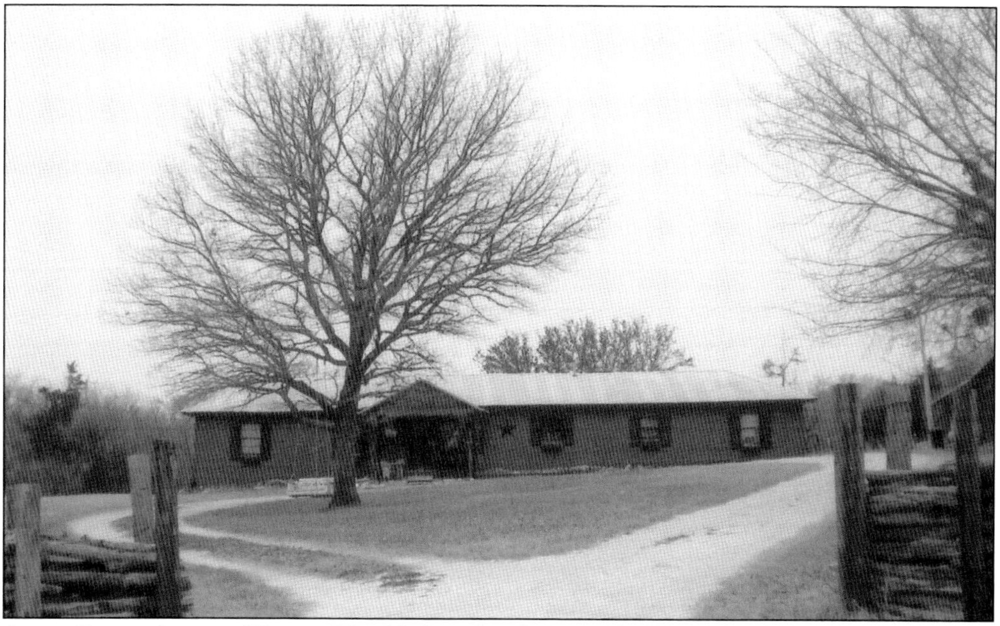

Aledo Depot Section House. The Aledo railroad section foreman lived in this home, originally located on the north side of the Texas and Pacific tracks west of North Front Street in Aledo. The structure was moved to Annetta around 1960 and became a private residence. (Courtesy of the author.)

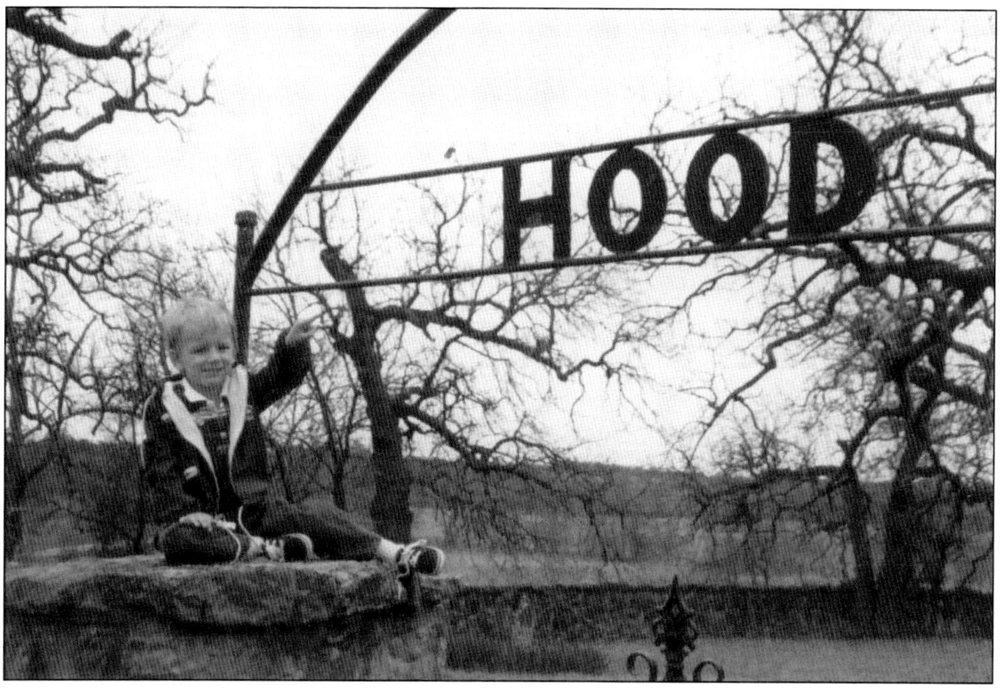

Hood Cemetery. Young Hood Whitson visits his family cemetery, first used in 1865 for the burial of Elizabeth McEwen, wife of A. J. Hood. Located on land near their original home, this site was her choice for the construction of a future house. Her grave is marked with a stone from the nearby creek. (Courtesy of Jackie McLennan.)

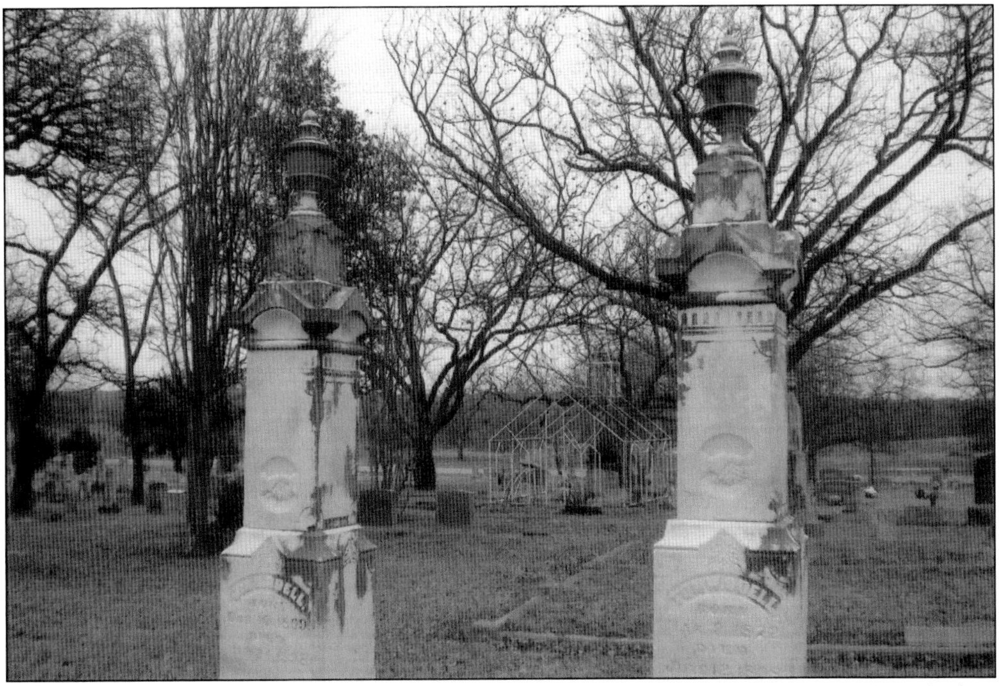

Annetta Cemetery. The earliest tombstone in the historic Annetta Cemetery is that of Edgar M. King, who died in 1882, although the location had been used as a burial site for some years before his death. Longtime Annetta resident Chester Tucker constructed the metalwork chapel. Inside, a small plaque honors "Wagon Train Baby," whose exact burial site in the cemetery is unknown. (Photograph by the author.)

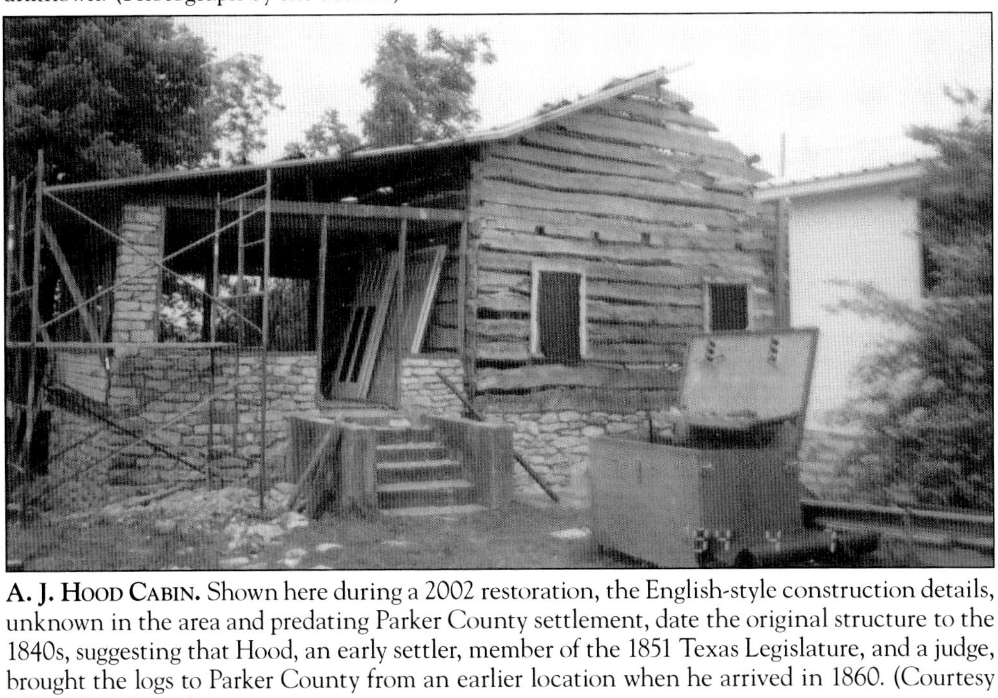

A. J. Hood Cabin. Shown here during a 2002 restoration, the English-style construction details, unknown in the area and predating Parker County settlement, date the original structure to the 1840s, suggesting that Hood, an early settler, member of the 1851 Texas Legislature, and a judge, brought the logs to Parker County from an earlier location when he arrived in 1860. (Courtesy of Jan Orr-Harter.)

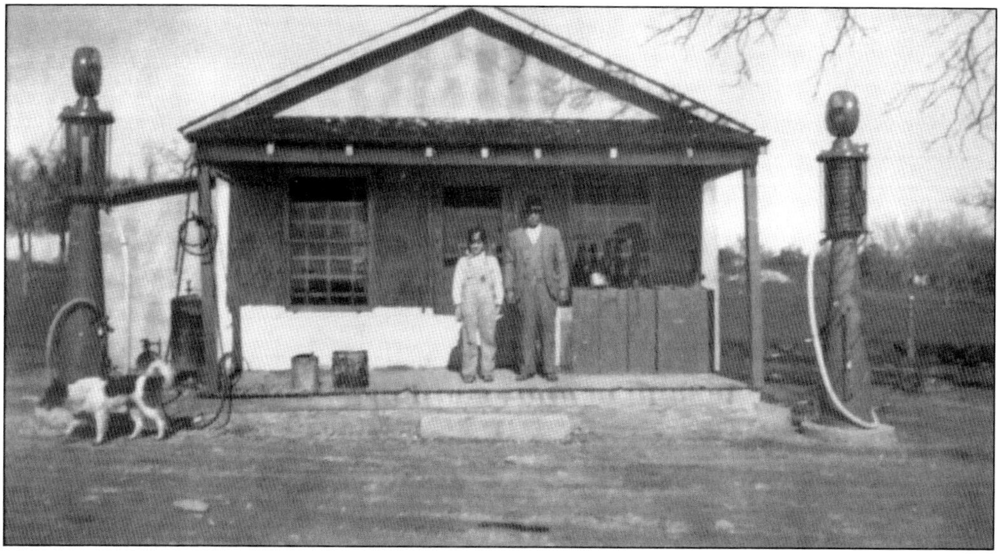

DICEY STORE, 1936. E. A. Spann and grandson William Wythe (Bill) Roberts stand in front of a Dicey landmark, the gas station and store owned by Roberts. Much of Dicey now lies under Lake Weatherford, which was built by the City of Weatherford in 1957. (Courtesy of Mary Roberts.)

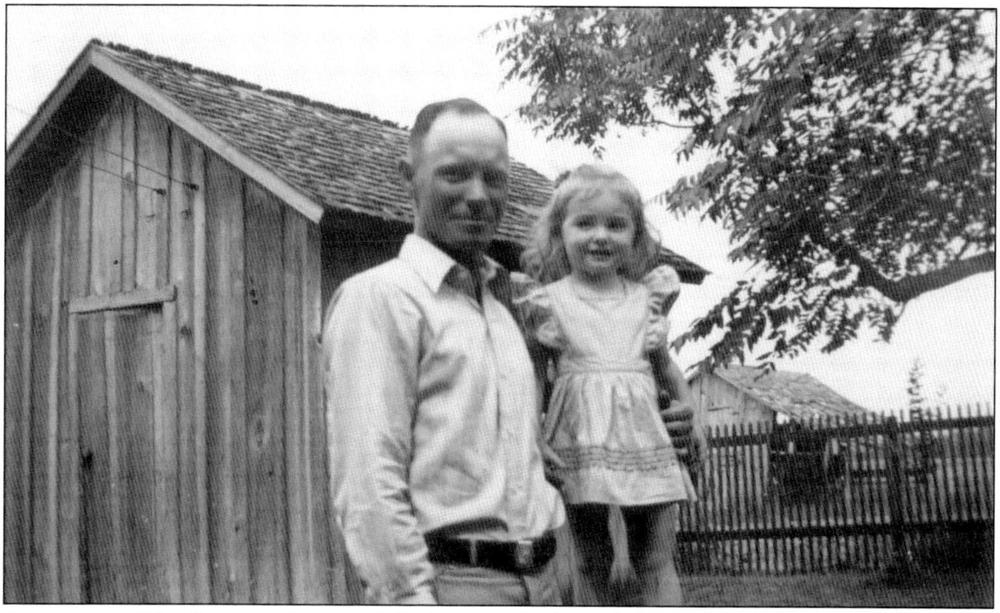

STAGECOACH WAY STATION. In this 1942 photograph, the only known photograph of the structure, young Betsy Coder and her uncle Bud are pictured at the Coder home, which was situated on land crossed by a 19th-century stagecoach trail. In the far background one can glimpse the stagecoach way station's barn. On the north side, a covered passageway allowed drivers to change horses in bad weather. A corncrib was located in the center of the building. Four horse stalls and a harness closet lined the south end. During the height of the buffalo trade, eastward-bound freight wagons hauling 15-foot stacks of buffalo hides would pass through this station. Roy Coder once showed Homer Norris a nearby spot where three horsemen had robbed a stagecoach. Coder tore down the barn in 1943. (Photograph from the Mattie Coder Collection; courtesy of the Doss Cultural and Heritage Center.)

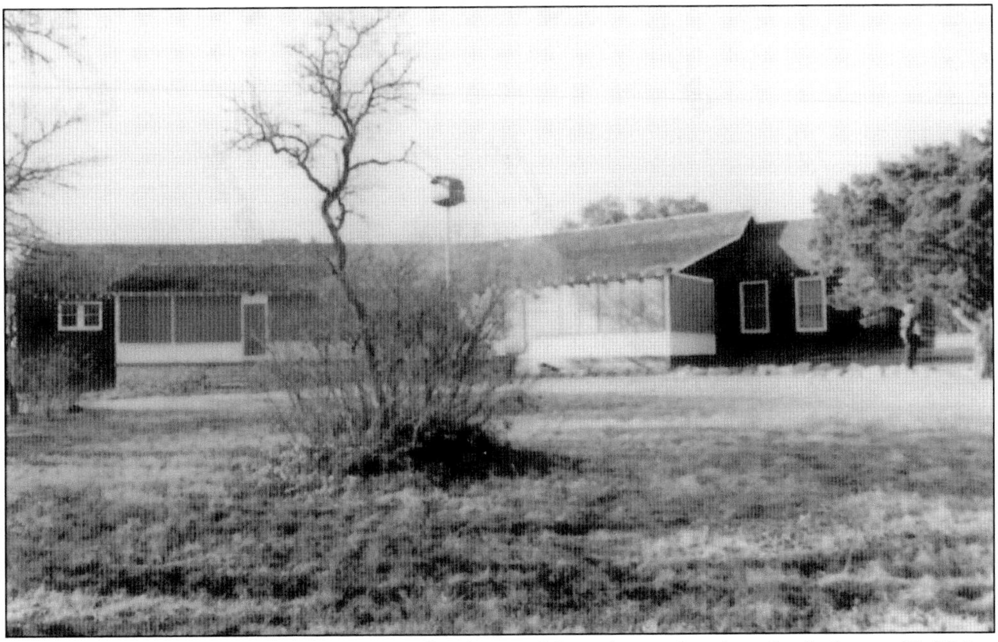

EL CHICO LODGE, 1935. Once a retreat for the wealthy, after its heyday, the lodge on El Chico Ranch served as a city hall for Willow Park and welcomed two church congregations before its purchase and current use as a private home. Curby and Vera Mirike developed the surrounding ranchland into El Chico Estates, the foundation of the modern-day Willow Park. (Courtesy of Stephen Bolton.)

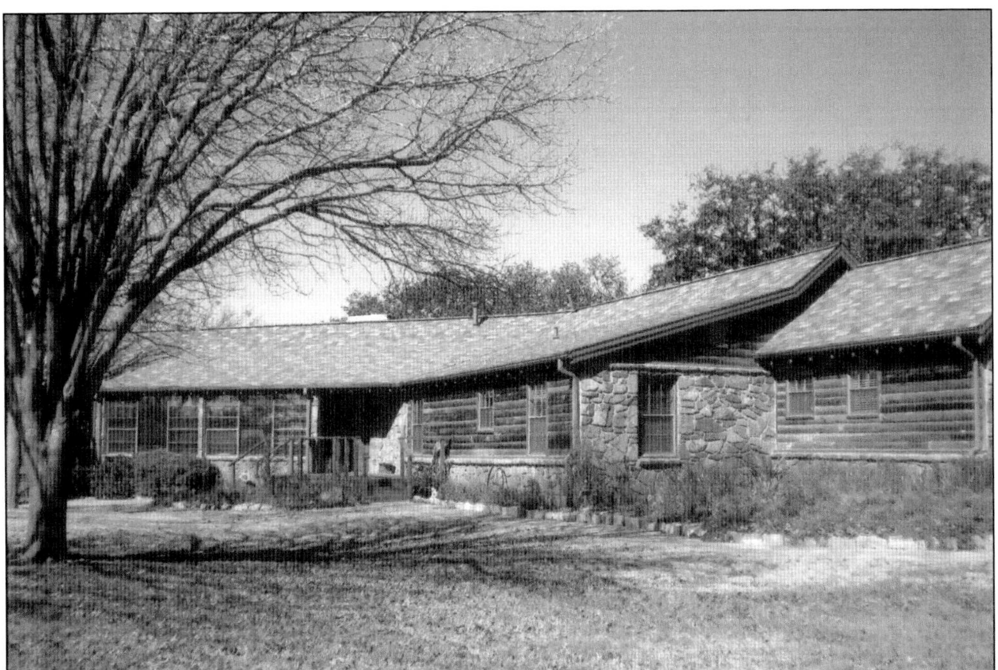

EL CHICO LODGE, 2010. This structure is now a private residence. (Photograph by the author.)

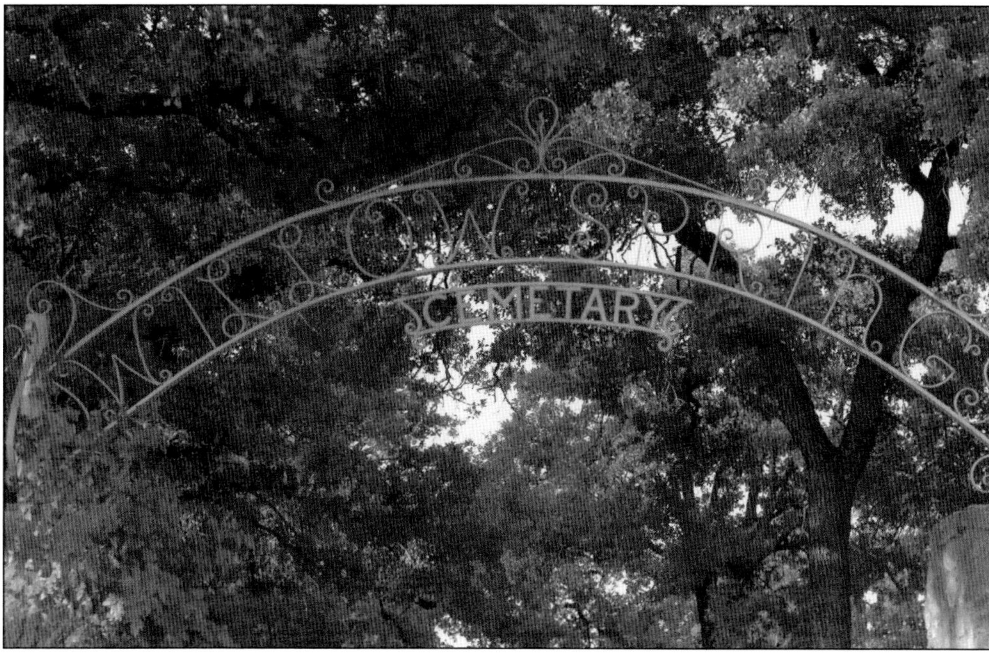

Willow Springs Monuments. Willow Springs Cemetery once served as a "whites-only" cemetery, with an adjacent cemetery reserved for those of African descent. In 1860, the tiny community, consisting of a church, school, and cemetery, attracted statewide attention as pioneer Martha Sherman was laid to rest in Willow Springs Cemetery. The victim of a brutal raid led by Chief Peta Nocona suffered for several days and bore a stillborn infant before dying. Martha asked to be buried near a church. Her ordeal galvanized action against the raiding bands of Plains warriors that led to the recapture of Cynthia Ann Parker, a white woman taken by Comanches as a child. (Photographs by Thomas Peipert; courtesy of Randy Keck/*Community News*.)

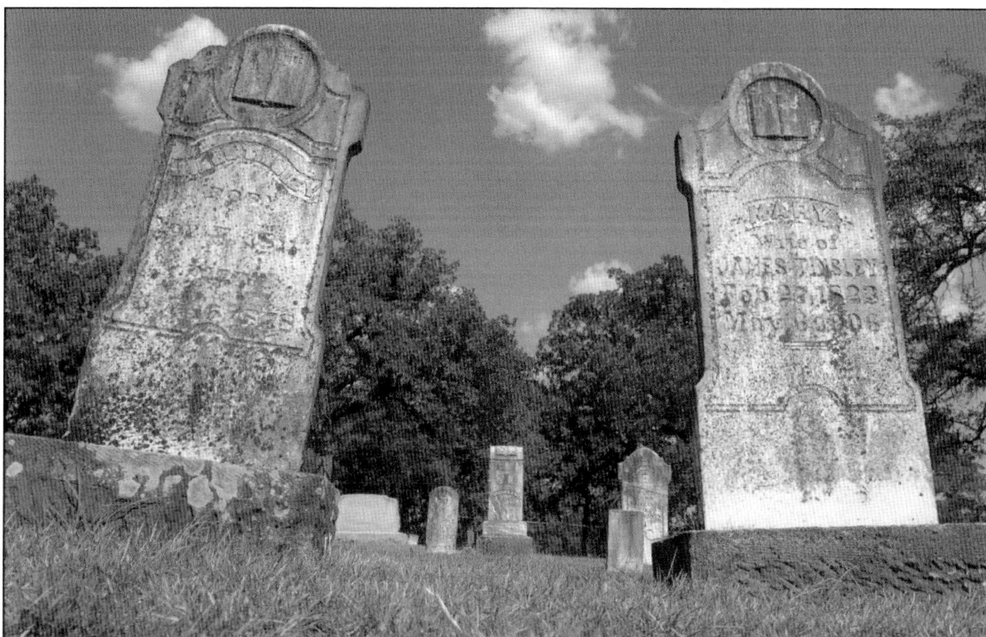

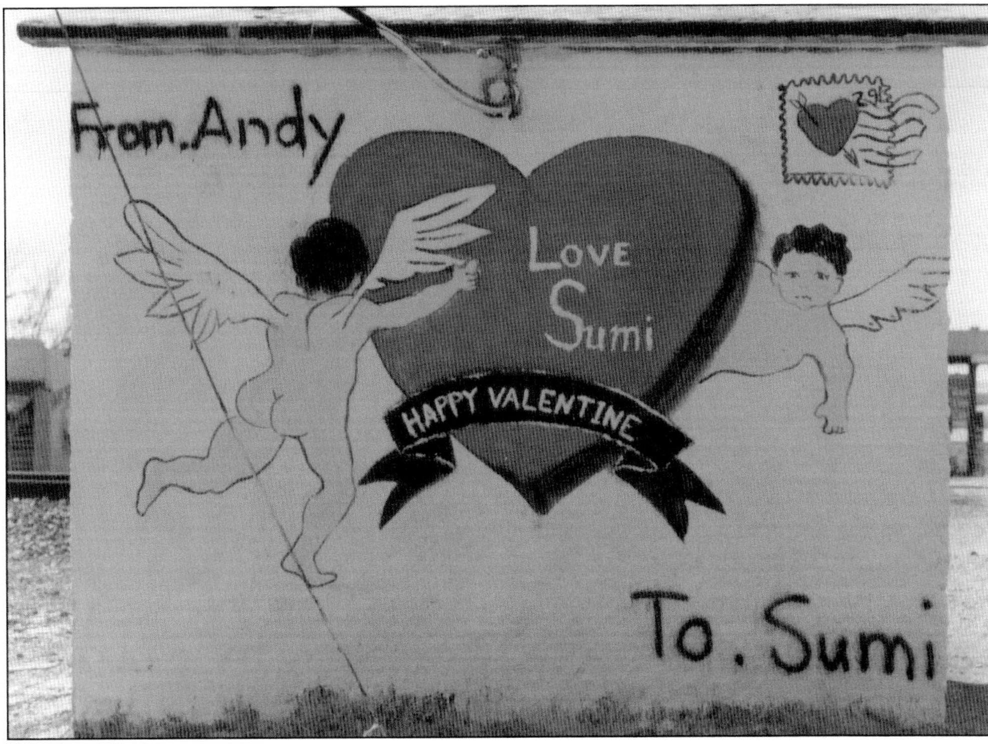

Paint Shack. For many years, Aledo residents have used the retired railroad signal bungalow as a modern telegraph. Messages change almost on a daily basis and range from birthday wishes to congratulations to cheers for the Aledo Bearcats and more. (Above, courtesy of John Chase; below, courtesy of Randy Keck/*Community News*.)

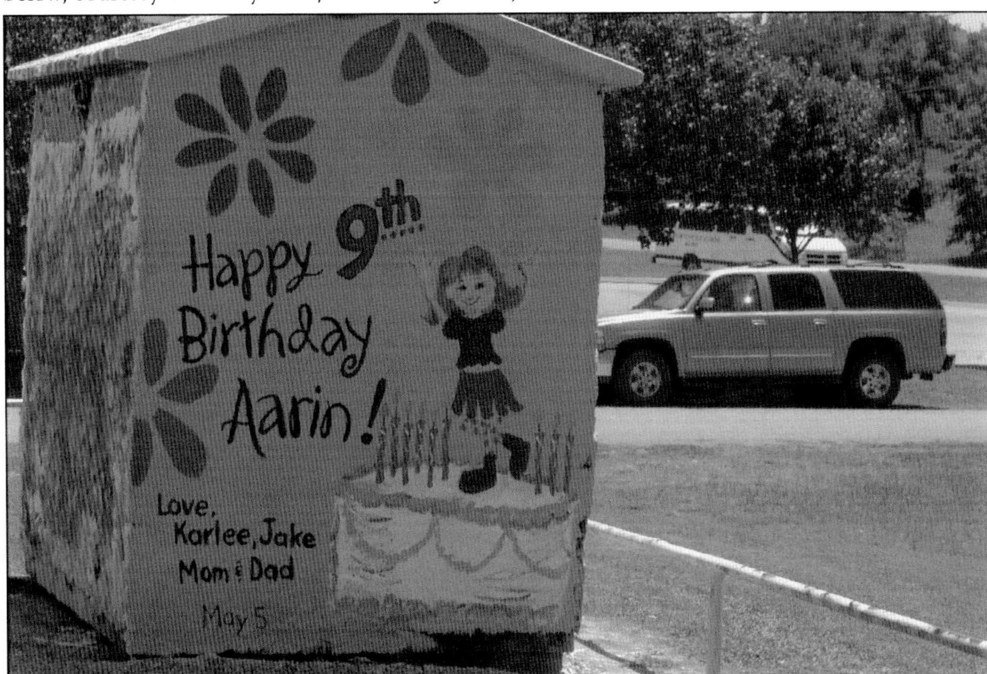

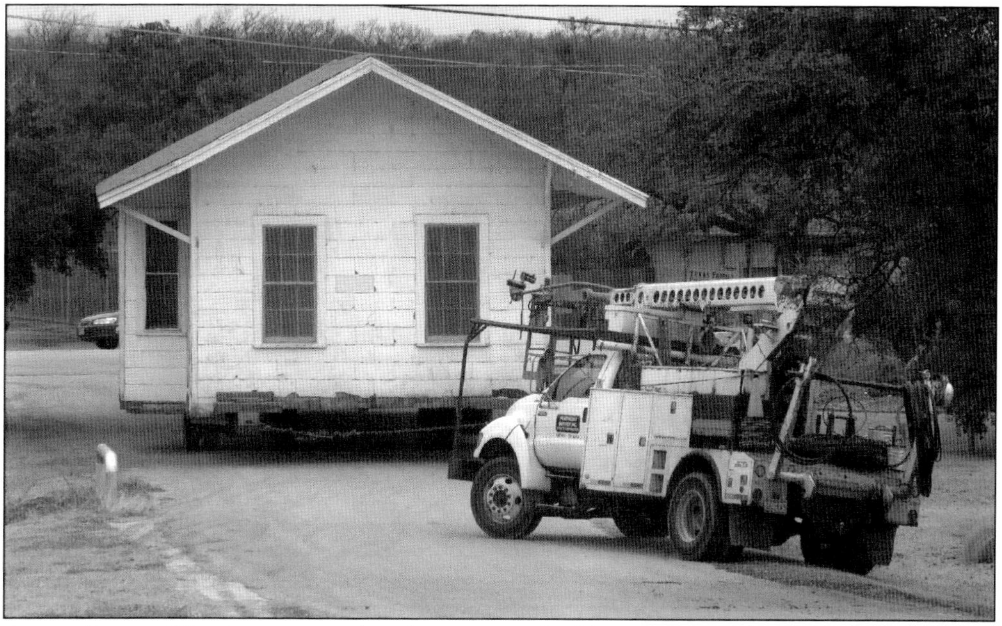

Aledo Depot. The depot spent decades as an outbuilding that stored tires at an automotive repair business until the Bennett family, which owned the property, donated the structure to the City of Aledo. Here the depot is moved to its new site at Aledo City Hall. (Courtesy of Randy Keck/*Community News*.)

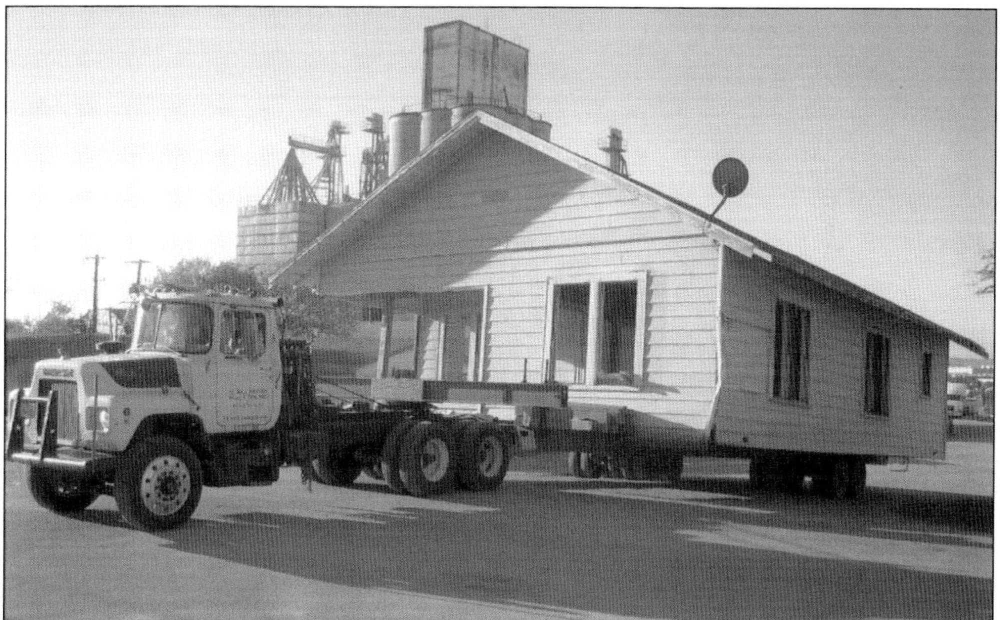

Burton Coder Home. Coder and his wife lived on South Front Street, now Old Annetta Road, next door to his barbershop. When a new owner requested city approval to raze the structure, businesswoman Kimberly Hardick bought the house and relocated it within the historic town plat, shown here. The house now has a new life as a commercial building. (Courtesy of Kimberly Hardick.)

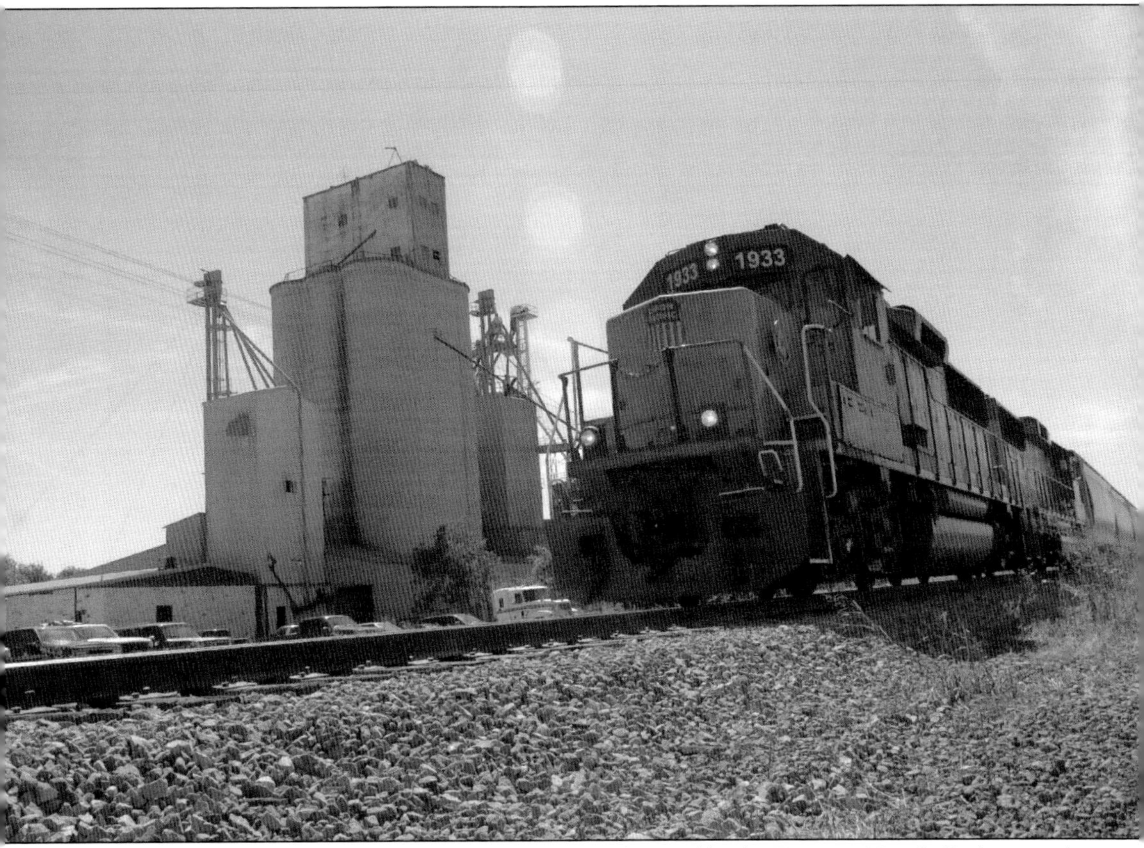

Railroad Town. Since its inception, Aledo has been bisected by the Texas and Pacific Railway tracks. Shown is a familiar sight to residents: a train running through town, parallel to North and South Front streets. (Photograph by Thomas Peipert, courtesy of Randy Keck/*Community News*.)

Eight

Personalities

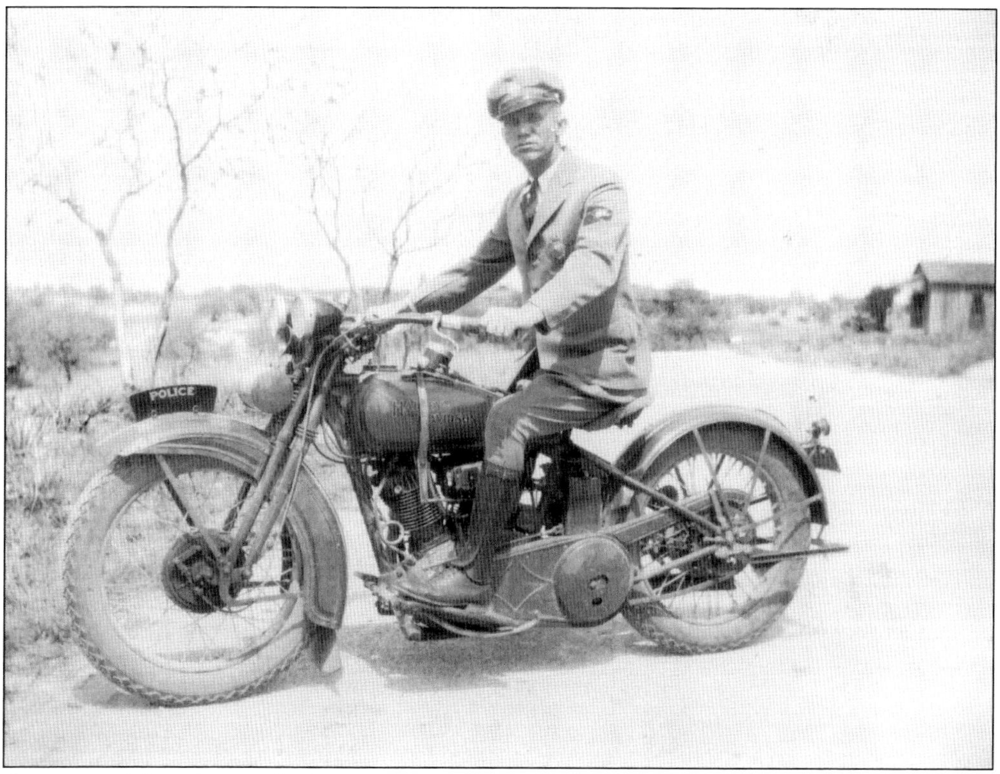

Constable Tom Gray. The lawman's courageous exploits made headlines and thrilled young boys like author and artist Homer Norris, whose private collection includes Gray's brass knuckles and blackjack. Gray is pictured near the Henry Norris home at the Tarrant–Parker County line in 1932. After halting a bank robbery in Aledo in a blaze of shooting, shutting down a still that had 5,000 gallons of mash cooking, and more, Gray became sheriff of Fort Davis County and a Texas Ranger. (Courtesy of Homer Norris.)

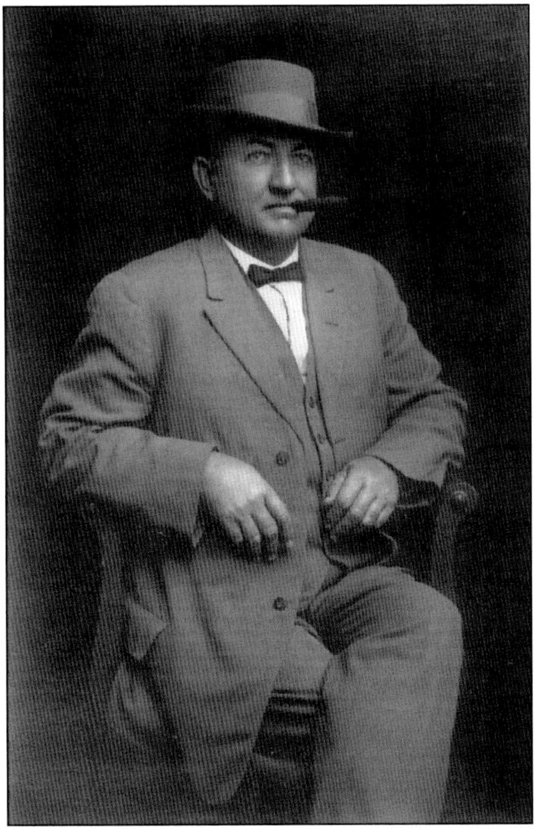

Charles Templeton McFarland. Dr. J. P. McFarland parlayed payments in gold from his patients during California's Gold Rush into profitable land speculation, including an 1883 acquisition of a 5,600-acre ranch along Bear Creek that his son, Charles McFarland, managed. In 1898, Charles bought the ranch from his father and built it into a 7,400-acre Durham Shorthorn and, later, Hereford operation. (Courtesy of Diane McFarland Cornwall.)

Stock Show Barons. An enduring tradition since 1896 in nearby Fort Worth is the Stock Show and Rodeo, the brainchild of Charles McFarland, who suggested an exhibition of stock to promote the industry. Around 1906, at what is believed to be the 10th anniversary show, are, from left to right, Hayes McFarland, Aledo resident Babe Woodhouse, Sonny Fain, Ben Woodhouse, Parker County real estate magnate and philanthropist E. D. Farmer, and Asa N. Grant. (Courtesy of Diane McFarland Cornwall.)

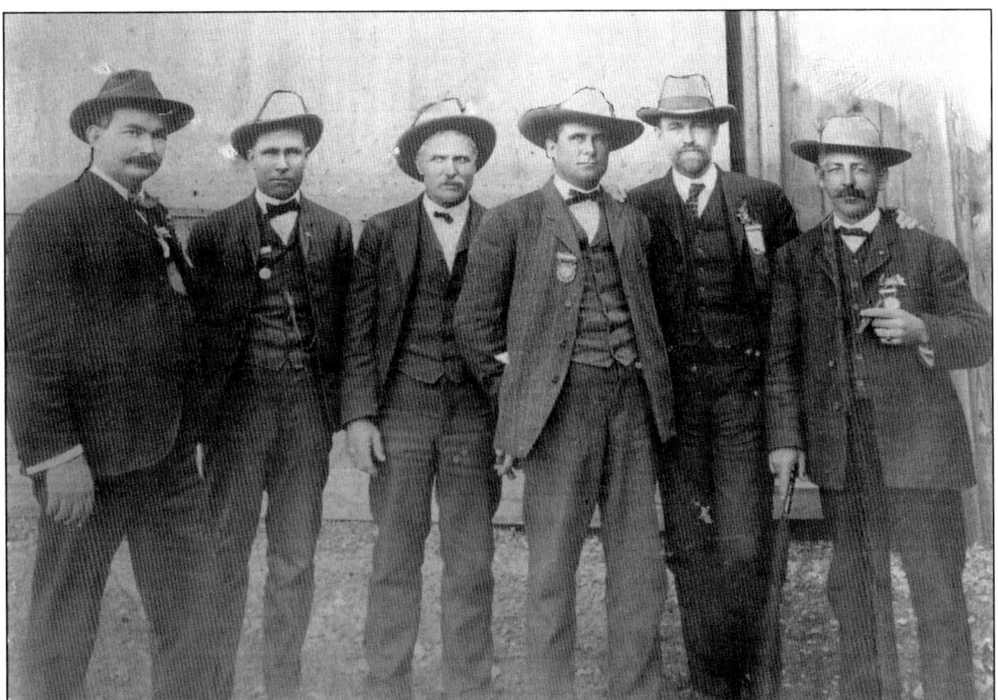

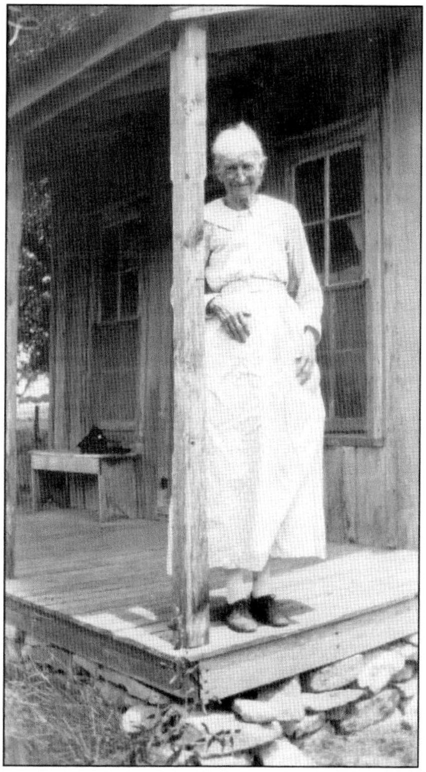

PERMELIA "MEALIE" STONE, 1936. Permelia married John Stone in 1879; by 1890, she was widowed. Upon her deathbed, she claimed to have killed her husband and buried him under her door stoop, but folks discounted her tale. (Courtesy of Evlyn Wiley Broumley.)

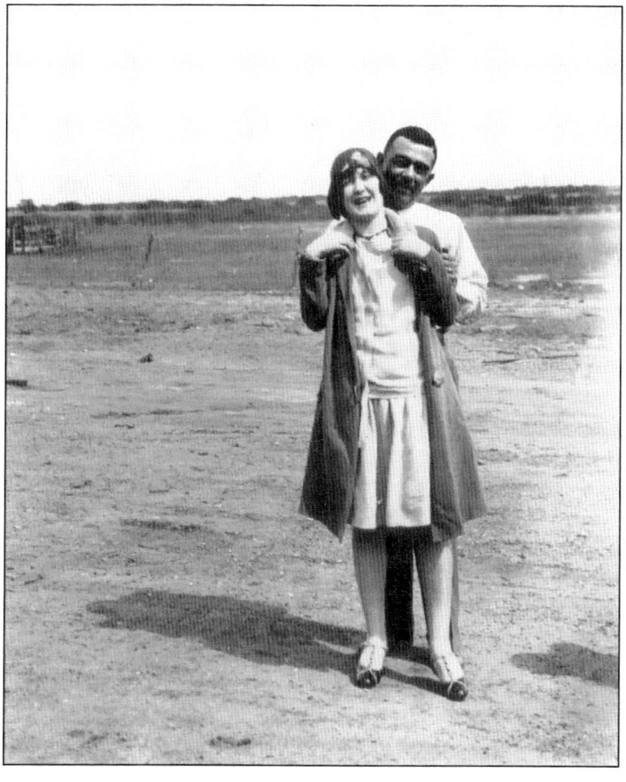

DOT AND JOE WINSTON. During the Great Depression, Winston bought 3,000 acres in southeastern Parker County for his cattle ranch. Men hiked from Fort Worth and camped on the banks of Bear Creek for the opportunity to work for wages building the Winston home. The Winstons are shown at the home site shortly after their wedding. (Courtesy of Jerry Reid.)

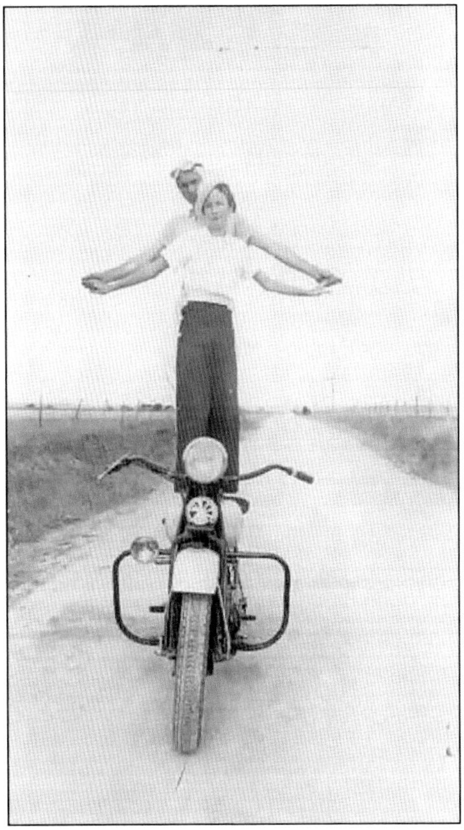

Riding High, 1936. Clara Lee Ball, daughter of R. J. Ball, poses with her fiancé, Joe Hunter. (Courtesy of Homer Norris.)

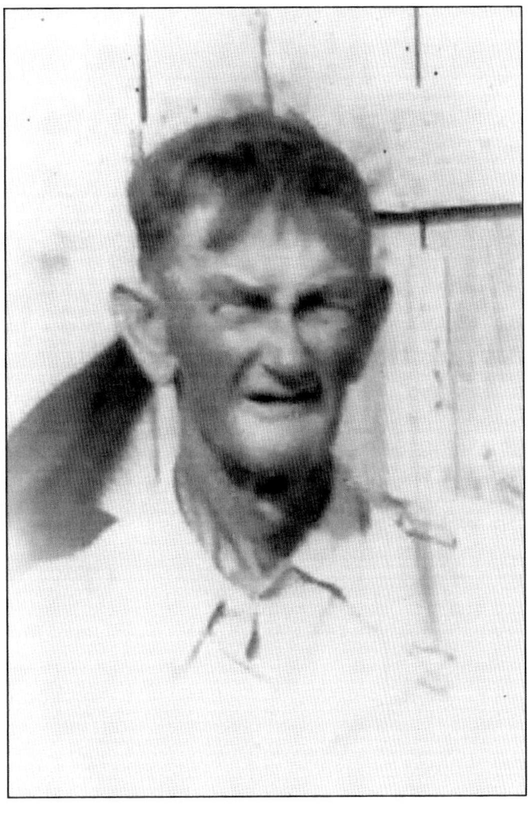

Robert Jordan "R. J." Ball, around 1947. Ball was a cattle drover before running a wagon freight service between Plano and Dallas. He went armed. "When I helped him kill hogs," Homer Norris recalls, "he unsheathed a Colt and blasted them." This is the only known photograph of Ball. (Courtesy of Homer Norris.)

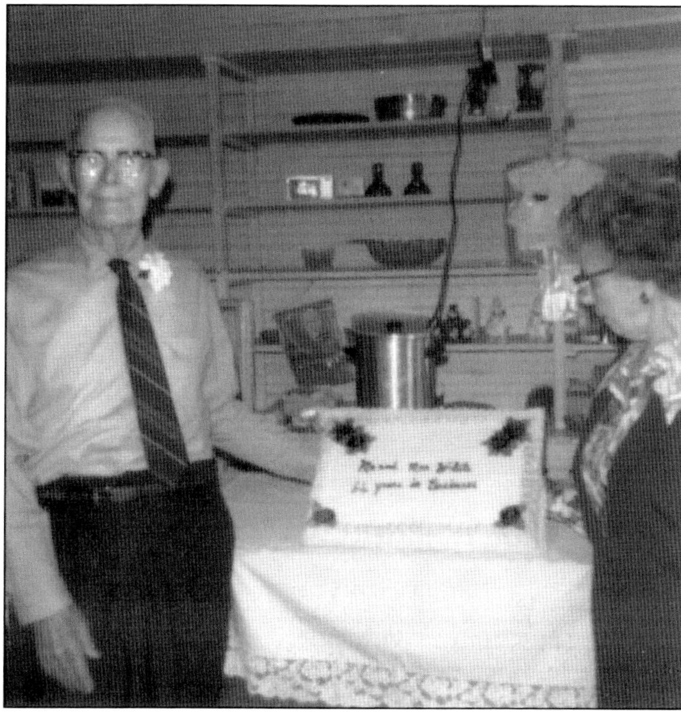

EMERSON AND JEWEL WHITE. White's Variety Store was a fixture on North Front Street in Aledo. White purchased an interest in the J. J. Sears Store in 1920; by 1930, he was its sole owner. The inscription on the cake—"Mr. and Mrs. White, 64 years in business"—reflected a long-held philosophy of the proprietor. "When you retire, you soon die or become disabled," White once said. "Unless we have a long spell of sickness, we'll die on the job." (Courtesy of Vickie Ballow Slagle.)

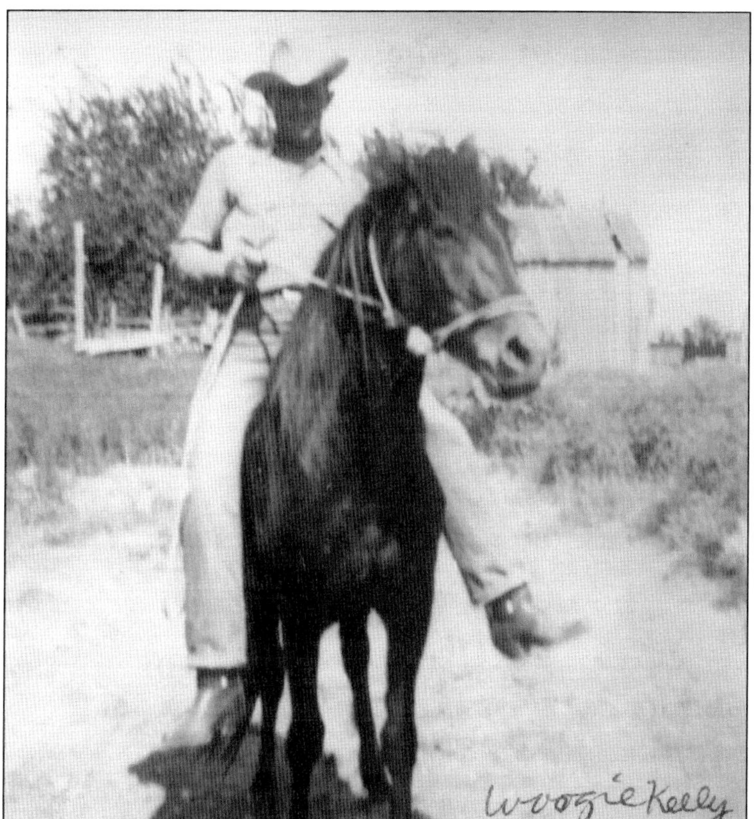

KENDALL "WOOGIE" KELLY. A beloved figure in Aledo, Woogie would pitch in on any job and deliver twice the production of his fellow workers. Only two hazy photographs of Woogie are known to exist today. (Courtesy of Homer Norris.)

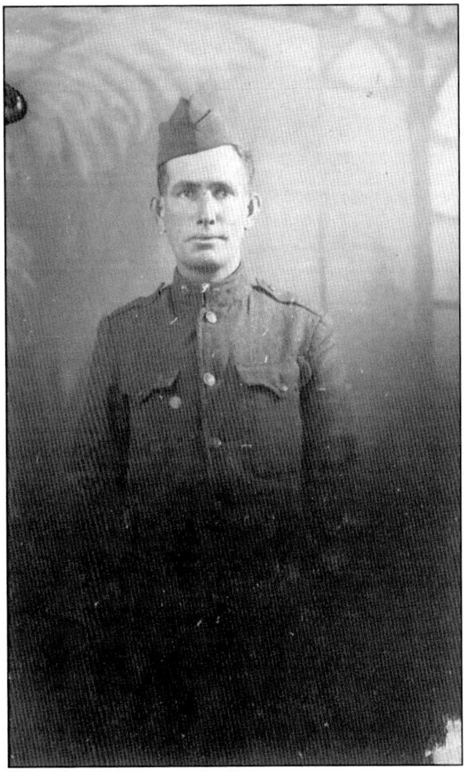

James Parnell McGlinchey, 1918 or 1919. Parnell served in France during World War I, driving a lorry to transport troops. (Courtesy of Don Collins.)

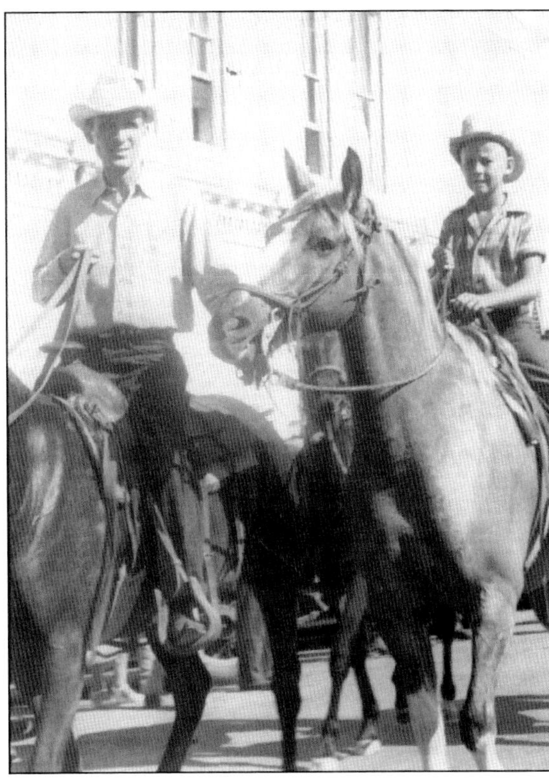

Horseman and Future Cattleman. John Chapman was a young boy when he proudly rode his horse in a Weatherford parade along legendary horseman Homer Dixon. Considered a great cowboy, Dixon won numerous cutting competitions, including first place at the Fort Worth Stock Show Rodeo on Miss Aledo, a bald-faced paint mare with little or no pedigree that he and his brother Shorty had trained. (Courtesy of John Chapman.)

BARNEY R. HOLLAND, 1949. Founder of Barney Holland Oil Company and son of Weatherford mayor, banker, and historian G. A. Holland, Barney poses here with Roby Jr. Holland married Ellen Bowie of Weatherford, author of *Gay as a Grig*, a memoir of her father's emigration from Scotland to Texas. The Hollands built a country home in Annetta. (Photograph by W. D. Smith, courtesy of Barney B. Holland Jr.)

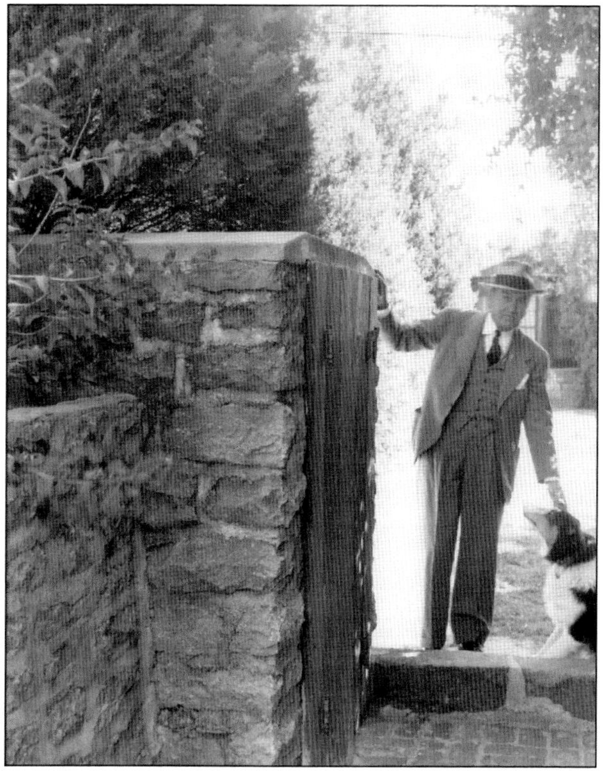

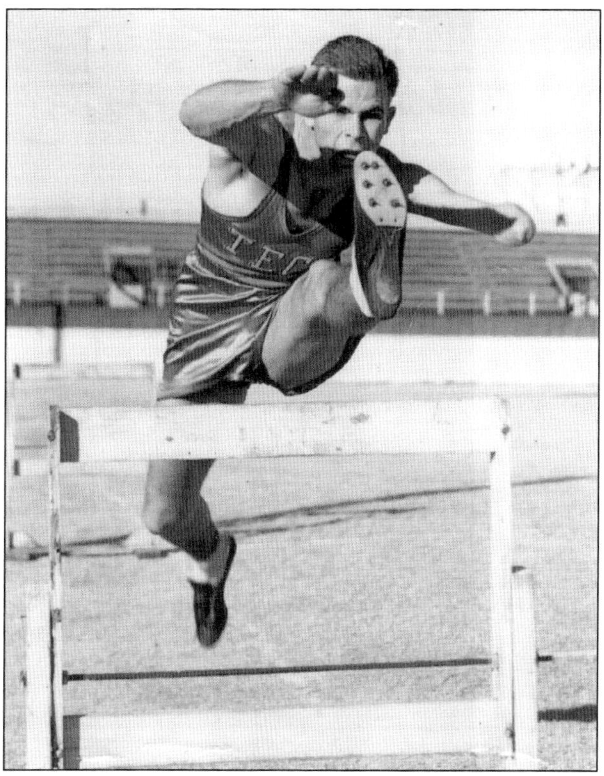

MARSH FARMER, TRACK STAR. As a member of the Texas Tech track team from 1938 to 1940, Marsh set world and collegiate hurdle records and was considered one of the finest track stars of the day. A partial left arm from birth was inconsequential to the All-American at Texas Tech. Farmer and track experts always believed he would have been a member of the 1940 U.S. Olympic team, but the Olympics were cancelled during the buildup to World War II. (Courtesy of Jon Vandagriff.)

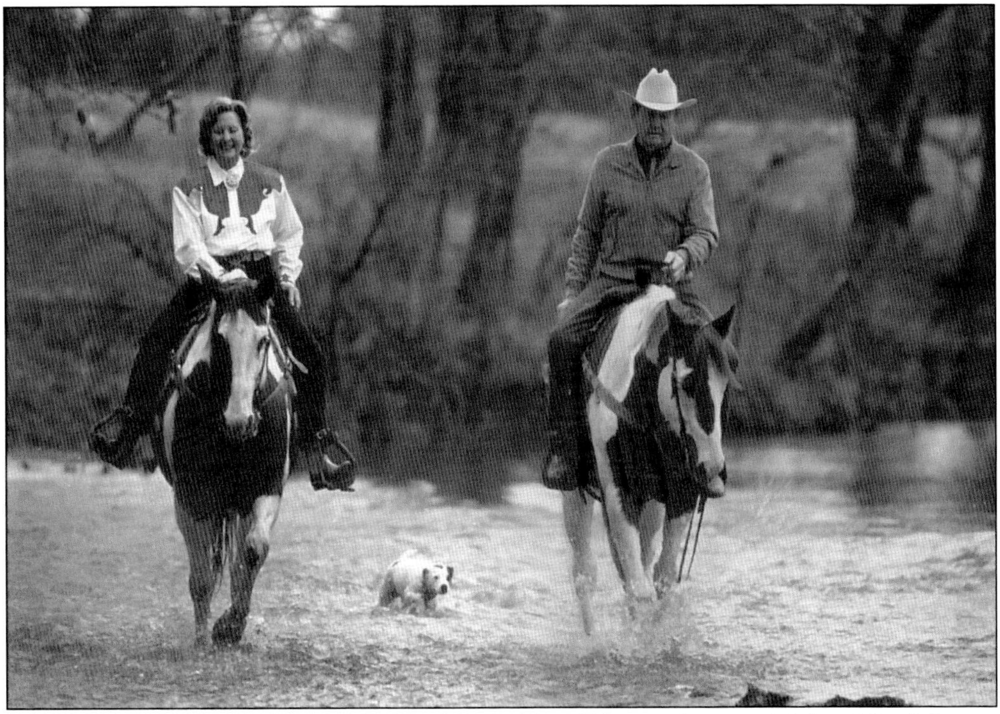

Mitzi and Lanham Riley. Like her mother and her father, rodeo stars Tad and Buck Lucas, trick rider Mitzi Lucas Riley and her husband (champion calf roper and horse trainer Lanham Riley) were stars during the heyday of Wild West and rodeo shows, and they were inducted into numerous halls of fame. In 1961, the Rileys bought a ranch near Aledo where they reared five children. Lanham Riley served on the boards of the county hospital and Aledo school districts. (Courtesy of Mitzi Riley.)

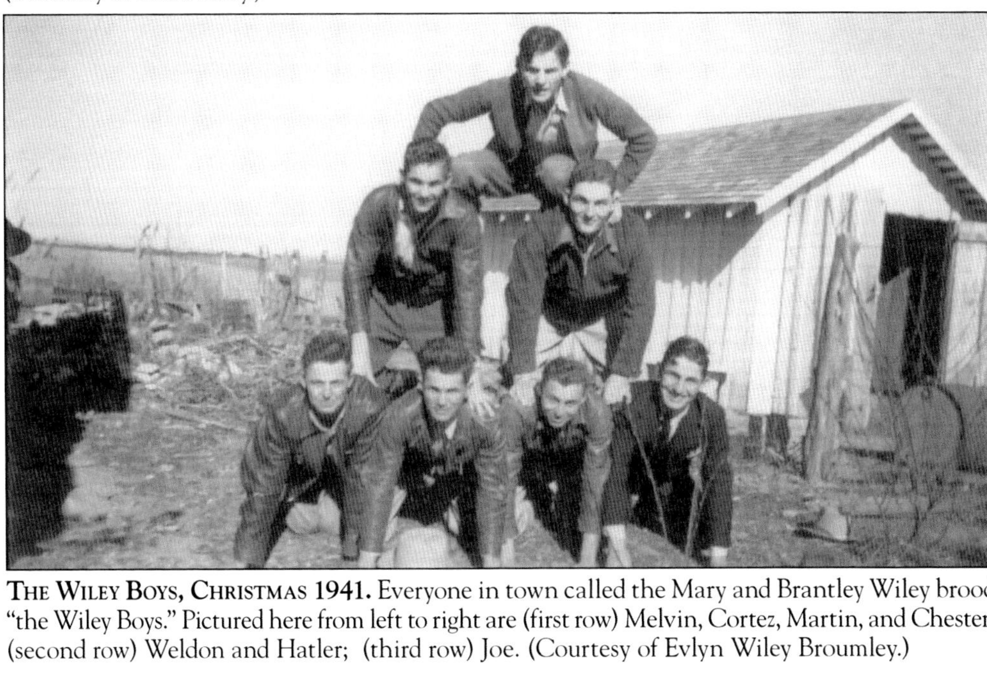

The Wiley Boys, Christmas 1941. Everyone in town called the Mary and Brantley Wiley brood "the Wiley Boys." Pictured here from left to right are (first row) Melvin, Cortez, Martin, and Chester; (second row) Weldon and Hatler; (third row) Joe. (Courtesy of Evlyn Wiley Broumley.)

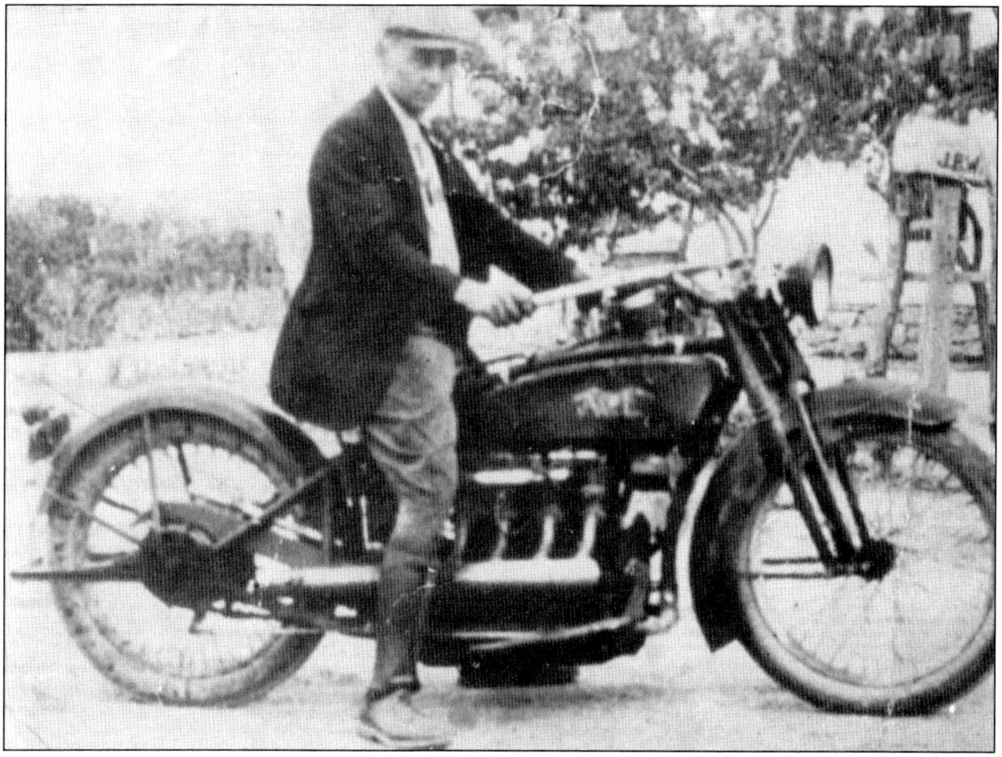

Henry Norris, around 1927. Norris, posing on his four-cylinder "Ace," was an inventive and resourceful man. A welder by trade, he once startled townsfolk by drilling a well with his 1932 Chevrolet. With his automobile on blocks, Norris ran a cable from a drum to an eccentric on a rear wheel, over a pulley atop a tower, and down to a drill bit in a hole. Tending to his project night after night, Norris drilled a 100-foot-deep, Chevy-powered well. (Courtesy of Homer Norris.)

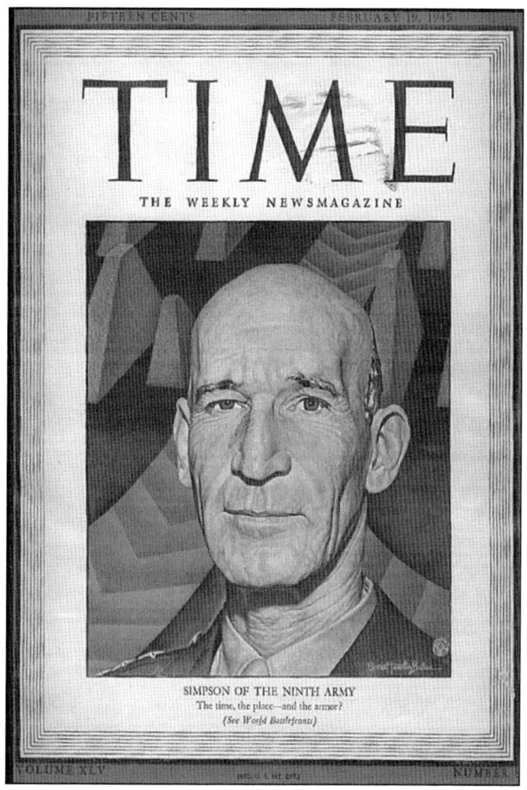

Gen. William Hood Simpson. A descendant of early settler A. J. Hood, Simpson served the nation from World War I through World War II, when he commanded the Ninth Army as part of Gen. Omar Bradley's Twelfth Army Group. His men faced some of the heaviest fighting of the war from the Ardennes to the Ruhr River and were the first to cross the Elbe River. General Simpson and his wife, Ruth, are buried at Arlington National Cemetery. (Courtesy of Jackie McLennan.)

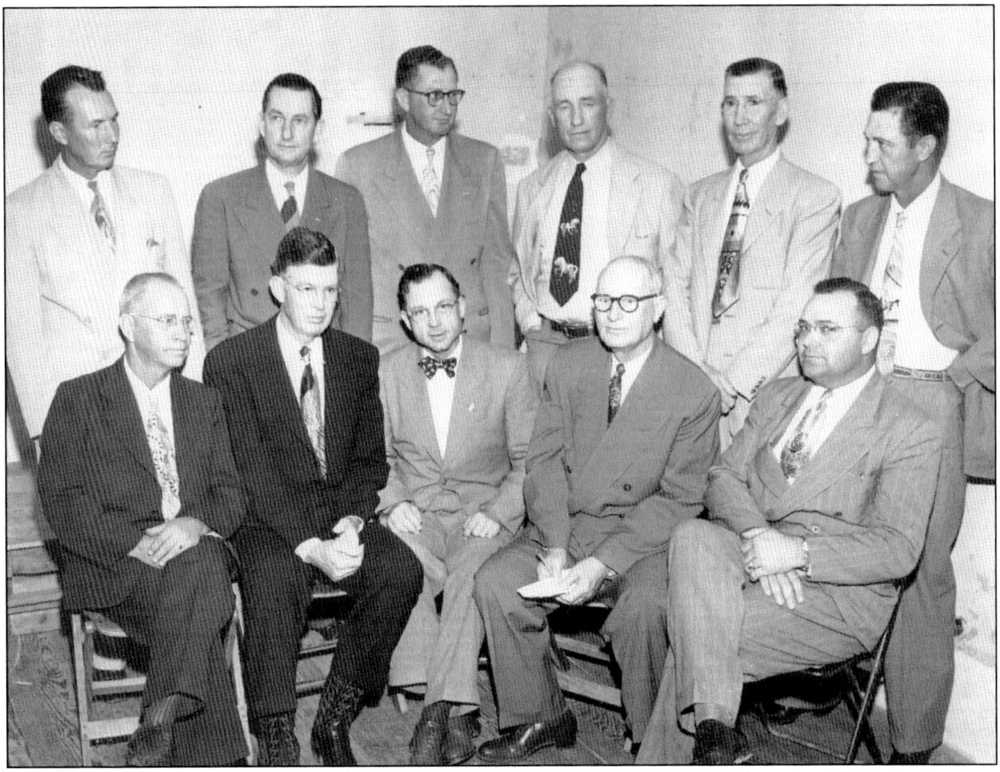

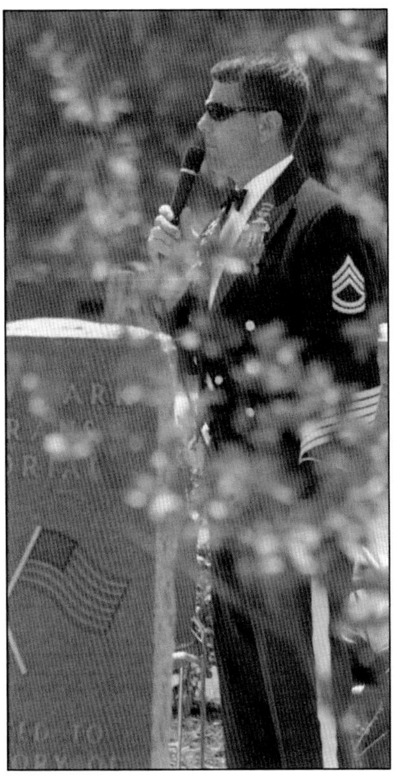

Aledo Civic Club. Organized in the 1940s, before Aledo was incorporated, the club contributed to community improvements, including the donation of land for the Aledo Community Center and the first fire station, and offered its facility for community gatherings and as a polling place. Members met in the old Sears bank building on North Front Street. Around 1950, the club's directors were, from left to right, (first row) Duke Medford, feed mill owner and rancher Ray Smyth, Fort Worth typewriter salesman J. Eldon Whalin, Lou Abbott, and school superintendent Willis Apple; (second row) First Baptist Church of Aledo pastor Frank Haynes, barber Burton Coder, mechanic Marvin Bennett, rancher Volney Hildreth, insurance broker Zan McGlinchey, and rancher Pete Kelly. (Courtesy of Vickie Ballow Slagle.)

Dana Bowman. Sfc. Dana Bowman of Willow Park was a decorated veteran of the U.S. Army's elite Special Forces and member of the legendary Golden Knights parachute team when an accident left him a double amputee. After his rehabilitation, he rejoined the U.S. Armed Forces and now serves as a motivational speaker who often enters his venue by skydiving into it. (Photograph by Brad Holt, courtesy of Randy Keck/*Community News*.)

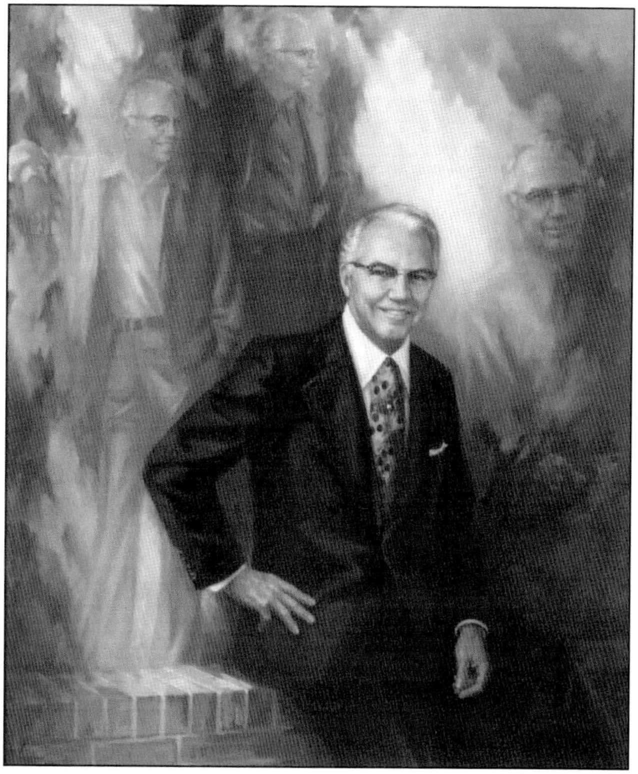

F. HOWARD WALSH AND MARY D. WALSH. The owners of the Walsh Ranches were recognized for their cattle operations and also for philanthropy. The couple's generosity helped to establish the Fort Worth Academy of Fine Arts, a library at the Tarrant County Community College Northwest Campus, and a counseling center at Southwestern Theological Center. The Mary D. and F. Howard Walsh Center for Performing Arts, the Walsh Physical Performance Center, and the Walsh Sports Medicine Center at Texas Christian University reflect the couple's support of the school. (Both, courtesy of the Walsh Foundation.)

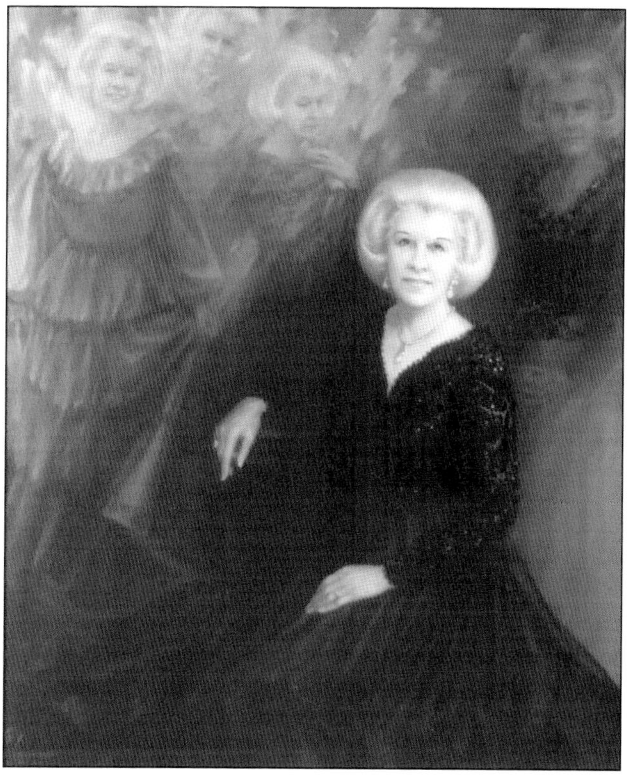

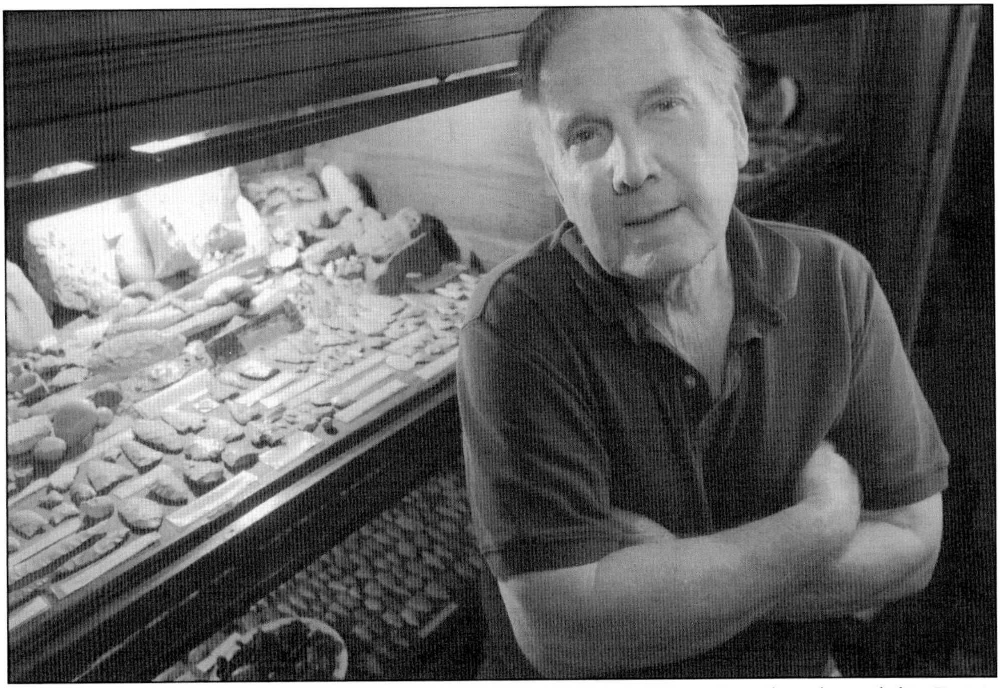

HOMER NORRIS. A commercial artist by training, Norris has enchanted readers through his *Prairie Sketchbook* series, books devoted to the area's story. His engaging, detailed, and accurate stories and sketches of the community, many from the oral histories of old-timers, are often the only surviving record. (Courtesy of Randy Keck/*Community News*.)

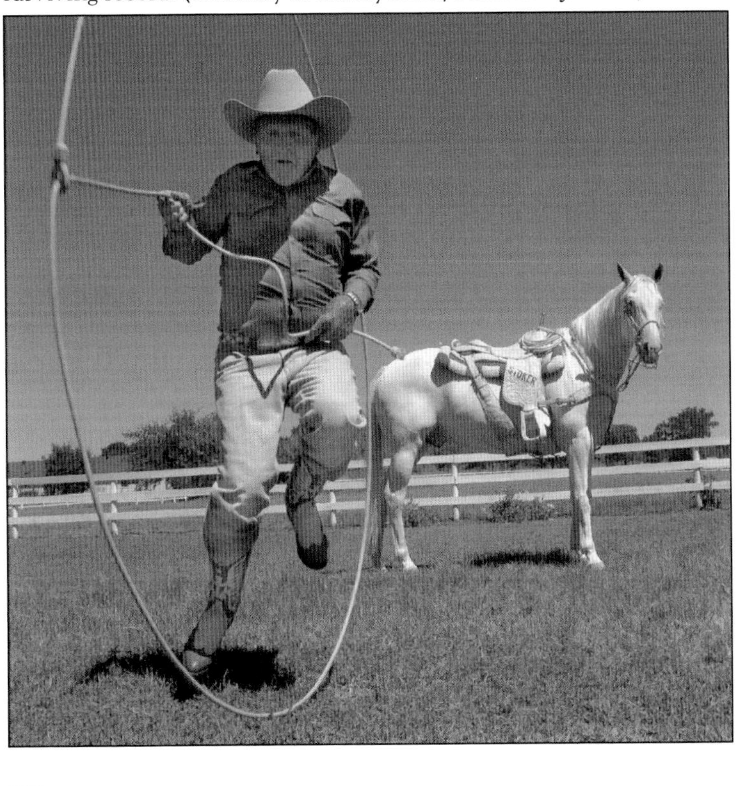

J. W. STOKER. Featured on the cover of Wheaties™ at age 12 as the Juvenile World Champion Trick Rider, the trick rider and roper appeared in such films as *Bus Stop*, starring Marilyn Monroe, and *Bronco Billy* with Clint Eastwood. Twice named Professional Rodeo Cowboys Association Entertainer of the Year, Stoker was inducted into the Cowboy and Western Heritage Hall of Fame in 1999. (Photograph by Thomas Peipert, courtesy of Randy Keck/*Community News*.)

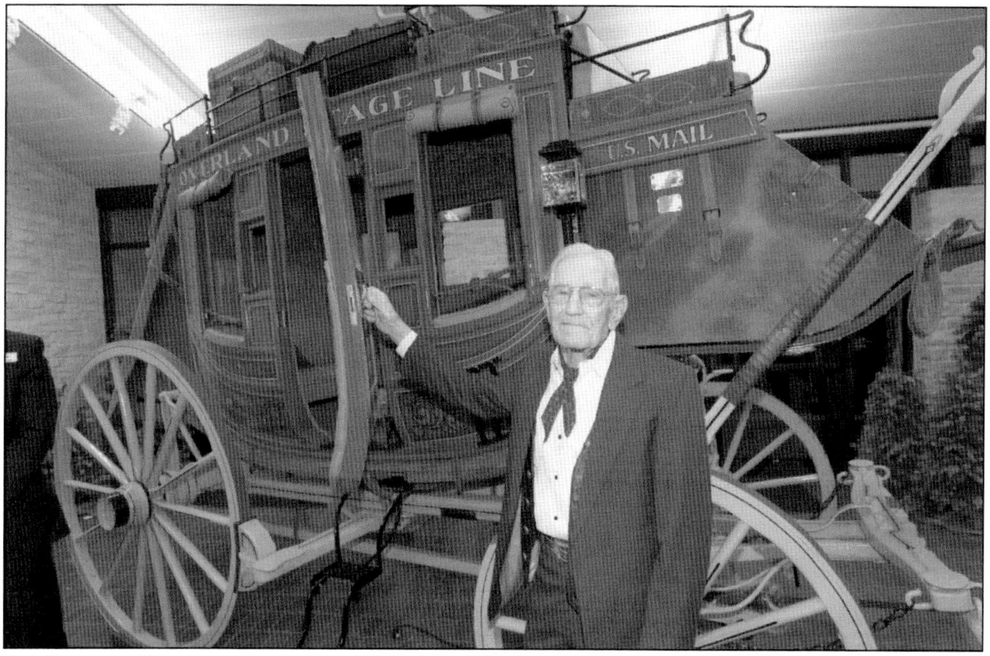

Jay Brown. True to every period detail and built with an artisan's skill, Brown's handsome stagecoaches have appeared in movies and national advertising campaigns. Brown is standing beside an example of his work now on permanent display at the Doss Heritage and Cultural Center in Weatherford. (Courtesy of the Doss Heritage and Cultural Center.)

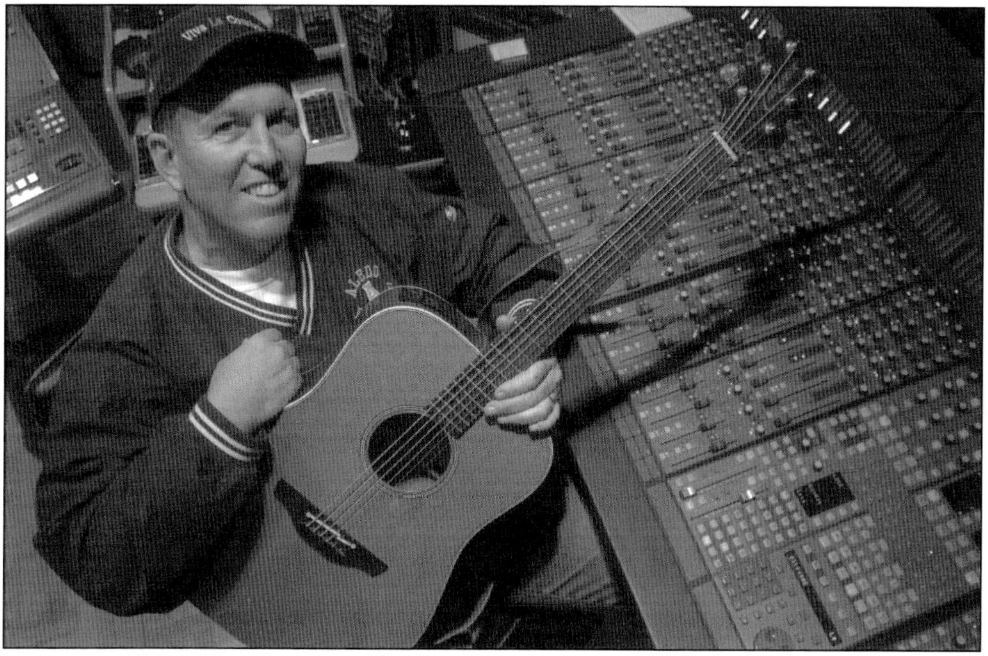

Dan Roberts. Musician, songwriter, performer, and East Parker County resident Dan Roberts opened for Garth Brooks's world tour in 1996 and 1997. Roberts was awarded Male Vocalist of the Year 2001 and Entertainer of the Year 2002 from the Academy of Western Artists. His third CD received three Grammy nominations. (Courtesy of Randy Keck/*Community News*.)

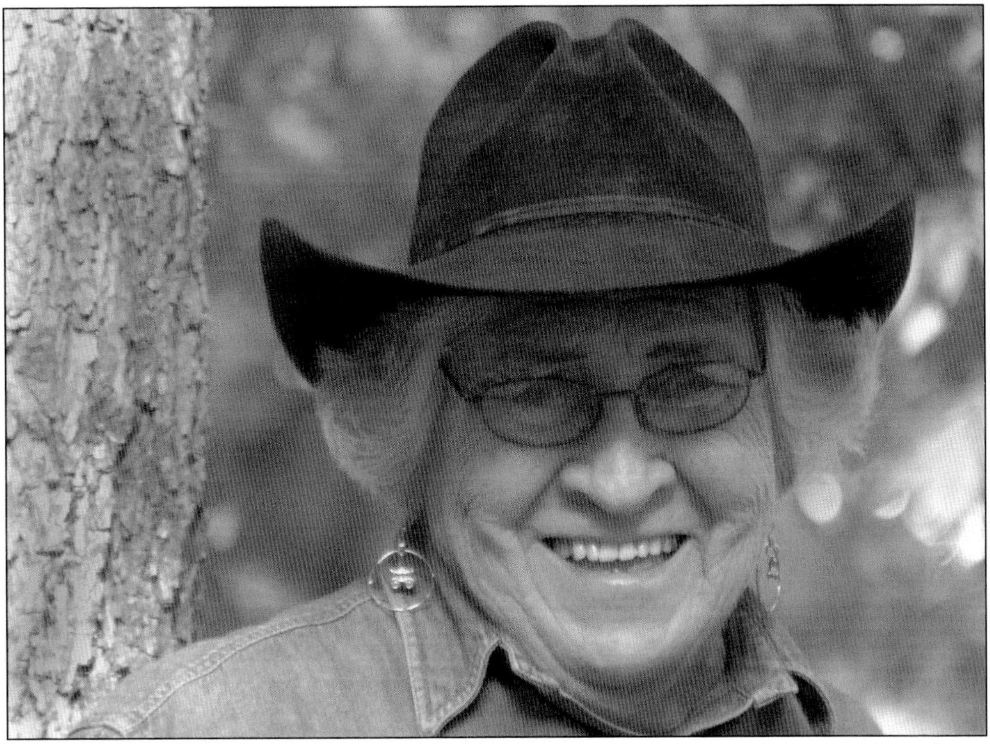

RAMBLIN' REUBENE. For almost three decades, Reubene Gressett Scott has penned a column for the weekly *Community News*. Her topics often include Texas history, adventures on the Texas Sesquicentennial wagon train, European tours, her idyllic childhood in Archer City, and interesting folks around town. *Ramblin' Reubene* columns have become a fixture in the community. (Photograph by Vikiann Gunter; courtesy of Vikiann Gunter.)

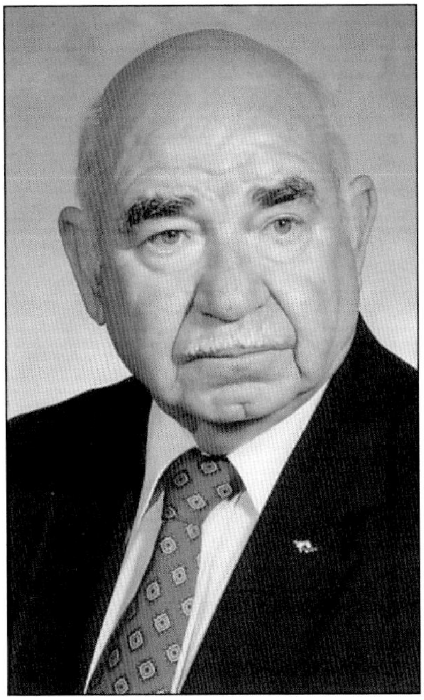

PAPPY THOMPSON. Retired U.S. Air Force lieutenant colonel Forrest Graham "Pappy" Thompson is considered the father of Hudson Oaks. A cofounder of the city, he served as mayor, alderman, and beloved mentor to many other civic leaders. He was a board member of the East Parker County Library and an active member of the East Parker County and Weatherford Chambers of Commerce. (Courtesy of Randy Keck/*Community News*.)

Bibliography

Bennett, Bobby Wayne. *Threshing Oats.* Privately published family memoir, 2005.

Handbook of Texas Online. http://www.tshaonline.org/handbook/online.

Holland, G. A. *The Double Log Cabin.* Weatherford, TX: Herald Publishing Company, 1937.

Jordan-Borden, Edith. *History of Parker County Texas Prior to 1936.* Weatherford, TX: Nebo Valley Press, 2006.

Kemp, Mary Estelle, and Billie Ruth Bell, eds. *Pictorial History of Parker County, Vol. II.* Weatherford, TX: Parker County Historical Commission, 1985.

Marshall, Doyle. *A Cry Unheard: The Story of Indian Attacks in and around Parker County, Texas, 1858–1872.* Aledo, TX: Annetta Valley Farm Press, 1990.

———. *Aledo Country Sketchbook.* Illustrated by Homer Norris. Aledo, TX: Annetta Valley Farm Press, 1987.

Newberry, Barbara Y., and David W. Aiken. *Weatherford, Texas.* Charleston, SC: Arcadia Publishing, 1999.

Norris, Homer. *Parker County Prairie Sketchbook.* Aledo, TX: Waya Press, 2006.

———. *Parker County Sketchbook.* 2nd ed. Aledo, TX: Waya Press, 2004.

Parker County Historical Commission. *History of Parker County.* Weatherford, TX: Parker County Historical Commission, 1980.

Portal to Texas History. http://texashistory.unt.edu.

Scott, Reubene Gressett. *Ramblin' Reubene, Book I.* Aledo, TX: Poverty Knob Press, 2003.

———. *Ramblin' Reubene, Book II.* Aledo, TX: Poverty Knob Press, 2004.

Smythe, H. *Historical Sketch of Parker County and Weatherford.* St. Louis: Louis A. Lavate Press, 1877.

Star-Telegram archives, University of Texas at Arlington.

Tanner, Leon, and Mary Kemp, eds. *Texas as It Is, Main Facts in a Nutshell!* Weatherford, TX: 2008. (Reprint of a 1876 publication.)

Vandagriff, Jon. *The Story of Parker County, Texas: 1852–1956.* Virginia Beach: Donning Company, 2010.

Vertical files, Weatherford Public Library.